Traveling with Man's Best Friend

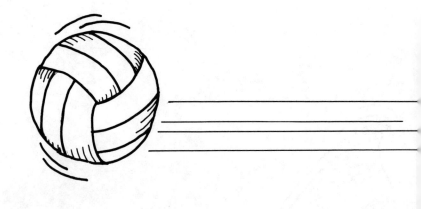

Traveling with Man's Best Friend

A Selective Guide to New England's Bed and Breakfasts, Inns, Hotels, and Resorts that Welcome You and Your Dog

Robert Habgood
and Dawn Habgood

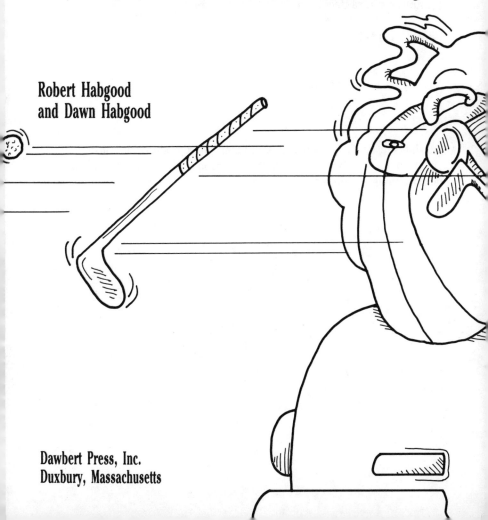

Dawbert Press, Inc.
Duxbury, Massachusetts

Cover Design: Cindy Frost

Illustrations: Lisa Beerntsen

Editor: Ruth W. Somerville

Dawbert Press, Inc.
P.O. Box 2758
Duxbury, Massachusetts 02331

ISBN 0-933603-20-7
First Edition/First Printing

TO HENRY

CONTENTS

INTRODUCTION
x

TIPS FOR THE TRAVELING DOG
xi

CONNECTICUT
1

RHODE ISLAND
15

MASSACHUSETTS
23

VERMONT
78

NEW HAMPSHIRE
139

MAINE
184

APPENDIX
239

B&B RESERVATION SERVICES
241

ADDITIONAL ACCOMMODATIONS
245

INTRODUCTION

Americans love their dogs and more often than not treat them like members of the family. We give them endless amounts of love and attention and the end result is terrific companionship. However, should you decide to leave home or bring your dog on a trip, problems suddenly arise: none of the charming inns seem to want you and your well-behaved dog. Armed with a plethora of guide books, you sort through them until, hours later, you finally locate a bed and breakfast (B&B) or inn that will accept a dog. Or, after extensive telephoning, you may finally discover an acceptable spot, only to find it does not feature the amenities that you would normally require when traveling without your furry friend. A simple vacation has suddenly turned into an arduous task. Must dog owners resign themselves to making compromising accommodation selections or traveling without their canine companions?

"Traveling with Man's Best Friend" is a selective guide to New England's B&Bs, inns, hotels, and resorts that welcome guests *and* their dogs. The selections should be acceptable to both you and your dog. (We have created a universal dog who goes by the name of "Bowser.") This book makes it easy to include Bowser on overnight or extended excursions.

After personally visiting hundreds of inns and B&Bs throughout New England, we have compiled a diversified guide to New England's finer accommodations, as well as an appendix of motels and hotels, that also cordially welcome your "canine companion." Some of these establishments have size requirements for visiting dogs, and others accept everything from a toy poodle to a Newfoundland. The only prerequisite is that prospective guests always inform the innkeeper or host about their traveling companion. The owners may then ask a few questions about your pet (i.e.: is he/she small or large, well behaved, a show dog, sociable, etc.). Please be honest. A dog who constantly barks or is unruly at home cannot be expected to change his behavior when traveling. Thus, rather than jeopardize the good nature of the manager or host, please refrain from bringing an unmanageable dog. More times than not, the inns and B&Bs that formerly accepted well-behaved dogs have changed their policies due to previous bad experiences. We cannot stress enough that traveling with a dog can be a lot of fun for both dog and master, but it is also a responsibility that, if misused, can ruin the opportunity for others.

Please remember that the innkeepers are under no obligation to accept your dog. They have both verbally and in writing stated that they have welcomed dogs in the past, had positive experiences, and will accept them in the future provided the "canine companions" are very well behaved. It is of course up to you to be considerate of other guests and be responsible for your dog's actions.

KEY TO ABBREVIATIONS

RATES:
Range from the least expensive to the most expensive bedroom and/or suite. Sales tax has not been included in the rate schedules (the tax rates vary from state to state). Special discounts or packages are often available—you may wish to inquire about these when making reservations.

PLANS:
(B&B): Bed and Breakfast; usually includes a Continental breakfast.
(EP): European Plan; does not include any meals.
(MAP): Modified American Plan: rates are often listed on a per person basis and include both breakfast and dinner.

PAYMENT:
AE: American Express; MC: Master Card; DC: Diners Club; VISA: Visa. When no credit cards are accepted, guests may pay their deposit or final bill with personal checks, traveler's checks, or cash.

TIPS FOR THE TRAVELING DOG

Just as you would plan to bring certain clothes and accessories for a personal trip, you may also wish to include many of the items listed below to ensure that Bowser has a comfortable and enjoyable vacation too:
* A leash and collar with ID tags.
* A few play toys, chew bones, treats, etc.
* A container of fresh drinking water.
* Food and water bowls.
* Dog bedding (towel, mat, pillow) or travel crate (kennel) if appropriate.
* Grooming aids (comb, brush, or flea powder).
* Prescription medication. If your dog is currently on any medication or is a nervous traveler, you may want to consult your veterinarian prior to departure.
* As an added precaution, many choose to bring their dogs' vaccination records in case of an emergency.

WHILE TRAVELING

* Do not permit the dog to interfere with your driving. Many choose to keep their dogs in the back seat, or in some cases, in their travel crate.
* Plan frequent stops (every two hours or so). During these breaks, you should leash your dog so he does not disturb others, run away, or inadvertently wander into the road.
* If you must leave your dog in the car during the warm weather months (a car can heat up almost as fast as an oven to temperatures in excess of 100 degrees), please take the following precautions with your dog to prevent heat stroke, brain damage, or possible death:
    1. Try to park the car in the shade and leave the windows open enough to provide ample ventilation.
    2. If you have to leave your dog for any length of time please be sure to check on him frequently.
    3. Before you leave the car, you may wish to fill his bowl with cold water to ease the effects of the heat.

ARRIVAL AT YOUR DESTINATION

To ensure that your visit is a completely enjoyable one, we thought it appropriate to list a few of the general concerns expressed by the hosts and innkeepers:

* Guests should keep their dogs leashed while on the grounds.
* Dogs should not be left alone in the bedrooms.
* Owners should try to walk their dogs away from the main grounds and clean up after their dogs.
* At night, please use the dog's bedding to keep him comfortable and lessen the chance of any damage to the furniture. Dogs should never be allowed to sit or lie on any furnishings.

We do not want to diminish the fun you can experience when traveling with Bowser. We feel that an informed pet owner will have a more pleasant vacation than one who is uninformed and inadvertently angers the hosts or other guests. We trust this guide will be informative and helpful, and hope you will truly enjoy traveling with your dogs as much as we do with ours.

CONNECTICUT

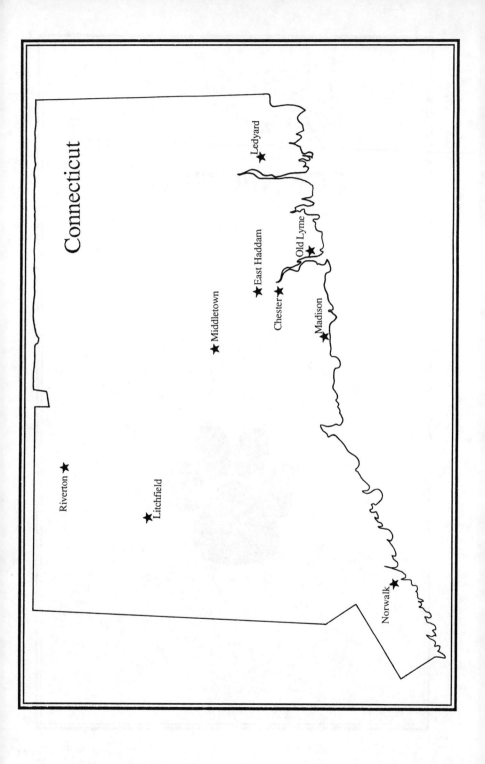

APPLEWOOD FARMS INN

528 Colonel Ledyard Highway
Ledyard, Connecticut 06339
(203) 536-2022
Innkeepers: Frankie and Tom Betz
Rooms: 7 doubles
Rates: $50-95
Payment: MC, VISA
Children: Two years and older welcome
Dogs: Welcome with prior approval
Open: All year

Deacon Russell Gallup built this center-chimney Colonial in 1826 for his wife Hannah and their children. The times have changed, but this somewhat rural country setting has remained much the same, physically and in spirit. The main road leading to the inn is lined by mature trees and ancient stone walls. Endless white fences encircle fields with grazing horses. Although five generations of Gallups grew up on this enormous farm, the tremendous cost of upkeep became a burden and they were forced to sell half of the land to Arabian horse breeders. Today, the Betz family owns the original house and remainder of the farm.

During the last two years, the interior of the inn has all been painstakingly refurbished. The Colonial charm has been maintained through the use of Williamsburg paints on decorative wainscottings, floral country wallpapers, and interesting stenciling. The wide board floors covered in dhurrie rugs creak as guests make their way through the rooms. Canopy or four-poster beds are adorned with white eyelet or nubbly spreads. The Ben Adams room is said to have the largest antique bed Tom has ever seen. It is an enormous white king-size bed made from two double beds. Laura Ashley-style prints and antique furnishings are in evidence throughout the inn's guest quarters. For those who are looking for a little added romance, four of the inn's six fireplaces are in guest rooms.

Although each bedroom has its own unique charm and personality, visitors will also enjoy the cozy parlor with its weaving loom and piano. Beyond it is the breakfast room, where a full country breakfast is served each morning. Although Bowser can participate on most of the excursions, there is a five-by eight-foot kennel behind the barn, should you need to leave him behind.

FRISKY FRIVOLITIES:
* There are over 33 acres of meandering trails for guests to explore with Bowser.
* Old Mystic offers walking tours of the town's historic homes (maps available from the Chamber of Commerce).
* The roads running by and adjacent to the inn are perfect for early morning country walks.

OLD LYME INN

Lyme Street
Old Lyme, Connecticut 06371
(203) 434-2600
Innkeeper: Diana Field Atwood
Rooms: 13 doubles
Rates: $85-115
Payment: Major credit cards
Children: Welcome
Dogs: Welcome, not to be left alone in rooms
Open: All year, except January 1-15

Whether people have heard about the Old Lyme Inn from the *New York Times, Travel & Leisure, Town & Country,* or *Bon Appetit,* they will surely find that it meets most expectations. The home was originally built by the Champlin family in 1850 as a working farm with some 300 acres. Years later, the family sold the farm and it was turned into a restaurant. Finally, in 1976, the old homestead was purchased and gradually restored.

Today, the inn is comprised of five guest bedrooms in the main farmhouse and eight additional suites in the north wing. A quaint farmyard scene of cows, horses, and dogs has been painted on the wall of the staircase leading to the second floor. The first set of rooms are simply furnished in a mix of Empire and Victorian styles. Bright colors contrast with the Bates bedspreads; comfortable sitting chairs are lit by brass lamps. Other modern conveniences include clock radios and individual air conditioning. The bathrooms are well equipped and offer extra amenities such as shampoos, fragrant soaps, and locally made witch hazel. Heat lamps and thick towels are enough to warm anybody.

The new wing houses the second set of guest quarters. These rooms are a bit larger, allowing ample space for canopy beds. Antique marble-topped bedside tables, love seats, and armoires are just a few of the elegant furnishings.

4

These bathrooms are also spacious and modern.

If the accommodations are not tantalizing enough, a delicious meal in the Empire Room will definitely top off the night. Entrees vary from Irish smoked salmon to lobster in a brandy cream sauce. Fresh native pheasant and roasted chicken are also specialties.

FRISKY FRIVOLITIES:
* Nearby Essex is a picturesque seaport town offering interesting shops to explore and a waterfront to amble along.
* There are many local parks (i.e.: Devil's Hopyard or Rocky Neck) that would be fun for picnicking or hiking with Bowser.
* In the summertime, you can take the ferry from New London to the eastern tip of Long Island. This is a secenic area that has charming farms and vineyards.

THE MADISON BEACH HOTEL

94 West Wharf Road
Madison, Connecticut 06443
(203) 245-1404
Manager: Lorraine Casula
Rooms: 26 doubles, 6 suites
Rates: Doubles: $60-120; Suites: $125-195
Payment: Most major credit cards
Children: Welcome
Dogs: Welcome
Open: April 1 to October 31

The Madison Beach Hotel boasts of being Connecticut's only hotel and restaurant on the beach. Years ago, during the whaling era, the hotel was used as a boarding house for shipbuilders. From 1922 to this day, the hotel has maintained much of its former charm and character, seeking only occasionally to increase the number of guest rooms and update the decor.

Most of the guest chambers have terrific views of the Long Island Sound through the sliding glass doors and from private decks. The rooms are on three different levels with the uppermost offering the most space and privacy. The decor emphasizes simplicity and comfort, with color accents on airy blues and yellows. The hardwood floors are painted a barn red and are covered with either dhurries or throw rugs. Brass and white wicker predominate. The floral wallpapers are contrasted by cream-colored chair rails. The modern private bathrooms are centered around a seaside theme.

In addition to the wonderful views and comfortable guest rooms, the hotel has a restaurant called The Wharf, which serves American cuisine. The Crow's Nest, located on the upper deck, is a terrific place to enjoy a drink and watch the evening glow reflecting off the water. In the morning, a Continental breakfast is served in the lobby. Guests may either eat this on the porch or, if they prefer, take it back to their bedrooms.

FRISKY FRIVOLITIES:

* The Long Island Sound is in front of the hotel and offers both sandy beaches and rock jetties for Bowser to explore.
* Historic Madison's quiet side streets lend themselves to a delightful stroll.
* A terrific walk from the inn leads down the beach road and by many of the historic homes.

THE INN AT CHESTER

318 West Main Street
Chester, Connecticut 06412
(203) 526-4961
Innkeeper: David Joslow
Rooms: 48 doubles
Rates: $80
Payment: Major credit cards, personal checks
Children: Over five years old welcome
Dogs: Welcome
Open: All year

The Inn at Chester is a welcome retreat for any traveler. Located in the rural Connecticut countryside, it sits off the road, tucked behind a grove of trees. State forest borders the acreage. A sense of tranquility pervades, aided by the mature trees and plantings of lilacs, evergreens, and roses.

The inn is actually a group of buildings, including the restored farmhouse and two newer wings. An antique barn houses the beautiful dining rooms. Handsome period antiques and oriental rugs are found throughout the inn, in the common rooms as well as the hallways. The bedrooms are spacious, with high ceilings, antique furniture, televisions, and private baths. All of the guest rooms are air conditioned for summer comfort.

The common rooms are very comfortable. Guests are frequently found gathered around the enormous stone fireplace in the lounge. Attached to this room is the barn, whose spacious first floor and hayloft are now used as the formal dining rooms, where there is nightly entertainment on the piano. After a savory gourmet meal, guests frequently gravitate to either the antique-laden balcony for drinks or to the Billiard Room for a game of backgammon, cards, or, of course, billiards.

The inn does have a tennis court and some walking trails through the woods. A pond, dug by the Parmelee's, the first owners, provides swimming in the summer and skating in the winter. A "joggercise" course and exercise facilities are available for those who want a more formal workout. There is also a sauna for use by the guests.

FRISKY FRIVOLITIES:
* Take a stroll with Bowser along the nature trails at the inn and through the state forest.
* For those who prefer a more strenuous workout, the road along the front of the inn is ideal for running or jogging.
* Ask the chef to pack a picnic lunch and set off to explore the Connecticut countryside. The Connecticut River is not far, nor are sailing and fishing.

THE GELSTON HOUSE

The Inn at Goodspeed's Landing
East Haddam, Connecticut 06423
(203) 873-1411
Innkeeper: David Joslow
Rooms: 7 doubles and suites
Rates: Doubles: $80; Suites: $125
Payment: Major credit cards
Children: Welcome
Dogs: Welcome with prior approval
Open: All year

The Gelston House was originally built through the combined efforts of entrepreneur William Goodspeed and his financial backers George and Hugh Gelston. An elegant ball on June 28, 1854, marked not only the opening of the house but also the beginning of the Connecticut River Valley's development. Unfortunately, over the years the house fell victim to the elements and a mild case of neglect. This came to a sudden halt when, in 1984, layers of paint were scraped off, the grand staircase was replaced, and the dining room and guest bedrooms were all restored to their original elegance.

Guests ascend the magnificent spiral staircase, past the floor-to-ceiling mirrors, to the second-and third-floor bedrooms and suites. Grand views of the river are found in each of the guest chambers. Each bedroom is furnished in the Italianate style with original antiques and reproductions. The bathrooms are all modern with amenities such as fragrant soaps, lotions, thick towels, and telephones.

Downstairs, visitors will want to spend time in the intimate Little Bar. Drinks are served from the full-length, pewter-topped bar, or they can be ordered from the small, cloth-covered tables. Antique sconces dot the mirrored walls. Two state-of-the-art kitchens will serve guests in one of the four dining rooms. The porch, with its hardwood floors, high ceilings, and dramatic views of the river through the floor-to-ceiling windows, will surely set the tone for a delightful dining experience. There are a myriad of choices for other dining experiences within the Gelston House's confines. The Summer Garden has a German beer garden atmosphere with its enormous shade trees, bright umbrellas, and views of the river. A light menu offers a wide selection of sandwiches (bratwurst is the specialty) and other treats as well as pitchers of beer. The restaurant serves lunch and dinner. Opera House patrons are also invited to drop by after the theater for libations.

FRISKY FRIVOLITIES:

* East Haddam is a nice old town that maintains much of its original charm while keeping pace with some of today's trends.
* A walk by the river will surely invigorate even the most sated guest. Many stop and admire the old Opera House.
* Should you be on an extended vacation, a fun way to spend the day is to take a ferry from nearby New London to Orient Point (Long Island, N.Y.), Block Island, or even Fishers Island to gain a greater appreciation of Long Island Sound.

TOWN FARMS INN

River Road and Silver Street
Middletown, Connecticut 06457
(203) 347-7438
Innkeeper: Adele Morgan
Rooms: 48 doubles
Rates: $80
Payment: All major credit cards
Children: Welcome
Dogs: Welcome
Open: All year

Squire Thomas Griswold Mather built this splendid Federal house for his family in 1839. Some 14 years later the squire sold his home to the town, whose town fathers chose to use the house as the poor farm for the next 91 years. Then in 1946, the home was transformed into the Commodore McDonough Inn, at which point the south wing was added. Finally, in 1985, it became the Town Farms Inn. The building also has the distinction of being listed on the National Register of Historic Places. Recently completed is a separate gambrel-style wing housing both conference and guest rooms. There is also an exercise facility and sauna.

The reception area and restaurant are found in the original building. An elegant ambiance is created through the use of oriental rugs, Queen Anne furnishings, and deep, comfortable sofas. Guests need little excuse to secure a drink at the intimate bar, settle down in front of the crackling fireplace, and listen to melodies emanating from the piano.

The dining rooms overlook the Connecticut River. The Indian Room has two fireplaces that cast a warm glow upon the low ceilings and hardwood floors. Two Indian portraits look down from barn red walls. Elegantly set tables with white tablecloths complete the effect. The adjacent brick-faced Captain Mather Library is a cozier dining room with views of the hills. However, the inn's most formal dining room is the Commodore McDonough. Guests will choose from gourmet delicacies such as baked brie, quail, oysters Elise, and smoked goose breast. The service is impeccable and the food innovative.

The guest accommodations are all furnished and decorated in the same simple but handsome fashion. The high ceilings allow space for the large, small-paned windows that look out onto the river or hillsides. The furnishings are Queen Anne in style, with four-poster beds and overstuffed wing chairs set on plush camel colored wall-to-wall carpeting. Fresh flowers complete the effect. The bathrooms are modern, finished with off-white tiles. Fragrant soaps and shampoos, as well as luxuriously thick towels, ensure that guests are comfortable.

FRISKY FRIVOLITIES:
* Even if Bowser does not become instant friends with Raffles (the owner's dog), there are ample grounds for frolicking.
* The banks of the river offer plenty of opportunities for long walks. The chef will even pack a picnic lunch for those who want to take an extended jaunt.
* Wesleyan University is close to the inn. Drive over and explore this scenic campus. Maybe a collegian or two will toss a frisbee for Bowser.

OLD RIVERTON INN

Route 20
Riverton, Connecticut 06065
(203) 379-8678
Innkeeper: Mark A. Telford
Rooms: 11 doubles, 1 suite
Rates: Doubles: $35-76; Suite: $125
Payment: All major credit cards
Children: Welcome
Dogs: Welcome with prior approval
Open: All year

The Old Riverton Inn has been in existence since 1796, serving the "The Hungry, Thirsty, and Sleepy." To this day, it has managed to retain much of its original ambiance. Hardwood floors slope steeply in many of the guest rooms. The furnishings are simple with upholstered arm chairs, comfortable couches, and Bates spreads covering maple bedsteads. Luggage racks are thoughtfully provided in each room. Iron fixtures are found on the doors and wainscotting adds dimension to the walls. The bathrooms are dated but clean. One even has a unique step-up bathtub. The most stately guest bedroom is the spacious suite. Its canopy bed, marble-topped table, Victorian couch, and matching armchair all lend elegance to this chamber. A fireplace warms the sometimes brisk night air. A terrific view of the river can be had from the suite and several of the other guest quarters.

Guests like to congregate in the comfortably furnished upstairs sitting area. In addition to an assortment of games and puzzles, there is a great selection of magazines for those who prefer a quieter pastime. Lunch and dinner are served in the beamed-ceiling dining room. The restaurant prides itself on offering a hearty New England fare. Across the way is a flagstone porch housing a small bar and brick fireplace. Sitting in front of the crackling fire and sipping a hot toddy is an appropriate way to end any winter evening.

FRISKY FRIVOLITIES:
* Visitors to the area should take the time to explore this quaint historic town and its surrounding back roads.
* There are terrific areas for cross-country skiing and scenic picnic sites and foliage trails to discover in the 2,954-acre People's State Forest.
* Canoeing and tubing in the river are favorite pastimes. Inquire with the innkeepers for local outfitters.

11

TOLL GATE HILL INN AND RESTAURANT

Route 202, P.O. Box 39
Litchfield, Connecticut 06759
(203) 567-4545
Innkeeper: Frederick J. Zivic
Rooms: 8 doubles, 2 suites
Rates: Doubles: $85-95; Suites: $125
Payment: Major credit cards
Children: Welcome
Dogs: Welcome; owners are responsible for any damage
Open: All year

The Toll Gate Hill Inn was originally built as the Captain William Bull Tavern in 1745. It was used primarily as a way station for travelers en route between Hartford and Litchfield. In 1923, Frederick Fussenich moved this "publick house" to Toll Gate Hill. Approximately 50 years later the inn was restored, with an emphasis on preserving its historical heritage. Today, Toll Gate Hill holds a coveted place in the annals of the National Register of Historic Places.

Guests will find that the charm of the inn is quick to unfold. A long, narrow, wood-paneled hallway leads to the handcrafted cherry bar. A crackling fire warms the room. A glance into the two dining rooms reveals corner cupboards, wide pine floors, beamed ceilings, and traditional American prints.

The extremely narrow back stairway leads guests to the intimate second floor sitting area and bedrooms. These chambers are individually decorated with an emphasis on country simplicity. Antique clocks, chintz-covered armchairs, and canopy or four-poster beds are the norm. The rooms on the top floor have been recently renovated, utilizing the steep eves and exposed rough-hewn beams to create cathedral ceilings. These guest bedrooms are small but appear spacious due to the high ceilings and use of color. Fireplaces keep three of the chambers particularly cozy. The bathrooms are modern and provide guests with amenities such as potpourri, bay rum tonic, and fragrant soaps. For those who wish to enjoy a glass of wine in their room, a brass ice bucket and corkscrew are thoughtfully provided. There are also four spacious rooms in the carriage house offering more privacy and equally as luxurious accommodations.

The inn has appeared in many gourmet magazines because of its fine cuisine and unique setting. The original Tavern Room and more formal dining room are limited only by their size. Whether guests choose oysters on the half shell as an appetizer, or shrimp and scallops Grand Marnier, roast duckling, venison, or boneless prime rib as the entree, they are sure to be delighted. In the morning, a Continental breakfast is served in either the guest's room or on the patio. It usually consists of fresh orange juice, fruit breads and muffins, and coffee.

FRISKY FRIVOLITIES:
* White Memorial Foundation and Conservation Center is a 4,000-acre area that is great for hiking or cross-country skiing with Bowser.
* Litchfield is one of the more interesting Connecticut towns to explore. It is noted for its Colonial homes. Some exploration can be done on foot and others by car.
* Bantam Lake is only four miles from the inn. It offers a number of recreational activities including swimming and boating (boat rentals are available).

SILVERMINE TAVERN

Silvermine and Perry avenues
Norwalk, Connecticut 06850
(203) 847-4558
Innkeeper: Frank C. Whitman Jr.
Rooms: 10 doubles
Rates: $52-74
Payment: Major credit cards, personal checks

Children: Welcome
Dogs: Welcome with prior approval
Open: All year, except Tuesdays September to May

The Silvermine Tavern is located on the banks of the Silvermine River and Mill Pond. It is actually made up of four buildings, each housing a fine collection of early American antiques. Tools, lamps, and other memorabilia hang from beamed ceilings or are placed on the various cupboards and shelves.The fireplaced common rooms are inviting with oriental rugs covering the hardwood floors and oil paintings adorning the walls. In one nook a grandfather clock keeps time amid wrought iron lamps, ladder-back chairs, and a harvest table.

The guest quarters reflect an authentic early American motif. Antique beds, bureaus, and side tables are set alongside chintz-covered armchairs. Braided rugs cover painted narrow-board floors. Favorite guest rooms are those with antique or canopy beds and screened-in porches overlooking the Silvermine River. All of the bathrooms are private and a some have special features such as claw-footed bathtubs.

The restaurant is composed of different rooms, all overlooking Mill Pond. In the summer, meals are often served on the terrace. In the winter, guests opt for dinner in front of the crackling fireplaces. The inn offers a wide selection of New England favorites such as lobster, steak, chicken, and various soups and chowders. Whether guests are watching the swans on Mill Pond or the trees swaying in the breeze, their dining experience will definitely be enhanced by this special setting.

FRISKY FRIVOLITIES:
* The nearby towns of Wilton, Greenwich, Darien, and Westport offer a varied impression of this scenic portion of western Connecticut.
* In addition to the many beaches and charming parks, visitors also enjoy walking the picturesque back roads surrounding the inn.
* Terrific cross-country skiing is available on many of the golf courses and nearby trails.

RHODE ISLAND

Rhode Island

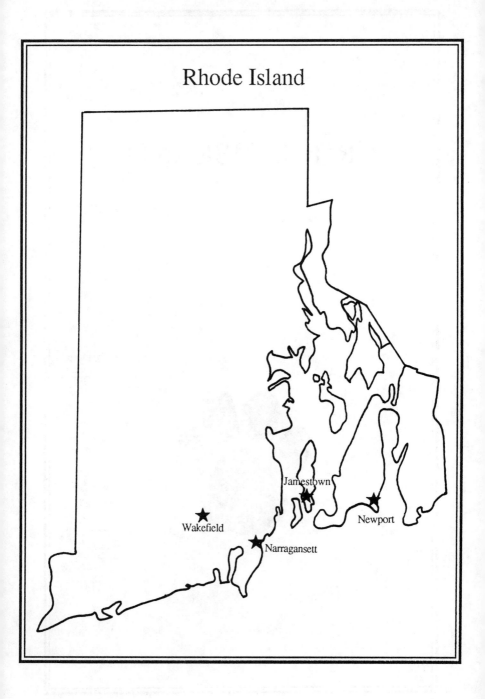

THE FOUR GABLES

12 South Pier Road
Narraganset, Rhode Island 02882
(401) 789-6948
Hosts: Joyce and Peter Turco
Rooms: 2 doubles
Rates: $45
Payment: Personal checks
Children: Welcome
Dogs: Welcome with prior approval
Open: All year

The Four Gables is a fine example of the classic Rhode Island summer homes that were built in the late 1890s. The four gambrel roof lines and gray-weathered shingles make this home particularly appealing. It is set behind a large, well-manicured hedge; planters of flowers are placed at the entrance to the driveway. The Turcos have been operating this charming home as a B&B for just over five years.

Once inside, guests will be greeted by Reuben, the loveable resident dachshund. This is a traditional home with antiques displayed in combination with more contemporary furnishings. Guests will soon feel at home as Joyce and Peter are good at making people welcome. A sitting room with its fireplace is quite inviting; however, many choose to relax in the larger living room. Here they will find a brick fireplace, a cable television, and a fine selection of reading material lining the bookshelves.

The two guest rooms are upstairs. One is decorated in vibrant green; the focal point being a pink and green handmade quilt on the double bed. The four pillows are covered with ruffled shams, and mints are placed on them at night. A white wicker bureau, rocking chair, and wall stenciling complete the effect. A standing rack is draped with towels. The second guest chamber is also quite cheery, with cornflower blue curtains accenting the colorful handmade quilt. This bedroom is also stenciled and offers guests a small television and a day bed for children. Both bedrooms share a large, very attractively decorated bathroom, complete with a blue claw-footed bathtub.

Each morning, guests are treated to a Continental breakfast in the cozy dining room. Fresh fruit, juice, and an assortment of homemade breads and muffins are placed out on the small dining room table, sometimes set with English country-patterned placemats. Afterwards, guests might want to take a walk along the ocean. The house is a half block from the water, making it an easy stroll. Croquet and badminton are also enjoyable afternoon activities.

17

FRISKY FRIVOLITIES:
* The ocean is down the street, with sidewalks to wander along as well as rock jetties to fish upon, and more distant lighthouses to visit.
* There are several great beaches a few minutes drive from the inn. The swimming is safe, and you and Bowser will appreciate the warm water.
* Many just enjoy walking the charming residential lanes or strolling by the boutiques, cafes, and historical sites.

LARCHWOOD INN

176 Main Street
Wakefield, Rhode Island 02879
(401) 783-5454
Innkeepers: Frank and Diann Browning
Rooms: 12 inn rooms, 7 Holly House rooms
Rates: $40-75 (off-season rates available)
Payment: All major credit cards
Children: Welcome
Dogs: Welcome, not to be left alone in room; $5 fee
Open: All year

For over 150 years, the Larchwood Inn has stood in this quiet section of Wakefield Village. The newly renovated Holly House, built during the same era as the inn, stands just across the street. The 12 rooms in the manor house look

18

out over three acres of land covered with mature oak, cherry, maple, pine, and dogwood trees.

Sloping and creaking hardwood floors lead to the individually furnished guest quarters. Antique and four-poster or canopy beds are covered with white Bates spreads. Comfortable, well-worn sofas and wingback chairs grace some of the larger rooms. All have antique tables, mirrors, and bureaus. Full-length floral-patterned draperies hang at the windows. Many of the rooms are perfect for families because of the double and single bed configurations. Most of the bed-chambers have tiled private baths that are dated but extremely clean. The rooms are reminiscent of an old-fashioned summer home.

The inn's public rooms have a distinctly Scottish flavor. Writings by the poet, Robert Burns, can be found throughout. Each year, on his birthday, the innkeepers celebrate with a festive party. They import a piper and offer traditional Scottish dishes which include "Haggis" (a true treat for the daring). The menu during the year is much tamer and consists of swordfish, lobster, and beef. In the summer months, the Larchwood Inn is a favorite among yachtsman, who dock in nearby Point Judith Pond and make the short journey to the inn for dinner. Before heading back to their boats, many like to visit either the Tam O'Shanter lounge or relax in the cozy fireplaced living room. A piano beckons those who enjoy tickling the ivories. Chester, the resident bird, will undoubtedly chirp along with the music.

FRISKY FRIVOLITIES:
* Many of the beaches in the area are public and uncrowded. Bowser should enjoy the romp, while you relax in the sun.
* Newport is a short distance from the inn. The drive is scenic and the opportunities for exploring are unlimited. The cliff walk, located next to The Breakers, is particularly nice for an afternoon stroll.
* Historic Jamestown is accessible to Wakefield by a number of bridges. In Jamestown is the original Beaver Tail Lighthouse and a few historic homes (the British burned much of the town in 1775). Watson Farm is a working farm with animals. Pack a picnic and go for the day.

THE CALICO CAT GUEST HOUSE

14 Union Street
Jamestown, Rhode Island 02835
(401) 423-2641

19

Host: Lori Lacaille
Rooms: 10 doubles
Rates: $35-75
Payment: AE, MC, VISA, personal checks
Children: Welcome (children under 12 years old free)
Dogs: Smaller dogs welcome with prior approval
Open: All year

The Calico Cat Guest House is located in a quiet residential area, just a block from Jamestown's waterfront and small village. This unassuming gray-shingled home offers guests comfortable accommodations as well as being convenient to the area's beaches (both large and small). Chrissy, the resident dog, will undoubtedly welcome newcomers into her home.

There are several common rooms and porches available to guests. Whether relaxing on the informal enclosed porch or watching television in the sitting room, one will find this B&B's ambiance to be casual. The bed chambers are located on all three floors; however, the stenciled third floor rooms are usually rented to long-term guests. Thus, one will most likely choose from any of the five or six remaining guest bedrooms and three shared baths.

Each guest room is individually decorated and features brass or wooden bedsteads and traditional furnishings. Hardwood floors and wainscottings add definition to the rooms, softened by floral wallpapers, sheer curtains, and dried flower arrangements. Fold-out sofa beds allow flexibility for families. Air conditioning is an added modern convenience found in all the rooms.

A Continental breakfast is offered each morning on the porch, overlooking the water. Afterwards, a refreshing walk down to the ocean is invigorating. This might also be a good time to fish or just walk on the beach and listen to the sounds of the foghorn.

FRISKY FRIVOLITIES:
* Just two blocks from the B&B is a small park alongside the ocean. After a quick romp and or swim for Bowser, maybe both of you would like to relax on the East Ferry Market & Deli's brick patio and watch the world pass by.
* Even the most "laid-back" people crave a little city life from time to time. A quick jaunt over the bridge brings you to the bustling town of Newport with its harbor, shops, and mansions.
* If you are a fisherman you might want to try catching a striped bass or bluefish. Walkers will find the beaches and coastal paths to be therapeutic

ELLERY PARK HOUSE

44 Farewell Street
Newport, Rhode Island 02840
(401) 847-6320
Host: Margo Waite
Rooms: 1 single, 1 double
Rates: $50
Payment: Personal checks
Children: Older children preferred
Dogs: Smaller dogs preferred with prior approval
Open: All year

The Ellery Park House is located just four blocks from the busy Newport waterfront and downtown. The 1900's gray clapboard and shingled Victorian-style home is in the heart of Newport's residential and historic Point neighborhood. A rather small house, in comparison to the famed Newport mansions, this B&B offers a relaxed environment with comfortable furnishings.

Once inside, guests naturally gravitate to the living room with its cozy window seat tucked into a bay window. The decor is elegantly simple with an oriental rug setting the tone for the handsome sofa and arm chair. An archway leads to the adjoining dining room where a formal antique two-pedestal table is surrounded by a matched set of chairs. The cushions are coordinated with the draperies and pale green trim.

Upstairs, the two guest rooms are also tastefully decorated. The first bedroom is furnished with two single beds with interesting turnings on the maple head and foot boards. A matching bedside table is topped with magazines, a potted geranium, and a brass lamp. The dark red curtains pick up the colors from an oriental runner between the two beds. The second dove-gray bedroom also has hardwood floors. A Sheraton-style bedside table rests alongside an antique sleigh-bed covered with a blue and white patterned spread. The bedside table also has a pot of geraniums and interesting reading material. A wall-mounted brass lamp swings away from the wall to provide light for reading. Tie-back curtains frame the window.

Morning brings a Continental breakfast from Margo's enormous Garland stove. Guests may take their muffins, breads, juice, and coffee either in the dining room or out on the small brick patio. The latter is quite charming as it is located behind a white board fence amidst her herb gardens. After a good night's rest, a filling breakfast, and some friendly conversation, guests will be ready for an exciting day exploring the wonderful sights in Newport.

FRISKY FRIVOLITIES:

* The waterfront is filled with terrific shops, boutiques, and restaurants. Early morning fishing boats dock at the pier and unload their catch.
* The Cliff Walk provides a different vantage point for viewing the mansions. The path meanders along the ocean and is quite scenic. There are even areas for Bowser to take a quick dip.
* In addition to the Tennis Hall of Fame, Hammersmith Farm, and a ferryboat trip out to Block Island, many choose to visit the other scenic towns in this tiny state, such as Watch Hill, Narragansett, and Little Compton (to mention a few).

MASSACHUSETTS

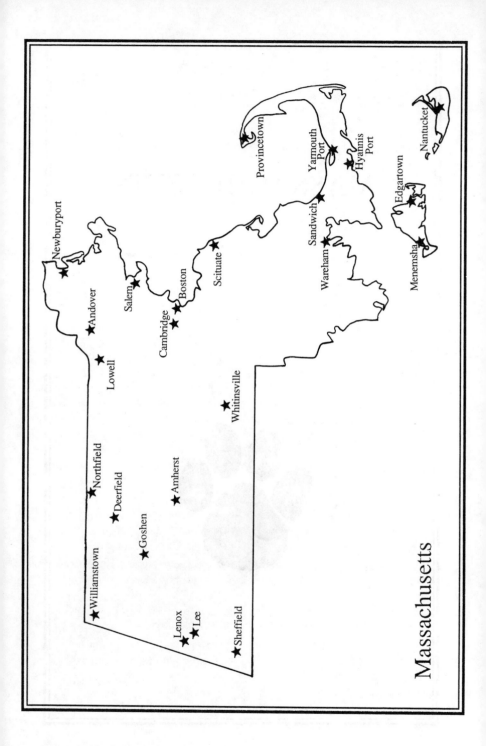

Massachusetts

Newburyport
Andover
Salem
Boston
Cambridge
Scituate
Lowell
Whitinsville
Northfield
Deerfield
Amherst
Goshen
Williamstown
Lenox
Lee
Sheffield
Provincetown
Yarmouth Port
Hyannis Port
Sandwich
Wareham
Edgartown
Nantucket
Menemsha

THE WILLIAMS INN

On the Green
Williamstown, Massachusetts 01267
(413) 458-9371
General Manager: Carl J. Falkner
Rooms: 100 doubles, 5 suites
Rates: Doubles: $68-90; Suites: $175 (packages available)
Payment: Most major credit cards
Children: Welcome
Dogs: Accepted in the first floor rooms only
Open: All year

From the outside, The Williams Inn looks like a large motor lodge, and initially we were hesitant to include it under this inn and B&B listing. It has, in fact, just undergone a substantial renovation, which has converted the interior of the building into a charming inn not unlike the Middlebury Inn in Middlebury, Vermont. The only feature that could not be duplicated was the sloping creaky floors.

The public areas have been painted in traditional Williamsburg blues and greens and are furnished with reproduction English antiques and period furniture. Although the dining room, as of this writing, has a bold red wall treatment, it has a very gracious quality. The adjacent Tavern is more contemporary with large windows overlooking the grounds. The bar is a favorite gathering spot for Williams College alumnae and guests of the inn.

The bedrooms have been very tastefully decorated in several color combinations. Mauve tones are combined with either pale greens or blues. Coordinated quilted and fitted chintz coverlets and dust ruffles encase the beds. Brass floor and table-top lamps are well located next to wing chairs and bedside tables. The bathrooms have been updated with new fixtures, Corian sinks, and heat lamps.

The Williams Inn, while not offering the antiquity found in many classic New England inns, has been able to successfully reproduce most of the charming amenities guests have come to expect. The inn also offers features that many smaller inns cannot. Those wishing to get some exercise or unwind after a long day will find a heated indoor swimming pool, jacuzzi, and individual men's and women's saunas. Guests who prefer to relax during their vacations will enjoy the comfortable sitting room with its blazing fireplace. This is the perfect place to spend some time after a long day of shopping, touring, or cross-country skiing.

FRISKY FRIVOLITIES:

* The Berkshires are an outdoorsman's paradise. Spend the day fishing with your faithful companion in one of the area's many lakes or streams.
* Cross-country skiing is available just outside of town.
* Williams College has extensive and beautiful grounds for walking, as well as sporting events, art festivals, and a summer theater

---

WALKER HOUSE

74 Walker Street
Lenox, Massachusetts 01240
(413) 637-1271
Innkeepers: Peggy and Richard Houdek
Rooms: 8 doubles
Rates: $45-120 (Weekly discounts available)
Payment: Personal checks
Children: Over eight years old welcome
Dogs: Accepted with prior approval
Open: All year

Western Massachusetts, and particularly the Lenox area, is a wonderful spot for visitors in any season. The Walker House, built in the early 1800s, exudes a warm grace that is typically reflected in many of the Lenox "summer houses." Upon entering the foyer, guests will notice the high, detailed ceilings and a long graceful staircase. Further down the hall, a large dining/breakfast room will be found with its invitingly blazing fireplace. In the morning, guests will gather around the large dining room table for a generous Continental breakfast. The windows dominating the end of the room provide beautiful views of the lovely formal gardens, with gently swaying pine and cedar trees serving as a backdrop. A massive sliding wood door leads into the formal living room. This spacious forest green room has an old music box, a piano, and deep comfortable sofas facing the large fireplace.

Each guest room is named after a famous composer and furnished in a style that adheres to his or her personality (the Houdeks have many musical interests and their inn reflects these in every nook and cranny). This creates a variety of room decors and moods. One may find a canopy bed, Victorian antiques (acquired at auctions), a gigantic brass bed facing a cozy fireplace (supplied with Duraflame logs), or perhaps a green and white wicker garden room motif. The bedrooms in the back of the house are particularly bright and sunny, whereas the rooms in the front are a bit more formal. All of the bathrooms are spacious and private, and each is unique. Some have a circular shower curtain, others have four-pedestal bathtubs. A split of white wine (which your hosts will gladly chill) and two glasses await guests of the inn.

Lastly, the deputy innkeepers have a very friendly dog, Woody, who will greet guests upon their arrival. At the time of our visit there were also six cats living in and around the house; however, they were quite inconspicuous.

FRISKY FRIVOLITIES:
* The Lenox area provides wonderful hiking trails. October Mountain is a nice option with a moderately difficult trail leading to the top and a terrific view.
* The Walker House is centrally located in the town of Lenox, where many enjoy exploring the quaint side streets and many interesting shops. Complimentary bicycles are also available.
* The local lakes are great for swimming in the summer and ice skating in the winter.

THE MORGAN HOUSE

Main Street
Lee, Massachusetts 01238
(413) 243-0181
Innkeepers: Beth and Bill Orford
Rooms: 13 doubles

Rates: $30-90
Payment: Most major credit cards
Children: Welcome
Dogs: Welcome
Open: All year

The Morgan House is located on the main street in Lee, only minutes from Lenox, Tanglewood, and the historic town of Stockbridge. The inn itself boasts quite an interesting history, dating back to 1817. Originally, the house was owned by William Porter, a local lawyer and marble quarrier. Edwin Morgan, who was sent out to find stone for the west wing of the nation's Capitol, discovered that Lee was an ideal location for excavating marble and subsequently became a business partner with Mr. Porter. When Mr. Porter died in 1853, Morgan bought the house. He eventually began accepting guests when The Housatonic House, a neighboring inn, burned down.

It was not until 1981 that Beth and Bill Orford purchased the house from Mrs. "Nat King" Cole, who had been running the inn for almost eight years. Aside from several additions and modifications, much of the original exterior structure and rustic charm are still intact. The guest bedrooms are furnished in an early American decor with an assortment of brass or maple beds covered with fluffy comforters. Towels are neatly folded at the ends of the beds, for all but one guest room shares a bath. Rocking chairs rest in the corners awaiting evening readers. Decorative touches are many, including delicate country floral wallpapers and braided rugs covering hardwood floors. The one guest room that does have a private bath was our favorite because of its particularly pretty furnishings and its quiet corner location.

Downstairs, guests will surely enjoy the nostalgia of the tavern and adjacent dining room, reminiscent of the old west or Gold Country of California. A few standouts among the assortment of collectibles are the original pages of the guest ledger posted on the walls and the old photographs of the inn through the years. The tavern is a nice place for a leisurely drink before sitting down to a delectable dinner selection of New England duckling, medallions of veal, prime rib, or filet mignon. Each morning, guests are invited to partake of a complimentary breakfast of homemade cinnamon buns, juice, cereals, eggs, and coffee or tea.

Any reason will suffice for visiting the Berkshires; the Morgan House is a treat for those who appreciate good hospitality coupled with the charm of the rustic historic past.

FRISKY FRIVOLITIES:
* A visit to scenic Lenox is a must. For those heartier souls, a long walk or run along Upper Mountain Road to Tanglewood is both exhilarating and peaceful.

* Many visitors come for the beautiful fall foliage and/or the winter activities which include cross-country skiing and ice skating on the many local lakes.
* Whether interests lie in the entertainment of the Williamstown Summer Theater or Tanglewood, exploring quaint New England towns along scenic Route 7, or taking advantage of the many outdoor activities available, a visit to this region is well worthwhile.

IVANHOE COUNTRY HOUSE

Undermountain Road
Sheffield, Massachusetts 01257
(413) 229-2143
Innkeepers: Carole and Dick Maghery
Rooms: 7 doubles, 1 suite
Rates: Doubles: $47-82; Suite: $95-135
Payment: Personal checks
Children: Welcome
Dogs: Well-behaved dogs accepted with a $10-per-day charge. They must be leashed and walked away from the lawns.
Open: All year

Whether guests have a child attending nearby Berkshire School, tickets to a Tanglewood concert, or enjoy the local outdoor activities, they will find the Ivanhoe Country House to be a welcoming country inn. Built in 1780, this house looks rather imposing from the outside, but once inside guests will find it is quite cozy and comfortably rambling. Down each hallway and around every corner are hidden alcoves, creaky hardwood floors, distinctive moldings, and interesting collectibles from another era.

The rooms are individually and tastefully decorated reflecting the Colonial period. Nubbly bedspreads adorn antique bedsteads, and furnishings complement the small floral print wallpaper covering the walls. Some of the rooms are very cozy, and others are quite spacious. The first-floor room (set off the beaten track) even has a screened in-porch. Many of the rooms have working fireplaces; a rarity in today's country inns. You would expect the baths in an old home to be antiquated; however, guests are pleasantly surprised to find nice modern facilities with charming antique features such as four pedestal bathtubs.

After a good night's sleep, guests will be treated to a lovely Continental breakfast awaiting them on their doorstep. Hot chocolate, coffee, and a choice of teas are always available, as well as an ever-changing selection of muffins. There are also mini refrigerators in the hallways for guests who wish to bring perishables and drinks for picnics or outings. The Maghery's are also more than happy to do anything they can to ensure a comfortable and memorable stay.

FRISKY FRIVOLITIES:
* Hiking on the Appalachian Trail or up local Mt. Everett is a terrific way to spend the day.
* Ask the Maghery's for directions to Race Brook Falls or Bartholomew's Cobble. These are excellent areas for energetic walks and peaceful picnics.
* In the winter, there are miles of cross-country ski trails for both adventurous and novice skiers.

CENTENNIAL HOUSE

94 Main Street
Northfield, Massachusetts 01360
(413) 498-5921
Innkeeper: Marguerite L. Lentz
Rooms: 5 doubles
Rates: $40-50
Payment: Personal checks
Children: Well-behaved children welcome
Dogs: Welcome with a $10 deposit and prior approval
Open: All year

The Centennial House was built in 1811 by the Stearn family, and for many years thereafter was owned by the Northfield Mt. Herman School. In 1982, Marguerite Lentz purchased the home and turned it into a B&B. This massive blue-grey Colonial fronts Northfield's Main Street and stretches back almost half a block. Guests enter through a side door into a glassed-in porch that looks out over the expansive gardens and lawn down to the bend of the Connecticut River.

The enormous dark wood-paneled and beamed-ceiling library is the first room guests enter. This was a later addition to the house, but still has a sense of history. On cold days, a fire is roaring in the huge fireplace at the end of this long room. There are various games scattered about and comfortable sofas for reading and relaxing on after an energetic day. Beyond this chamber lies the main portion of the house, which is as architecturally interesting as it is historic.

Unique parallel staircases lead up to the guest rooms. Each of the spacious guest quarters is individually decorated in old-fashioned prints and subdued colors. Full-length floral draperies frame some of the small-paned windows; others have simpler sheer white curtains. Large oval braided or rag rugs cover the hardwood floors. Simple furnishings are enhanced by brass beds and some period furniture. The five bedrooms share three-and-a-half baths.

A Continental breakfast is served each morning in the front parlor. The aroma of homebaked bread and muffins manages to waft upstairs from the kitchen. Hot chocolate is offered to guests as well as coffee, tea, and juice.

FRISKY FRIVOLITIES:
* Many enjoy the wonderful cross-country skiing this region has to offer. Others prefer to drive along scenic Routes 9 and 119 (traversing the Green Mountain National Park), especially during the foliage season.
* The Connecticut River runs by Northfield and the Northfield Mt. Herman School. Take Bowser over to explore the campus and then for a picnic along the river.
* A 10-minute drive will bring you to both the historic town of Deerfield and Deerfield Academy. There are quiet picturesque streets for walking Bowser.

DEERFIELD INN

The Street
Deerfield, Massachusetts 01342
(413) 774-5587
General Manager: Paul J. Burns
Rooms: 23 doubles
Rates: $72-80 (packages are available)
Payment: All major credit cards
Children: Welcome
Dogs: Welcome
Open: All year, except Christmas

The Deerfield Inn is located on probably one of the most beautifully preserved historic streets in New England. The inn, built in 1884 by George A. Arms of Greenfield, is only one of the many exquisitely restored homes in this quaint town. With the exception of a fire in the main building in 1979 (closing the inn until 1981), the inn has been serving the public since 1885. This, in itself, is no small feat.

The Beehive Parlor is the first room weary travelers will see. With its long-case clock, navy chintz-covered sofas, English reproduction antiques, wingback chairs, and writing tables, this is indeed a cozy place to while away the hours. Guests may be tempted to drop everything in the parlor, but should ignore the urge as they will be pleased upon entering the bedrooms.

All of the rooms are individually decorated with reproduction antiques. Some have brass lamps with handmade cut and pierced lampshades, a butler's table, a tiny Queen Anne mirror, and an overstuffed chintz couch. Others have Bates bedspreads or bright flowered coverlets and matching draperies. Each is unique, cozy, and very intimate. Modern amenities include individually controlled thermostats, but, in keeping with the Colonial feeling, the floors are appropriately squeaky and sloping. The South Wing is a 1981 addition, containing 12 guest rooms connected to the inn by a covered walkway. From the outside it resembles an antique barn; however, all of the rooms have the same cozy, Colonial ambiance found in the main building.

Guests will enjoy dining in the Charles Phillips restaurant, where the entrees range from succulent rack of lamb to delicate salmon and shrimp dishes. The pastry chef concocts delicious homemade desserts that will surely tempt even the most conscientious weight watchers. Guests who have really enjoyed these treats can visit the bakery and pick up an assortment of freshly baked cookies, apple crisp, pecan sweet rolls, or Indian pudding. Sweet tooths will not be disappointed, although your waistline may be.

FRISKY FRIVOLITIES:
* The Deerfield Academy is practically next door to the inn. You will enjoy

taking Bowser for a walk on campus and out to the fields for a run or game of catch.
* There are a number of historic houses all within walking distance of the inn. You will enjoy exploring the small town via the picturesque streets.
* Deerfield has a Valley Art Association sale every July and August, for those who arrive too early to enjoy the spectacular fall foliage.

THE WHALE INN

Route 9, Box 66
Goshen, Massachusetts 01032
(413) 268-7246
Innkeeper: Kenneth T. Walden
Rooms: 4 doubles, 1 suite
Rates: Doubles: $25-45; Suite: $65
Payment: Personal checks
Children: Welcome
Dogs: Welcome
Open: All year

The Whale Inn lies just off the scenic Berkshire trail. This 200-year old, yellow center-chimney cape is surrounded by a spacious lawn and wooded area. The inn is primarily known for its generous and tasty New England fare; however, there are also five rooms on the second floor for travelers. Although not well advertised, guests will find extremely clean, comfortable, and homey accommodations.

Wide pine floors covered with braided or rag rugs are found in each guest chamber. The furnishings are early-American antiques. Many of the beds are quite high, including a wonderful canopy bed. Floral wallpapers cover the walls and white nubbly spreads adorn the beds. Windsor and wing chairs sit off to the side. The rooms are simply decorated but very clean, including the private bathrooms. There is one suite accommodation providing ample room, as well as a television and refrigerator.

Many come to the Berkshire area to see the vibrant fall foliage or to cross-country or downhill ski. Skating is a wonderful winter treat on ice-covered lakes, and in the spring it is fun to watch the maple sugaring process. Visitors find a number of excuses for wanting to see this region and the Whale Inn is certainly a comfortable and peaceful stop along the way.

FRISKY FRIVOLITIES:
* Some of the most scenic and historic New England towns are just a short drive away: Stockbridge, Lenox, Deerfield, and Amherst, to mention a few.
* Others crave the serenity and adventure of the many nearby parks: DAR State Forest, Winsor State Forest, and Mohawk Trail State Forest.
* Cross-country skiing is available throughout the area on groomed and ungroomed trails. Ask the innkeeper for his favorite spots.

THE LORD JEFFERY INN

30 Boltwood Avenue
Amherst, Massachusetts 01002
(413) 253-2576
Innkeeper: David Joslow
Rooms: 50 doubles
Rates: $70-80
Payment: Major credit cards, personal checks
Children: Welcome
Dogs: One well-behaved dog per room
Open: All year

Located among five fine New England colleges, the Lord Jeffery Inn is an idyllic place to spend time, whether visiting a young collegian or just exploring the beautiful countryside. The inn is a perfect mix of history and subtle modern amenities.

From its construction in 1926 through 1986, the Lord Jeffery was owned and operated by Amherst College. Over the years it became increasingly difficult for the college to continue to maintain the inn, both physically and financially. Then, in 1986, David Joslow (the present owner) stepped in and began an overdue restoration process that both preserved the architectural integrity and improved the inn's facilities. After almost a year's work, the inn reopened in October of 1986, with a complete facelift to the public and guest rooms.

Once inside the inn, guests will delight in the number of cozy sitting areas, where they may enjoy a quiet game of backgammon, sit among the many fine antiques, or just visit with friends in front of the walk-in fireplace. The living room is a particularly cozy spot, especially in the brisker winter months. There are also several other alcoves scattered around the inn, where guests may stretch out in front of a warm fire or enjoy the sunlight streaming in through the small-paned windows.

The warmth of the public areas extends to the guest rooms as well. They are individually decorated in simple printed fabrics that nicely contrast with the Williamsburg blue and red wall treatments. Special architectural features include painted wainscottings and gabled ceilings in many of the third floor rooms, and interesting nooks and crannies. The bathrooms are all modern but differ in decor. Each offers guests baskets of Gilchrist and Soames fragrant soaps, shampoos, and other special goodies. The inn does not lack for modern conveniences either, as all bedrooms have direct-dial telephones, cable color televisions, and individual climate controls.

The Lord Jeffery's main dining room is inviting with its warm salmon-colored walls and hunter green accents. Box-beamed ceilings, bow back side chairs, and white tablecloths complete the intimate dining experience. The restaurant serves a wide variety of dishes, Continental in flavor. If guests do not elect to dine at the inn, there are a number of other terrific eateries within walking distance.

FRISKY FRIVOLITIES:
* The Amherst Common is just across the street from the inn. Those wanting a longer jaunt will find the Amherst College campus a terrific area for exercising Bowser.
* There are many historical houses in town within walking distance of the inn. Emily Dickinson's home is located on Main Street, the Robert Frost House in on Sunset, and the Strong House Museum is on Amity Street. (The Chamber of Commerce's *Guide to Sites* is very informative.)
* Northfield Mountain is 40 minutes north of Amherst. This is a terrific recreational area for hiking, picnicking in the summer, and cross-country skiing in the winter.

THE VICTORIAN

583 Linwood Avenue
Whitinsville, Massachusetts 01588
(617) 234-2500
Innkeeper: Rick Clarke
Rooms: 8 doubles
Rates: $90-120
Payment: Most major credit cards
Children: Welcome
Dogs: Welcome with prior approval
Open: All year

     The Victorian was originally built by James Fletcher Whitin in 1871. This 23-room mansion sits atop a knoll, and is flanked by a carriage house and gatehouse. The three-story main house still has a copper mansard roofline. The original 250 acres has dwindled to just 50 acres, but the elegant ambiance is still very much intact.

     Once inside, guests will be impressed with the carefully maintained leather wainscotting and polished walnut, cherry, and mahogany woodworking. Wallpapers are from the Victorian period, and are highlighted by crystal and brass sconces and oil paintings. Everything from the oriental rugs and grand piano to the marble fireplaces and antique furnishings recreate another era.

     Each of the bedrooms is named appropriately for its color scheme or view. Thus, guests who ask for the River Room or Pond Room will have water views. The only fireplace is found in the Armour Room. Most chambers have high ceilings and are very spacious. The king-size beds are often dwarfed by the enormous vertical windows. Additional furnishings of interest include Victorian settees, fainting couches, and highboys. Fresh flowers and live plants are also found in each chamber. The bathrooms are all private.

Continental breakfasts feature fresh baked breads and muffins, fruit, orange juice, coffee, and tea. More substantial meals can be requested at an additional charge. The Victorian is known for its delicious dinners. Guests may either dine in the Louis XV parlor with its romantic fireplace, or in the library amid the endless volumes of books. An ever-changing menu offers filet mignon, pheasant, rack of lamb, salmon in basil sauce, lobster, or roasted duckling. Once sated, guests may wish to take a pleasant walk along the grounds. Whatever your reason for visiting Whitinsville, a stay at The Victorian will transport you back to a truly splendid era.

FRISKY FRIVOLITIES:
* The region to the southwest of Whitinsville is dotted with small lakes as well as state forests and parks.
* Bowser can demonstrate his fishing expertise in the local pond.
* Whitinsville is a quiet area, making it perfect for walks in town or around the inn.

THE WINDSOR HOUSE

38 Federal Street
Newburyport, Massachusetts 01950
(617) 462-3778
Innkeeper: Judith Crumb
Rooms: 3 doubles, 3 suites
Rates: Doubles: $79; Suites: $85
Payment: MC, VISA, personal checks
Children: Welcome
Dogs: Welcome with prior approval
Open: All year

The Federal-style Windsor House was built by Lieutenant Aaron Pardee in 1787, just in time for his wedding. The final result was a combination of a mansion and ship's chandlery, architecturally combining three different styles. After years of assorted owners, the house was renamed the Windsor House in 1978. This sturdy brick building has withstood New England winters for many years, due in part to its massive 18-to-20 inch thick brick walls. However, once in a great while a strong "nor-easter" can actually blow rain into the house through fissures in the brick.

Two sitting rooms occupy the first floor, each simply decorated with period antiques. A wide stairway leads up to the guest bedrooms. Each chamber on the second floor has very high ceilings and is quite spacious. Wide-board floors are covered with area rugs. In addition to the period furnishings, each room is named after its original occupants. The bridal suite occupies one corner of the house, with a queen bed amid a few selected antiques.

The nursery, just across the hall, has floral wallpaper and two antique mahogany beds with carved pineapple finials. (It is interesting to note that all the mattresses in the house were specially made to fit the antique beds.) A crib rests in the corner alongside a comfortable rocking chair that will soothe even the most restless infant. The Nanny's bedroom, appropriately enough, is next to the nursery. This is beautifully and simply furnished. The standouts are the high double bed and Sheraton-style bureau. On the top floor rests Aaron's old study, which has a full wall of floor-to-ceiling bookshelves. From the double bed guests can catch a glimpse of the ocean in the distance. Of the six bedrooms, three share a bathroom and the others have private baths.

People who frequent B&B's have learned that the breakfasts vary greatly in quantity as well as quality. Judith's culinary delights are not to be missed. Breakfast is served around a large oval wooden table, which fills only a portion of the cavernous sunken kitchen. The setting is truly unique with exposed brick occupying an entire wall and huge racks of pots and pans hanging from the open beamed ceilings. Breakfast usually starts with a cup of specially blended coffee and assorted fresh fruit. Then Judith will seek guests' preferences for their eggs, her specialty being herb scrambled eggs with delicious (and spicy) homemade sausage on the side. On other days, she will serve pastries or maybe blueberry pancakes. Guests will definitely appreciate the time and effort Judith puts into her meals and certainly enjoy the conversation and hospitality she provides.

FRISKY FRIVOLITIES:
* After taking in the sights in Newburyport, many opt to visit one of the beaches in the state with the shortest coastline - - New Hampshire.
* If one has the desire to catch a glimpse of a few of New England's most charming and historical towns, a drive to Portsmouth, New Hampshire or Kennebunkport, Maine is worthwhile.
* The Windsor House is located in an historic part of Newburyport. The streets are quiet and inviting for walkers and Bowser.

THE ESSEX STREET INN

7 Essex Street
Newburyport, Massachusetts 01950
(617) 465-3148
Manager: Laurie Pearson Hay
Rooms: 17 doubles and suites
Rates: Doubles: $59-75; Suites: $135
Payment: All major credit cards
Children: Welcome
Dogs: Welcome
Open: All year

The Essex Street Inn was built in 1801 and is located on a quiet one-way street less than a block from Newburyport's main shopping area. This newly renovated old home appears to have been a duplex at one time with matching staircases climbing either side of the dividing center wall. The downstairs parlor has several comfortable couches for guests to relax on, and an antique clock ticks in the corner. Wall-to-wall carpeting is found throughout and wallpaper designs range from seashell patterns to floral prints.

The inn has accommodations to suit all travelers. Each room has air conditioning, a telephone, a color television, and a private bathroom. Some guest rooms are larger than others providing extra space for a sofa and rocking chair. The guest beds vary from four poster to canopy beds and are covered with either white nubbly spreads or Vermont quilts. Antique bureaus and old captain's chests are waiting to be filled with clothes.

Each suite also varies in size as well as furnishings. Fireplaces warm guests on cool nights and patios are refreshing on warm summer evenings. Other special features include gourmet kitchens and large whirlpool baths. There is even a two-bedroom suite, perfect for families, that has two fireplaces, a sitting room, and a loft. A separate building houses three apartments.

FRISKY FRIVOLITIES:
* Whether vistors wish to roam the historic streets of Newburyport, browse through the numerous shops, or just take a stroll down by the park on the waterfront, there is plenty to keep even the most active visitor satisfied.
* There are self-guided walking tours of Newburyport. These run along High Street and focus on housing styles ranging from the 17th to 19th centuries. The Maritime Museum and Chamber of Commerce have brochures and maps.
* Drive down the coast to Cape Ann and visit the historic towns of Rockport, Ipswich, and Annisquam.

THE MORRILL PLACE INN

209 High Street
Newburyport, Massachusetts 01950
(617) 462-2808
Innkeeper: Rose Ann Hunter
Rooms: 10 doubles
Rates: $40-70
Payment: AE, personal checks
Children: Not allowed
Dogs: Welcome with prior approval
Open: All year

The Morrill Place Inn is a beautiful example of one of the many distinguished sea captain's mansions that were built during Newburyport's heyday in the early 1800s. At that time, Newburyport was this country's seventh largest port; however, it soon lost its stature among the ocean-going vessels. Today, after years of struggle, Newburyport is undergoing a revitalization.

The Morrill Place has also recently had a facelift. Several years ago, this 26-room estate was the site of a decorator's showcase. Each of the decorators was responsible for a room in the house. As Rose is quick to point out, no expense was spared even when it came to spending many thousands of dollars to make the balloon curtains for the front living room. In any case, guests will be thoroughly comfortable and visually entranced, as every room is designed in a different classic style.

A dark green runner is a stark contrast to the white painted main staircase leading up to the second and third floor guest rooms. Beds run the gamut from antique four-poster to canopy to day beds. Wide-board floors are adorned with hand painted carpets. Vibrant chintz draperies are found framing the windows, while antique clocks tick amidst the Sheraton-style antiques.

An informal sunlit sitting room awaits people who want to visit with other guests or perhaps watch television. White wicker furniture rests below an enormous mirror framed in fabric, while a ceiling fan sends cool breezes through the room. For those who prefer to wander and find their own little nook, there is still the formal parlor, dining room, living room, and library to recuperate in after a long day.

In the morning, guests will enjoy a delightful Continental breakfast in the dining room. Make sure to look twice at the marble around the fireplace which is actually a "faux finish." This is the art of painting wood to look like marble. This technique has also been applied to the walls, where metal combs have etched out designs in the glaze.

FRISKY FRIVOLITIES:
* Newburyport is a lovely town that is still in transition. Much of the downtown has been beautifully restored and is great fun to wander through.
* In addition to this old New England town, it is well worth the trip to explore the scenic coastline and charming North Shore communities of Marblehead, Manchester, Gloucester, and Annisquam.
* The beaches in this area are beautiful (the water can be quite frosty though) and we recommend a day at Plum Island, Crane's Beach, or Singing Beach.

ANDOVER INN

Chapel Avenue
Andover, Massachusetts 01810
(617) 475-5903
Innkeeper: Henry Broekhoff
Rooms: 31 doubles, 2 suites
Rates: Doubles: $39-79; Suites: $120 per person
Payment: AE, MC, VISA
Children: Welcome
Dogs: "If you can't ride them in, they are welcome."
Open: All year, except the last two weeks in August

The Andover Inn is located on the picturesque campus of Phillips Academy. This traditional brick building is set amid mature trees and well-manicured grounds. A flower-lined brick pathway leads to the front portico. The huge reception area is tastefully decorated with antique furnishings, camelback sofas, and matching arm chairs.

A tiny elevator brings guests to their bedrooms. The second floor rooms have grass or floral wallpapers with contrasting wood paneling and wainscottings. Finial bedsteads are the focal points for the rooms, with writing desks, Queen Anne furnishings, and leather side chairs providing accents. Modern conveniences such as color televisions, air conditioning, radios, and private telephones are also included. The few guest bedrooms that do not have a private modern bathroom are provided with a wash sink. These bed chambers either share an adjoining bathroom or a separate facility is available down the hall. The guest rooms on the third floor are somewhat larger and have gabled or arched ceilings. Views of the campus, Cochran Chapel, and the arts building may be had out of both the second-and third-floor bedrooms.

The small, dark, wood-paneled bar is a favorite gathering place before dinner. Guests can also be found relaxing in one of the many comfortable sitting areas. Dining is a festive affair. Glass chandeliers accent the box-beamed ceilings in the dining room. Formal, full-length draperies and a grand piano enhance the elegant effect. During the week, dinner is accompanied by classical music playing softly in the background. A more exotic event takes place on Sunday nights when a traditional *Rijsttafel* is served. This is a multi-course Indonesian meal based around rice dishes and is very popular. Those desiring a more mild choice of entrees will find a wide selection available, which includes grilled swordfish, scampi flambe, duck a l'orange, and escallopes of veal "Chasseur."

FRISKY FRIVOLITIES:
* The Andover School has a beautiful campus that is perfect for leisurely walks. The buildings' classic architecture and school's expansive grounds are of interest to people and dogs alike.
* The North Shore is a short drive from Andover. Along the way, you will discover quaint coastal towns like Beverly Farms, Manchester, and Annis-quam.
* One of the best features of this area is the abundance of nearby maple sugaring houses and apple picking farms.

THE STEPHEN DANIELS HOUSE

1 Daniels Street
Salem, Massachusetts 01970
(617) 744-5709
Innkeeper: Catherine B. Gill
Rooms: 5 doubles
Rates: $45-65
Payment: Personal checks
Children: Welcome
Dogs: Welcome
Open: All year

The Stephen Daniels House has been in existence since 1667. Sea captain Daniels built the original four-room house. Almost 90 years later in 1756, Daniels' great grandson enlarged the house to its current size of 15 rooms. Remarkably, from 1756 until 1931 his descendants lived in the home. Fourteen years ago it was transformed into a guest house.

The Stephen Daniels House is centrally located to most of Salem's historical sights. It also offers guests the hospitality and comfort they would expect to find at a small New England inn. Walking inside is like taking a step back in time. Sloping wide pine floors creak as guests wander through the house. Years of wear are ingrained in the treads of the steep, winding staircase. Low box-beamed ceilings reflect the light from the enormous fireplaces. There is a true sense of history in the Stephen Daniels House.

Guest rooms are located throughout the inn. One bedroom has a canopied double bed covered with a white nubbly spread. The canopy fabric is also used in the dust ruffle and is draped at the windows. Oriental rugs cover the floors, an antique rocking chair sits off to one side, and a comb-back Windsor armchair sits off to another. Fresh flowers rest on bedside tables, amid period antiques. A Sheraton field bed, blanket and captain's chests, quilts, chairs of all shapes and sizes, muskets, and pewter plates all add to the feeling of antiquity. The house also has built-in alcoves and recessed bookcases holding other treasures.

The tiny back staircase is winding and worth at least one trip up or down. Shelves along the stairs hold a collection of duck decoys. At the base, guests will find an enormous walk-in hearth with iron cookware that looks as though it could still be used. The breakfast room, where a Continental breakfast is served each morning, is on the backside of the hearth. Guests may also choose to take their breakfast outside on the patio, where they can enjoy the surrounding garden and bask in the morning sunshine.

FRISKY FRIVOLITIES:
* Exploring historic Salem can take the better part of a day. A great way to unwind is a pleasant walk through the Salem Common, just a few blocks from the inn.
* Although Salem is indeed a beautiful historical spot, you might want to visit the picturesque towns of Marblehead, Hamilton, Manchester, and Beverly Farms, which are just down the road.
* A longer walk from the inn (although not much) is a trip down Chestnut Street where many sea captain's built their homes during the China Trade days.

SHERMAN-BERRY HOUSE

163 Dartmouth Street
Lowell, Massachusetts 01851
(617) 459-4760
Innkeepers: Susan Scott and David Strohmeyer
Rooms: 1 single, 1 double
Rates: Single: $40; Double: $45
Payment: Personal checks
Children: Welcome. "Children find our home tedious."
Dogs: Welcome with prior approval
Open: All year

The Sherman-Berry House was built in 1893. Its history can easily be traced through the images in the centennial stained-glass window just above the first floor landing. Susan Scott and David Strohmeyer are the fourth family to occupy the house. The Clapps were the original owners, and also opened the first auto repair shop in Lowell. In the window, next to the Clapp family name, is a little wrench. The Bayers had five daughters, and five symbolic balloons are next to their name. David Strohmeyer works with Wang Laboratories and has placed a Wang insignia next to his name.

The house has quite a history, and thanks to the current owners' determination and perseverance, the story will continue. The four-by four-foot stained-glass window is just one of 20 or so other stained-glass windows found throughout the house. Some of these are mounted in window frames and others hang by wires. Susan and David have also completely redecorated their house with a charming selection of wallpapers, antiques, and oriental rugs.

There are a number of common rooms guests will enjoy using. The parlor's hardwood floor is patterned with light and dark inlaid wood. An antique loveseat and intricately carved matching side chairs are upholstered in a soft hunter-green velvet. A marble bust and assorted plants sit atop pedestals. The living room is equally inviting with its sofa, armchairs, and rocking chairs. The fireplace mantle is set with tile and assorted Americana memorabilia is framed on the walls.

The guest chambers are on the second floor. The pink bedroom has a large oriental rug on the hardwood floor, and an antique white iron and brass bedstead covered with a handmade quilt. The second bedroom is similar in design with light streaming in from the windows. It is furnished with a brass trundle bed, antique bureau, and rocking chair. The two chambers share a bathroom.

Each morning guests will congregate in the dining room for a deluxe Continental breakfast. The surroundings are as interesting as the conversation and food. Decorative china lines the wainscotting, an assortment of plants surround the dining room table, and an 1885 Murphy bed resides in the corner. Susan said that the bed is in the process of being restored and will eventually be moved upstairs. We thought it made an excellent conversation piece.

FRISKY FRIVOLITIES:
* The neighborhood has quiet streets that are quite pleasant for early morning or evening walks.
* The inn is a stones' throw from Tyler Park. Those wishing to stray a bit further a field may visit the Lowell National and State Parks.
* Concord, Lexington, and Walden Pond are less than an hour's drive from the inn. These towns are of great historical interest as well as being good walking towns.

THE CHARLES HOTEL

One Bennett at Eliot Street
Cambridge, Massachusetts 02138
(800) 882-1818, (617) 864-1200
Rooms: 300 (inclusive of suites)
Rates: Doubles: $147-207; Suites: $250-1,200 (weekend packages)
Payment: All major credit cards
Children: Welcome
Dogs: Small dogs welcome accompanied by a $100 damage deposit
Open: All year

Harvard Square has always been a hub of activity for Cambridge, while still managing to hold onto its intimate community feeling. The Charles Hotel, just off the Square, exudes a similar ambiance. There is much going on within this well-defined complex in the way of jazz entertainment, fine restaurants, and distinctive stores; however, the hotel is run much like a small inn. There is incredible attention to detail and personal service.

The designers of the Charles Hotel have created interesting ell-shaped guest rooms, allowing for maximum privacy. Electric-blue down quilts have subtle triangular patterns of maroon and gray. Guest rooms are colored in soothing pale gray with maroon and white accents. Overstuffed sofas and matching armchairs allow for total relaxation. Traditional ladder-back chairs are pulled up to light oak writing tables and armoires. Some of the more elaborate suites have pencil post canopy beds, reproduction antique pine armoires, and wet bars. Live plants and arrangements of flowers can be found throughout. All guest rooms have three telephones and two televisions, one in the bedroom and the other in the bathroom. The bathroom also has an elaborate selection of soaps and shampoos. A thick terrycloth robe adds the final touch to this luxurious bathing experience.

The public areas are equally well appointed. Antique quilts hang on the walls throughout the hotel alongside original "realist" art. There is a feeling of light and space throughout the Charles Hotel. Atriums shed sunlight on the live plants; floor-to-ceiling glass windows open onto intimate courtyards. People enjoy sitting outside in the Courtyard Cafe at the end of the day. They can enjoy a casual meal here or perhaps later retreat to Rarities, a more elegant restaurant specializing in beautifully presented and eye appealing New England cuisine.

There is much to do in Cambridge. Harvard Square is a short walk from the hotel, as is the Harvard University campus. There are a myriad of stores, restaurants, and nightclubs all within walking distance. After a day of exploring, Le Pli awaits hotel guests. This is a private spa offering a sun-drenched indoor swimming pool, Nautilus equipment, and aerobic dancing, as well as a full range of herbal body wraps and body massages.

FRISKY FRIVOLITIES:
* The Charles River is a five-minute walk from the hotel. A nice route is down through the John F. Kennedy School of Government park to the river.
* Harvard University is also a few minutes from the hotel. It has a beautiful campus waiting to be explored.
* A walk along Brattle Street will yield numerous historic mansions. Information on these homes can usually be found on the front gates or on pedestals placed along the sidewalk.

HOTEL MERIDIEN

250 Franklin Street
Boston, Massachusetts 02110
(617) 451-1900
General Manager: Bernard Lambert
Rooms: 328 doubles and suites
Rates: Doubles: $170-190; Suites: $350-485 (weekend packages)
Payment: All major credit cards
Children: Welcome
Dogs: Small, very well-behaved dogs welcome
Open: All year

     The Hotel Meridien, housed in the old Federal Reserve Bank building, lies in the heart of Boston's financial district. It is also close to Faneuil Hall Marketplace and the Boston waterfront. The hotel has been deemed an historic landmark, thus the exterior facade cannot be altered. When it was being renovated this presented some interesting architectural problems, but they have been beautifully and creatively solved. The interior design is exquisite and, often times, awe-inspiring.

     Subsequently, the Hotel Meridien has earned a reputation as being one of Boston's most elegant hotels with a staff dedicated to attention to detail. Bedrooms are ell-shaped and some walls (where the old building meets the new) are of sloping glass. Guest rooms vary from the traditional to the modern with as many different decors as there are rooms. Some guests will find their bedroom in a loft with a downstairs sitting area naturally lit by floor-to-cathedral-ceiling windows. Other guest rooms have nooks and crannies housing soft comfortable sofas, canopy beds, live plants, and lovely flower arrangements. Heavy chintz draperies complement quilted bedspreads. Cream-colored walls are accented by warm earth tones people find very pleasing. Each of the guest chambers has a stocked mini bar, AM/FM radio, telephone, and large bathroom complete with a bathroom scale. For those on the move, there is same day valet dry cleaning, shoe shining, foreign currency exchange, and telex facilities.

     In the morning, guests may enjoy a breakfast ordered from room service, complete with a complimentary Wall Street Journal or Boston Globe, or they may choose to dine at the Cafe Fleuri. A six-story atrium filled with light graces those dining in the Cafe. The Cafe's Sunday brunch is notorious for having an extravagant selection of goodies, giving it the reputation as being one of the best brunches in Boston. Evenings at the Hotel Meridien can be spent at Julien's around the grand mahogany bar below the towering gold inlaid ceilings. The cuisine is nouvelle but the architecture is from another era. The narrow windows in the dining room were formerly gun ports guarding the entrance to the building. Today, the old vault once reserved for precious valuables is now the pastry pantry.

Whether one is relaxing in an intimate sitting area, a comfortable guest room, or at one of the Meridien's restaurants, guests are sure to enjoy a sense of privacy and luxury rarely experienced.

FRISKY FRIVOLITIES:
* Many visitors enjoy a walk down by Boston Harbor to the Waterfront Park and through famous Faneuil Hall.
* If you prefer a taste of old Boston, venture up towards the State House, Beacon Hill, and the Boston Common.
* For those who wish to see what is offered outside Boston, we suggest a visit to historic Concord and Lexington.

FOUR SEASONS HOTEL

200 Boylston Street
Boston, Massachusetts 02116
(617) 338-4400
General Manager: Hans Willimann
Rooms: 288 doubles and suites
Rates: Doubles: $150-235; Suites: $330-1,200 (weekend packages)
Payment: All major credit cards
Children: Welcome
Dogs: Small dogs welcome
Open: All year

The Four Seasons Hotel is one of the more recent additions to the Boston hotel scene. Ideally located across from the Boston Public Garden and close to the financial district, Copley Place, and Faneuil Hall, the Four Seasons will delight even the fussiest of travelers.

From the outside, the hotel appears quite modern, but step inside and the scene is one of elegant simplicity. Sitting areas are inviting with deep sofas, side chairs, traditional reproduction antiques, and lavish plantings and floral arrangements. Guests may find the front desk a little difficult to locate as it is unobtrusively tucked into a corner.

The bedrooms are equally as elegant as the public areas. Wallpapers are soft and neutral, and fitted chintz bed coverlets are coordinated with the draperies. Formal wing chairs, marble-topped coffee tables, and Sheraton-style writing tables are softly lit by brass standing lamps. The remote-controlled television lies hidden in a mahogany armoire. The management has tried to anticipate guests' needs by providing three telephones, terrycloth bathrobes, and a stocked mini bar with refrigerator. The rooms have even been designed with windows that actually open, an unusual feature in a city hotel. There are also a number of guest room configurations. The Four Seasons Rooms have parlors separated from the bedroom by folding doors, while standard doubles are spacious and airy. For the special occasion, full-size suites and the exquisite Presidential Suite are also available.

Guests have access to the spa, which is open from 6:00 a.m. to 9:00 p.m. The adjacent lap pool has a terrific view of the Boston Public Garden. Further rest and relaxation can be found in either the whirlpool or sauna. A professional massage is also a delightful option, for those who really want to be pampered.

FRISKY FRIVOLITIES:
* A walk in the Boston Public Garden with your leashed dog is a terrific way to while away the hours. The gardens are well kept and other dog walkers can usually be found there.
* For a more energetic workout, many jog down either Commonwealth Avenue or the Esplanade that parallels the Charles River.
* Should one wish to explore a little further afield, then a trip to Harvard University and Cambridge is always educational (early morning scullers and crew teams practice on the river).

THE LAFAYETTE HOTEL

One Avenue de Lafayette
Boston, Massachusetts 02111
(617) 451-2600
General Manager: Brian G. Kirby
Rooms: 500 doubles and suites
Rates: Doubles: $150-200; Suites: $250-400 (weekend packages)
Payment: Major credit cards
Children: Welcome
Dogs: Small dogs welcome after owners sign a damage release
Open: All year

The Lafayette Hotel is one of the newer hotels in Boston. Tucked away from the hustle and bustle of Boston's downtown, it is only minutes from the financial district, Government Center, and the Downtown Crossing's shopping area. From the outside, the hotel is rather severe and sterile but once inside this new "Swissotel," visitors are immediately met with an elegance, charm, and sophistication many hotels boast of but few can actually deliver. Crystal chandeliers in the capacious lobby cast a cheery glow over the marble floors and mahogany antiques. Magnificent fresh flower arrangements are placed throughout. Private sitting areas afford people an opportunity to visit comfortably.

Guests, after checking in and helping themselves to a Swiss chocolate (or two...), will be escorted to their rooms. Although there are 500 rooms in the building, guests will immediately sense a more intimate atmosphere. This is due, in part, to a tiering system. Each tier is four floors high with bedrooms forming the perimeter around a center atrium. Cozy sitting areas are attractively appointed with deep sofas and elegant reproductions. Warm earth tones predominate.

The bedrooms are also quite elegant although not necessarily spacious. Painted a subtle cream color and accented by green or rose tones, each is warm and welcoming. Beautiful mahogany reproduction English antiques are found in all the rooms. King-size beds are flanked by bedside tables with brass lamps. There are mahogany writing tables and armoires housing television sets alongside well-stocked mini bars. Telephones can be found in both the bedrooms and the well appointed bathrooms. In the evening, guests will return to their rooms to find the beds turned down and yet another Swiss chocolate nestled on the pillow.

A lap pool is available for those who want an early morning swim. There is also a sundeck on the roof for afternoon lounging. After an active or relaxing afternoon, many choose to dine at the Restaurant Le Marquis de Lafayette, which has received many awards for its fine French cuisine. Cafe Suisse is also available to people desiring a more informal and diverse dining experience. There are also a number of excellent restaurants within a block or two of the hotel.

FRISKY FRIVOLITIES:
* Enjoy an invigorating walk in the Boston Common and Boston Public Garden, where many local Back Bay and Beacon Hill residents also bring their dogs for a stroll.
* Should you wish a pleasant spot for an afternoon picnic, a good cross-country ski, or just a natural setting for a walk or jog, Fresh Pond in Cambridge is just the spot.
* Another scenic walk takes visitors to the State House, down Beacon Hill via Chestnut street, along Charles Street, and home via Louisburg Square.

THE RITZ CARLTON HOTEL

15 Arlington Street,
Boston, Massachusetts 02117
(617) 536-5700
Manager: Sigi Brauer
Rooms: 246 doubles, 41 suites

Rates: Doubles: $165-225; Suites: $295-1,000 (weekend packages)
Payment: All major credit cards, personal checks
Children: Welcome
Dogs: Small dogs welcome
Open: All year

The Ritz Carlton is one of Boston's finest landmarks with a reputation for impeccable service, fine food, and elegant accommodations for more than half a century. An extensive renovation was completed in 1985, when guest rooms were stripped down to the bare walls. Windows, wall moldings, plumbing, and ventilation systems were all updated. Even with extensive refurbishing, the charm and character of the grand old hotel remain intact. This is evident upon entering the lobby, where the elegant decor and furnishings can still transport one back to the days of Brahmin opulence. The ornate woodworking glows with renewed life and, of course, every ounce of brass has been polished to a brilliant luster. This is one of the few hotels left in the United States where white-gloved elevator operators and a butler on every floor are still fashionable.

The newly refurbished guest rooms are decorated in a French Provincial style, complete with an armoire housing a television set, fully stocked honor bar, and refrigerator. The effect would not be complete, however, without the crystal lamps, large beveled mirrors, and spacious bathrooms. Some of the suites overlook the Boston Public Garden and others the twinkling lights of Newbury Street. Suites with crackling fireplaces have warmed many a soul during cold New England nights.

The hotel offers many enticing excuses for venturing out of the cozy bedrooms. Guests may savor High Tea and dine on scones and delicate sandwiches while sipping imported teas in a traditional English fashion. Guests may also choose to eat either in the exquisite dining room or the less formal Ritz Cafe (serving breakfast, lunch, dinner, and after-theatre supper). The Ritz Bar is an institution, one that local Bostonians typically frequent after a workday.

The Ritz is indeed a special spot, consistently and conscientiously making an effort to meet guests' every need. It also happens to be centrally located to most of Boston's cultural and tourist attractions.

FRISKY FRIVOLITIES:
* Boston is a walking city. One of the nicest and most educational walks is along the Freedom Trail. Sturdy walking shoes are in order as the hills, cobblestoned streets, and length of the trail can be tough on the feet.
* Wander across the Boston Public Garden, to shops and restaurants on

Charles Street and then up onto Beacon Hill.
* The Boston Common is the place for dog lovers in the early morning and evening hours. The local residents of both the Back Bay and Beacon Hill frequently meet here to let their dogs frolic together while they talk (corner of Beacon and Charles streets).

RASBERRY INK

748 Country Way
North Scituate, Massachusetts 02060
(617) 545-6629
Hosts: Frances Honkonen and Carol Hoban
Rooms: 2 doubles
Rates: $50
Payment: Personal checks

Children: Permitted on occasion
Dogs: Welcome with prior approval
Open: All year

Located in a small South Shore coastal town, the Rasberry Ink is a beautiful 19th-century white clapboard farmhouse with raspberry colored shutters. Set behind spruces, pines, and a red maple tree, the small front yard is nicely landscaped. The brass wind chimes and American flag blowing in the breeze catch guests' attention until Carol and her dog come to greet them.

The foyer leads guests either off to the left into the dining room or directly upstairs to the bedrooms. Ascending the naturally stained stairs, one cannot help but notice how light and airy the house appears. The floral-wallpapered hallway leads to the Yellow Room. This bed chamber has hardwood floors covered with braided rugs and warm grasspaper-covered walls. The mahogany dresser nicely complements the large four-poster bed in this simply furnished room. Further down the hall, guests come to the Oak Room named for its large carved oak headboard. This bedroom has a pretty armoire with a mirror and marble top and a comfortable loveseat. Both guest rooms share a modern white and black tiled bathroom, which features a circular brass shower curtain rod above the tub. There is also an inviting sitting room just down the hall.

Each morning, guests are served breakfast at the large dining room table. They can expect a fruit salad, juice, cereal, eggs or an omelet of their choice, fresh muffins or breads, pancakes, or possibly some other surprise from Carol's culinary bag of tricks. While conversing with the other guests, take a moment to look at the mirror set into the carved wood mantle over the brick fireplace.

The rest of the morning could be spent leisurely reading the paper in the Presidential rockers on the porch. Others may wish to stretch their legs with a pleasant walk to the village. Whatever one's reason for visiting this historic area, the simple charm and elegance of Rasberry Ink will surely have guests returning before too long.

FRISKY FRIVOLITIES:
* The South Shore has many small, picturesque towns with interesting histories and walkable streets. You may wish to visit Hingham, Cohasset, and Plymouth.
* The beach is only a few minutes away from the B&B, with an even wider selection scattered north and south of Scituate.
* Duxbury offers visitors panoramic views of the South Shore from the top of Myles Standish Monument. You may also enjoy a picnic in the park beneath the monument.

LITTLE HARBOR GUEST HOUSE

20 Stockton Shortcut Road
Wareham, Massachusetts 02571
(617) 295-6329
Host: Dennis Coppola
Rooms: 4 doubles, 1 suite
Rates: $47-67 (off-season rates available)
Payment: Personal checks
Children: Welcome
Dogs: Welcome with prior approval
Open: All year

The Little Harbor Guest House is a rambling red Cape Cod-style home built around 1700. For those who love the quiet, like to play a little golf, and want to be within walking distance of the beach, this is just the place. The guest house is located on the road leading to the Little Harbor Country Club and is surrounded on all sides by green fairways. Despite what some may think, the house has never been hit by a golf ball (nor have the guests).

The first floor of the house is comprised of spacious living and dining rooms. A sectional sofa and chairs are grouped around the enormous hearth in the living room, where the ticking of clocks can be heard in the background. The inn's clock collection is quite extensive and will surely be of interest to aficionados. The adjacent dining room is painted a warm pink, and delicate roses and other flowers are painted on the fireplace mantle and around the base of the chandelier. Breakfast consists of handmade pastries, fresh fruits, and coffee and tea.

The upstairs guest bedrooms are separated into two clusters. The two chambers at the top of the stairs are decorated in pinks and greens and are comfortably furnished. The two other rooms are found down a rambling hallway. One of these bedrooms has a canopy bed with a floral bedspread matching the canopy coverlet. Pink pencil-thin lines have been painted on the bed posts, accenting the pink on the fireplace mantle. The last room could be called the Yellow Room. This has two double beds and an extensive array of white wicker furniture. A view of the front yard and golf course can be had through the small-paned windows.

The inn has a good-sized pool on the grounds and three acres of property to enjoy. Guests might also be interested in the golf or just the beauty of nearby Mattapoiset, Marion, or the Cape Cod area. The Little Harbor Guest House is a pleasant retreat after an active day exploring this scenic region.

FRISKY FRIVOLITIES:
* You may opt to either take a pleasant walk down the road toward the beach or along the dirt road to the left of the inn.
* For those who are anxious to explore historic New Bedford (Whaling City) the entire downtown has been refurbished with cobblestone streets leading to many quaint shops and cafes.
* Marion is a short drive from the inn. The harbor, Tabor Academy, the town's shops and historic district are all within easy walking distance from one another.

HAWTHORNE HILL B&B

P.O. Box 777, Grove Street
Sandwich, Massachusetts 02563
(617) 888-3336
Host: Maxime Caron
Rooms: 2 doubles
Rates: $60
Payment: Personal checks
Children: Small children not accepted
Dogs: Welcome with prior approval
Open: May through November

Some eight years ago, Roger and Maxime Caron discovered a picturesque location, overlooking Shawmee Pond, for their new home. After painstaking clearing, grading, and landscaping this overgrown lot, Roger began building the house himself. All of these major projects took longer than expected but the final result is a custom-built home on a lovely piece of property.

A long gravel driveway leads visitors a half mile or so back onto the property. Guests begin to appreciate the calm and tranquility of this intimate B&B almost immediately. The house is set atop a small knoll, and is surrounded by a sloping lawn and garden in the front and woods leading down to the dock and the pond in the back. The guest rooms and living areas occupy the entire left-hand wing of the house. There is a living room (solarium) used both as a comfortable sitting area and a breakfast room. When the weather is agreeable, breakfast is served on the wraparound deck. The morning meal usually features a variety of fresh fruits, croissants, and muffins; however, for those hearty appetites Maxime is always willing to prepare larger meals. For early risers, there is always a pot of fresh coffee waiting.

The two cozy guest rooms should keep even the early birds comfortably in bed until the aroma of breakfast titillates their taste buds. The two rooms are similar in decor. Floral curtains hang at the windows, matching the dust ruffles and comforters. Each chamber has a private bath, although one must be reached by walking across the hall. The baths are modern and quite spacious, clean, and cheerfully decorated. Fragrant soaps enhance guests' showers, while heat lamps and nice thick towels warm chilly bodies.

Guests will most likely want to relax in the living room in front of the two crackling fireplaces, with terrific views of the pond and the woods surrounding it. Maxime will ensure that her guests' stay is both comfortable and rewarding. She can suggest several fun and interesting areas that she enjoys visiting, as well as mentioning activities that may be appropriate for her guests.

FRISKY FRIVOLITIES:
* This B&B has plenty of property for even the most active dog to play on (accompanied of course), not to mention a pond for swimming. Maxime has a large friendly dog named Fritz.
* Those who would prefer to walk a bit can reach the center of Sandwich in 15 minutes. Many of the local streets are very quiet and ideal for more introspective souls.
* Cape Cod and its various beaches provide peaceful walks for a well-behaved canine companions. Maxime has several favorites and she will gladly pass them on.

THE SUMMER HOUSE

158 Main Street
Sandwich, Massachusetts 02563
Host: Pamela J. Hunt
(617) 888-4991
Rooms: 5 doubles
Rates: $50-60
Payment: MC, VISA
Children: Over 10 years old accepted
Dogs: Small dogs accepted with prior approval
Open: April through Thanksgiving

The Summer House is an exquisitely renovated 1800's Greek Revival home located in Sandwich, a Cape Cod town that has managed to retain much of its original charm. The innkeeper, Pamela Hunt, is personally responsible for much of the work that has gone into making the house a showplace. The inn is a true delight for those lucky people who discover it.

Pamela has dedicated a great amount of her time to restoring much of the inn's ornate woodwork and hardware. Fireplaces grace almost all of the rooms, lending an inviting charm and coziness. Pamela has called upon her artistic talent by handpainting beautiful designs and intricate rugs on the hardwood floors. Where she does not use vibrant, rich wallpapers, Pamela instead hangs gathered fabric on the walls. The spacious guest rooms are furnished with well-preserved antique furniture, including the beds, some of which are quite high. Simple Bates bedspreads or comforters cover them, which is appropriate as they do not detract from the other details in the rooms.

After a good night's sleep, a special treat awaits hearty breakfast appetites. An assortment of delicious homemade muffins and fresh fruit is presented to guests in the cheery breakfast room. The black-and-white checked floors contrast with the deep red walls and white trim, creating a dramatic effect. After breakfast, guests may pass through gigantic sliding, paneled wooden doors into a parlor painted in a deep forest green. Sated guests can settle onto two sofas there and enjoy one of the many books or games available.

Sandwich is a wonderful town to use as a base for exploring the Cape and the Summer House is a special place to come home to each day.

FRISKY FRIVOLITIES:
* The Cape offers a interesting selection of towns to explore, including Hyannis, Osterville, Chatham, and Provincetown.
* The many local beaches are quite inviting; however, guests should also try to explore the scenic back roads adjacent to King's Road (Route 6A).
* There are many interesting walks from the inn. One in particular takes people to Shawmee Pond with its green sloping banks and lush foliage overhanging the water.

HARBOR VILLAGE

P.O. Box 635
Hyannis Port, Massachusetts 02647
(617) 775-7581
Manager: Marijane Mahan
Rooms: 20 one-to four-bedroom cottages
Rates: $750-1,200 per week (daily rates available off-season)
Payment: Personal checks
Children: Welcome
Dogs: Welcome with prior approval
Open: May to mid-October

Over the years, Hyannis and Hyannis Port have received an inordinate amount of media attention due as much to their celebrated residents as to their white sand beaches and warm waters. As a result, this once sleepy summer community has become inundated with tourists and retirees. It is still a popular vacation spot; the trick is in finding a peaceful corner to call your own. The Harbor Village in Hyannis Port offers a solution.

The Harbor Village cottages are only a few minutes from downtown Hyannis, but the 17 acres surrounding this retreat make it seem more like a few hours. A black iron fence and cobblestone pillars flank the entrance to the gravel drive leading to the resort. Guests wend their way through groves of pine trees and planters overflowing with flowers until they arrive at their cottage, some of which are replicas of famous Cape Cod homes. Each is privately owned and thus unique in both design and decor. Split rail fences and decorative wells add character.

The exteriors vary from grey weathered shingles to painted clapboards and shutters. Some of the small-paned windows are decorated with window boxes overflowing with flowers. Yards are attractively landscaped; large decks offer views of the tidal cove or woods. Although the interior decor ranges from contemporary to a more simple and traditional New England look, all cottages do have special amenities. The kitchens are fully equipped (some have dishwashers) and have an adjacent dining room or separate eating area. Living rooms have fireplaces and cable television hook-ups. Linens, towels, and blankets are provided, as is daily maid service. Guests should, before making a reservation, decide which amenities and furnishings they prefer, and where they want to be located with respect to the water. (Each cottage has a water view, some more distant than others.)

The Harbor Village offers all guests direct access to the tidal cove, a private boathouse, and a sandy beach. It is ideal for those who prefer to be off the beaten track, but still close enough to the stores and restaurants.

FRISKY FRIVOLITIES:
* A footpath leads out to Quohog Beach. This is a favorite walk in the early morning and evening.
* The ferries leave from Hyannis Port for Nantucket and Martha's Vineyard. A day trip is feasible to both islands.
* A morning walk into Hyannis Port is a pleasant way to start the day. There is a small newsstand where you can get the paper, and the streets at this hour are uncrowded.

THE LAMB AND LION

Main Street
P.O. Box 511
Barnstable, Massachusetts 02630
(617) 362-6823
Innkeepers: Joanne and David Rice
Rooms: 10 doubles
Rates: $55-105 (weekly and off-season rates available)
Payment: MC, VISA
Children: Welcome
Dogs: Quiet, well-trained dogs welcome
Open: All year

The Lamb and Lion is located on the more tranquil north side of Cape Cod, yet it is only a few minutes from bustling Hyannis and the ferry boats taking visitors out to Martha's Vineyard and Nantucket. The inn consists of several buildings, each offering unique accommodations. The Colonial house, built in 1740, faces the road. Most of the guest rooms surround the outdoor swimming pool. Each of these bedrooms is bright and summery, bedspreads and cushions having matching floral prints. Country antiques and white wicker furniture complement the decor in these spacious rooms.

The solarium also has white wicker couches and chairs, dramatically appointed with black cushions with tiny bright flowers. The airy sensation of the room is enhanced by the views of the gardens and the pool through the floor-to-ceiling windows. In the morning, the solarium is used as the breakfast room, while at the end of the day it is a favorite gathering spot for cocktails.

For those desiring something more spacious or perhaps out of the ordinary, there is the honeymoon suite with a fireplace, sunken bathtub, and private deck. Families or groups of friends might want to take advantage of the converted barn, built in 1740. This exudes a more rustic, Colonial feeling and offers guests a variety of accommodations, along with a full kitchen, living room, and private patio. Finally, there is also a one-bedroom cottage with a sleeping loft. This has a separate entrance, affording guests the privacy they require.

The inn is ideal for those looking for a tranquil setting and a diversified selection of guest rooms. In addition to antiquing and playing golf, many guests just enjoy meeting new people and relaxing in true Cape Cod style.

FRISKY FRIVOLITIES:
* Visitors to this area may wish to visit the scenic towns of Sandwich, Osterville, and Hyannis.
* The Rices can suggest local beaches based on your need for warm or cold water and desire for privacy.
* Those who are looking for a full day trip should either venture out to Provincetown and the Cape Cod National Seashore or take a ferry to either Nantucket or Martha's Vineyard (from Hyannis).

THE VILLAGE INN

Box 1, Route 6A
Yarmouth Port, Massachusetts 02675
(617) 362-3182
Innkeepers: Mac and Esther Hickey
Rooms: 10 doubles
Rates: $36-60
Payment: Personal checks
Children: Welcome
Dogs: Well-behaved dogs accepted
Open: All year

Visitors to the villages along Cape Cod's King's Road (Route 6A) will be pleased to discover an area brimming with New England history. This part of the Cape remains relatively unspoiled and unchanged, one of the few exceptions being that many of the traditional sea captain's homes now house country inns or antique shops. The Village Inn is one such example. Built in 1795 for a local sea captain, this Colonial home stands in the heart of Yarmouth Port's historic district.

The Hickey's, have done much in the way of updating the inn, obviously bearing in mind its unique and special historical features. Guest rooms are simply decorated, with maple headboards crowning beds draped in calico coverlets. These country furnishings serve to highlight the natural beauty of the house. Wainscottings and ceiling moldings are found in some rooms and low beamed ceilings in others. Narrow fireplaces and built-in bookshelves all enhance the coziness of the inn. Wide-board floors are painted an avocado green. One particularly interesting bathroom on the first floor has an antique copper bathtub, a fireplace, and thick towels draped over a freestanding towel rack.

Guests will find themselves spending their time in the inviting living room, which is loaded with books and antiques. The front parlor is equally as charming but just a bit more secluded. Breakfast is served on the enclosed porch and consists of homemade breads, coffee, and juice. Should guests request it, a more substantial meal can be prepared.

After breakfast, many enjoy walking through the nicely landscaped back yard shaded by ancient elms. A leisurely drive down Route 6A will lead to one of the other charming historic villages, where guests may take advantage of the ponds and saltwater beaches.

FRISKY FRIVOLITIES:
* Yarmouth Port is an interesting town to walk through. The overall feeling is mostly residential with shops scattered along Main Street.
* Bustling Hyannis offers ferry trips to both Nantucket and Martha's Vineyard.
* A fun way to spend the day is to pick up bicycle map and ride along some of the more remote back roads on the Cape.

THE HARGOOD HOUSE

493 Commercial Street
Provincetown, Massachusetts 02657
(617) 487-1324
Owners: Harold Goodstein and Robert Harrison
Rooms: 17 apartment suites
Rates: $80-141 daily; $545-970 weekly (off-season rates available)
Payment: Travelers' and personal checks
Children: Well-behaved children over 10 years old welcome
Dogs: One small-to medium-sized dog accepted per apartment with prior approval
Open: All year

If your idea of a beach vacation is a fully equipped spacious apartment, an unobstructed water view, privacy, and self sufficiency, then the Hargood House is a terrific choice. Located on the water's edge in four buildings dating back to the 1800s, the complex provides a combination of old-fashioned grace and modern ingenuity. Fabulous bay views may be had through the floor-to-ceiling windows, which can be opened to allow the invigorating sea air to flow through the apartment. Of course, guests always have the option of resting in a hammock on their own private deck, or enjoying the warmth of a Franklin stove while watching the fog roll in on a cool New England evening.

It is difficult to describe the average apartment at the Hargood House, as each is unique. Your hosts have traveled the world, collecting additional antique furniture and knick knacks with each subsequent trip. Leather chairs from Spain might be mixed in with a more traditional English butler's tray table. The architectural design ranges from exposed beams in several apartments to a combination of brick and rough hewn wall boards in another guest room, creating the ambiance of a ship's cabin. Or, perhaps your unit will be decorated in bright floral patterns.

Thankfully, guests will always find the kitchens to be well stocked with matching china and good quality stemware and flatware. Dishwashers and large refrigerators complete the modern touches. Linens are included, and the daily maids do a great job of both meeting guests needs and keeping the apartments spic and span.

We suspect that the water lapping at the pilings will draw most people out of their apartments and into the sun. There is a green lawn and a small sand beach behind the seawall, for guests to enjoy. Hours may be spent here reading or just watching the tide come in and out of the bay.

The Hargood House offers something for everyone who wants to enjoy the benefits of being both close to the heart of a town and right on the water's edge. From its location on Commercial Street, the complex is within easy walking distance of the downtown art galleries, restaurants, and boutiques.

FRISKY FRIVOLITIES:
* Those who are on an extended stay and are craving the attractions of a major city may take a ferry directly to downtown Boston.
* After seeing the sights in Provincetown, many wish to savor some of the Cape's other quaint towns like Chatham, Bass River, Osterville, and Sandwich.
* There are many houses of historical interest, not to mention of architectural intrigue. The narrow winding streets are often quite uncrowded early in the morning, the best time of day for capturing a true impression of this town's character.

RED INN

15 Commercial Street
Provincetown, Massachusetts 02657
(617) 487-0050
Innkeepers: Duane and Mary-Jo Abare
Rooms: 3 doubles
Rates: $95-125
Payment: All major credit cards
Children: Not appropriate for children
Dogs: Small, well-behaved dogs welcome
Open: All year

We consider the Red Inn to be a rather special find. It combines a wonderful and intimate waterfront restaurant with the added bonus of three relatively undiscovered rooms. The Federal-style inn dates back to 1805 and everything has been done to preserve this feeling. Low ceilings serve to reflect the warmth of the fires burning in the many original fireplaces. Narrow hallways will either lead diners out into a cozy bar or into one of the elegant dining rooms. Tables encircled by Windsor chairs that rest on creaky wide pine floors enhance the historic feeling. Each common room has expansive views of the bay through floor-to-ceiling windows.

The Red Inn used to be known exclusively as a restaurant and had developed quite a reputation for its fine cuisine. Special lobster dishes are always on the menu, as is a wide selection of excellent beef entrees and even pork chops brought in from Vermont. Of course, the seafood is always plentiful with swordfish, Cape Cod scrod, and bluefish topping the list. Diners should show restraint on the main courses as the inn offers irresistible desserts. After dinner, sated guests may retire to their rooms, open a paned window, and drift off to sleep to the melodic sounds of the foghorn and the lulling effects of the crisp salt air.

The guest rooms can be reached by a very narrow staircase (in fact some people have to turn sideways to walk up it). Each of the bedrooms is located directly off the cozy, creaky hardwood-floored landing. Care has been taken to decorate each with interesting antiques and period furnishings. One room actually resembles a sitting room with a handsome Sheraton writing table set alongside a more rustic naturally finished sweater chest. The ceilings are a little (maybe a few inches) over six feet, which adds to the intimate feeling. A comfortable queen-size bed folds out of the couch. The bath is private and just across the hall, and since there are only these two rooms in this section of the inn, guests are assured of complete seclusion. The other bedrooms have either a canopied bed or twin beds adorned with handmade patchwork quilts.

FRISKY FRIVOLITIES:
* Visitors might wish to take a walk by the Seth Nickerson House (the oldest house) to see a 1746 classic cape, or if you prefer to see the town in a somewhat different fashion, pick up a horse-drawn carriage from Town Hall.
* There are several walking and bicycling trails along the beach and over the dunes to explore.
* If you have already completed the Historical Society's walking tour, there is always the Fall Arts Festival or the Fine Arts Work Center to give you new insights into the art world.

WHITE WIND INN

174 Commercial Street
Provincetown, Massachusetts 02657
(617) 487-1526
Innkeeper: Sandra Rich
Rooms: 13 doubles and suites
Rates: $24-85 (off-season rates available)
Payment: All major credit cards
Children: Welcome
Dogs: Welcome in first-floor rooms
Open: All year

Provincetown maintains much of its charm because of the quaint winding one-way streets; however, this can create quite a problem in the summertime as traffic tends to become quite congested. The White Wind Inn, with its in-town location, allows guests the luxury of parking their cars upon arrival and never having to use them again. Walking is the perfect mode of transportation to stores, restaurants, and the beach.

In the mid-1800s, the inn served as home to a wealthy shipbuilder, but for the last 17 years Sandra Rich has owned and operated it as a guest house. High ceilings create a sense of spaciousness in many of the rooms, and antiques and soft plush carpeting lend warmth to others. Each of the accommodations is individually and tastefully decorated. One has a mahogany four-poster bed with a forest green flowered spread, a fireplace, a refrigerator, and a television; and many of the other rooms have more of an art deco feeling created with ceiling fans and modern furnishings. If guests are craving balconies overlooking the water, a small sitting area, and a private entrance, the White Wind Inn can easily meet these needs.

Many like to gather in the morning on the front veranda to sit in the deck chairs, sip a cup of freshly brewed coffee, and watch the world pass by the inn. A small, quiet beach is located directly across the way for refreshing dips, and of course there are always the larger Provincetown beaches for a full day at the shore.

FRISKY FRIVOLITIES:
* The stores, galleries, and restaurants are all within easy walking distance of the inn.
* After visiting the monument depicting where the Pilgrims first landed, you may wish to try your hand at surf casting along the "back shore" for striped bass and blues.
* Should you not have access to the water by boat, many opt to take an excursion on the Portuguese Princess Whale Watch (which allows one or two dogs per boatride at no extra charge).

WATERMARK INN

603 Commercial Street
Provincetown, Massachusetts 02657
(617) 487-2506, 487-0165
Innkeepers: Kevin Shea and Judy Richland
Rooms: 10 doubles and suites
Rates: $95-170 (off-season and weekly rates available)
Payment: MC, VISA, personal checks

Children: Not accepted
Dogs: Welcome in first-level suites with hardwood floors
Open: All year

The Watermark Inn is on Commercial Street, a bit removed from the bustling center of Provincetown yet still within walking distance. A slate walkway leads guests into a grassy courtyard shaded by a large tree. The gray-shingled facade of a two-century-old building is all that remains unchanged today; the inside has been architecturally altered to make the most of the waterviews, sunlight, and ocean breezes.

The inn is comprised of spacious suites, each having a bedroom, living room, and private bath. Living rooms are placed where they can take maximum advantage of the water views. Guests in first-floor suites facing the water can even hear the waves lapping at the pilings supporting the sundeck. By opening the sliding glass doors, this mesmerizing sound can be heard throughout the apartment. The bedrooms have louvered doors allowing for both privacy and a nice air flow. The walls have been painted white and the hardwood floors are lightly stained. The boxed beams add further dimension to many of these architecturally interesting units. Sunny and airy rooms give guests the sense of being in a private summer house. The spaciousness is further enhanced with a simple decor of Scandinavian furnishings, Marimeko fabrics, and equally cheery paintings and wall coverings.

The inn has a private sandy beach, which at low tide extends almost a quarter mile out into the bay. Guests have been known to relax here for days, leaving only to slip back into the privacy of their suites. The modern simplicity of the accommodations combined with the tranquility of the ocean will surely make anybody's stay a most pleasant one.

FRISKY FRIVOLITIES:
* Provincetown is a fun artistic community to explore (there is an historical tour available) with good shops and restaurants, not to mention beaches.
* There are several self-guided nature trails that are quite enjoyable: one at Province Lands and two others at Pilgrim Heights.
* At low tide it is nice to walk along the bay with your dog. Watch the tide carefully though to make sure you can return safely.

POINT WAY INN

Corner of Main Street and Pease Point Way
Box 128
Edgartown, Massachusetts 02539
(617) 627-8633
Innkeepers: Linda and Ben Smith
Rooms: 14 doubles, 1 suite
Rates: Doubles: $55-165
Payment: AE, MC, VISA, personal checks
Children: Welcome
Dogs: Welcome in two of the guest rooms
Open: All year

A 150-year-old sea captain's house is an ideal and charming setting for Edgartown's Point Way Inn. Set at the top of Main Street and surrounded by high evergreen hedges, there is an aura of serenity about the inn even though the bustling downtown is just two blocks away. As you enter the courtyard, you will pass by a whitewashed gazebo set amid gardens and a large lawn (the site of many an afternoon croquet match). Step inside the door and you will feel as though you have jumped back in time, as the old photographs and news clippings recount the Smiths' family history.

Ben and Linda Smith bought the inn in the summer of 1979, after returning from a year-and-a-half cruise with their daughters, Leslie and Marni. The original structure and the end result of their intensive labor is a clear study in contrasts. They began their project with a rotten front porch, three bathrooms, a poor architectural layout, and an abundance of optimism. Today, they have a structurally sound house, 16 bathrooms (although some are quite tiny), and 15 well-planned, cozy guest chambers.

The bedrooms are individually decorated with antiques, interesting floral wallpapers, and assorted four-poster, canopy, and antique beds. The Smiths have included thoughtful touches such as pin cushions (for quick repairs), chocolates on the beds, sherry to warm the soul on those cool Martha's Vineyard nights, and an assortment of interesting books. Guests with dogs are welcome in two of the inn's bedrooms with private entrances. One cozy green and white bedroom is on the ground floor. Its bright summer cottage effect is created through the use of simple furnishings and a brass bed. Above this room is a more spacious suite with a woodstove, double bed, comfortable couch, and a private deck.

In the morning, a Continental breakfast is served either in the sunny garden or out in the gazebo. Fresh breads, juices, coffee/tea, and milk are a few of the offerings. Later, guests may want to join Ben as he ventures out to dig littlenecks. If the morning is chilly, some guests opt to settle down in the library with a good book in front of the Franklin stove. Those who are early to return from the beach or exploring the island will find afternoon tea awaiting them. Many are subsequently drawn into a spirited game of croquet.

FRISKY FRIVOLITIES:
* Mornings are a wonderful time to go on a quiet walk through Edgartown, down North Water Street to Lighthouse Beach. There you can walk and beachcomb, while Bowser enjoys a dip in the ocean.
* Another pleasant day trip is ferrying over to Chappaquidick and heading out to Wasque for a little surfcasting.
* After exploring the many shops and boutiques, many head up-island to Gay Head, West Tisbury, and Menemsha (where the lifestyle is a little less hectic and the towns far less commercial).

THE DR. SHIVERICK HOUSE

Box 640, Pent Lane
Edgartown, Massachusetts 02539
(617) 627-8497
Innkeeper: Tena McLoughlin Ramsdell
Rooms: 8 doubles, 2 suites
Rates: Doubles: $125; Suites: $350
Payment: MC, VISA, personal checks
Children: Welcome
Dogs: Welcome
Open: All year

The Dr. Shiverick House lies half a block from the head of Edgartown's charming Main Street. Originally built in 1840, Dr. Clement Shiverick soon after added a wing to accommodate his office and waiting room. After his death, his wife decided to incorporate a few of her favorite forms of southern architecture and design. In 1875, she had the house rotated, added another wing, and completely redecorated the interior. Over the years, this simple two story family residence has been added to and refurbished many times.

Upon entering the gracious hallway, guests will begin to appreciate not only the attention to detail in restoring this 19th-century mansion, but also the use of period antiques to recreate the ambiance of the 1800s. High ceilings are also found throughout. Each guest chamber is decorated a little bit differently with romantic floral wallpapers or perhaps cream-colored walls with contrasting mocha trim. The honey-hued pine floors are covered with oriental rugs. Resting upon these are Chippendale and Queen Anne-style antiques and high canopy or four-poster beds adorned with dust ruffles and pretty quilts. Brass fixtures softly illuminate the rooms at night. Crackling fireplaces warm cold toes, while dried wreaths and cheery prints hanging on the walls add color and whimsy. Guests will be happy to know that each of the bedrooms has a modern private bathroom.

Many people head in to the "sun-drenched solarium" after a hearty Continental breakfast and relax in one of the comfortable overstuffed chairs or sofas affording views of the brick patio and flower gardens. Although this is an ideal spot for afternoon reading or conversation, there is also a breezy second-floor porch that overlooks the rooftops of Edgartown. Whatever your reason is for visiting Martha's Vineyard, the Dr. Shiverick House will provide you all the hospitality and comfort desired; while the nearby sights, shops, and beaches will satisfy your yearning for a picturesque New England vacation.

FRISKY FRIVOLITIES:

* Light House Beach is only a 15-minute walk through town. On the return trip, a quick left down towards the Chappaquiddick ferry will bring you back along the harbor.
* Although visitors should definitely explore Edgartown and Vineyard Haven, they should not miss a trip up-island, where the beautiful natural surroundings, less commercial towns, and friendly people are the true heart and soul of the Vineyard.
* Water buffs, can rent a boat down by the harbor or try their hand at fishing for some bluefish.

CAPTAIN R. FLANDERS

North Road, #252
Menemsha, Massachusetts 02535
(617) 627-5544
Host: Elizabeth Flanders
Rooms: 2 singles, 4 doubles
Rates: Singles: $40; Doubles: $75-90
Payment: Personal checks
Children: Welcome
Dogs: Welcome
Open: April 15 to November 15

The Captain R. Flanders is located up-island from the larger and more crowded towns of Vineyard Haven, Oak Bluffs, and Edgartown. This part of Martha's Vineyard does not have ferry boats, expensive boutiques, or a plethora of restaurants. Instead, one will find winding back roads that pass by scenic ponds, remote beaches, and classic Vineyard homes. Stone walls covered in wild roses seem to meander for miles. "Up-island" has still managed to maintain the essence of the Vineyard. It is where people can find the true bohemians, as well as those seeking seclusion.

The Captain R. Flanders house is just off North Road, outside the fishing port of Menemsha. A small sandy lane leads guests by an old windmill and a gently sloping field with grazing horses. The Captain R. Flanders is primarily comprised of a few farm buildings, although the rooms are in the central house. From the outside it appears to be a little rustic, but once inside guests will have quite a different feeling. The original wide pine floors in the spacious living room are nicely complemented by a large brick fireplace. Ornamental plates are lined up along the pale blue molding on the near wall. A grandfather clock and some Queen Anne-style antiques add a touch of formality to the simply furnished home. There is a backgammon table for those who want to play board games, and for the more sedentary there is a soft sofa perfectly positioned to take advantage of the nice view of the pond. Just off the living room is a screened-in porch set with small tables and bow-back chairs. A Continental breakfast is served here each morning.

The bedrooms are individually decorated, some more simply than others. White walls are highlighted with yellow trim. One guest room has a double bed with a Bates spread, dhurrie rug, and a terrific old-fashioned painted rockinghorse. Creaky back stairs lead guests to the remaining rooms. Shared, as well as private, baths are available.

Guests will find their hosts willing to give them the run of the farm.

After serving breakfast, your chefs are off again and guests are welcome to make themselves at home.

FRISKY FRIVOLITIES:
* The Gay Head cliffs, Menemsha harbor and pond, and the Chilmark Store (site of a country fair each summer) are great places to visit.
* The Captain Flanders house is surrounded by farmland, which is fun for early morning explorations. The wildlife and wildfowl are plentiful in this area.
* The fishing village of Menemsha is within walking distance of the inn. The road is not terribly busy. Poole's Fish Market is fun to stop by, to check on the daily catch.

JARED COFFIN HOUSE

29 Broad Street
Nantucket, Massachusetts 02554
(617) 228-2405
Owner: Philip Whitney Read
Rooms: 8 singles, 50 doubles
Rates: Singles: $50; Doubles $90-135 (off-season rates available)
Payment: All major credit cards accepted
Children: Welcome
Dogs: Welcome
Open: All year

The Jared Coffin House occupies the upper corner of Broad and Center streets. It is comprised of six buildings; two are attached to the main mansion and the others, the Daniel Webster House, Harrison Gray House, and Henry Coffin House, are within a block. With the exception of the Daniel Webster House, all are antique mansions built in the early- to mid-1800s.

The elegance of this era has been graciously preserved in all of the buildings. The formal public areas are adorned with oriental rugs and impressive English antiques. The buildings' intrinsic features include handcarved woodworking, high ceilings, and marble fireplaces, all of which lend an even more elegant air to the inn.

Guest rooms are dramatically different from one another, each with their own special treasures. One of our favorites is on the second floor in the Jared Coffin House. This corner guest room is graced with many high windows that not only add an airy sensation, but also warm the room with streams of sunlight. A canopy bed with its hand-embroidered bedspread and matching canopy is the focal point of this bedroom. An elegant mahogany Chippendale bureau rests beside the bed, with a sofa against the far window.

Another interesting guest room can be found in the Harrison Gray House. The room has kept all of its antique features with the exception of a loft built into a cathedral ceiling. A mahogany canopy bed rests on an oriental rug, and two quilted twin beds are reached by ascending a wooden ladder to the loft (great for those with children). Those traveling with a dog or energetic children will appreciate the private second entrance leading out the back. This building is also a favorite as its parlor is both elegant and cozy with an antique grandfather clock ticking in the corner. Just beyond is a green and white sunroom.

Finally, for those yearning for modern appointments combined with classic antiques, there is the Daniel Webster House. Wide pine floors are covered with plush carpeting. Once again canopy beds are found, as well as an assortment of collectibles. All the guest rooms have modern amenities including a television, telephone, and spacious private bath.

Dining at the Jared Coffin House is a delightful experience. There is the dark, cozy Tap Room with its enormous mahogany bar, as well as the adjacent outside patio for summertime dining. There is also a more formal dining room, open for dinner. The Jared Coffin House offers guests all they could want in a quaint New England inn, while Nantucket provides a quintessential look into a picturesque old whaling town.

FRISKY FRIVOLITIES:
* The inn is in the heart of historic Nantucket. Window shopping as well as ventures up tiny side streets are a must.
* The beaches are well within walking, jogging, or bicycling distance from the inn. Put your "well-behaved" companion on a leash and head off to enjoy some of the softest sand on the East Coast.
* In addition to the informative Historical Society, enchanting old houses, terrific shops, and wonderful art exhibits, many just enjoy the peace and quiet of the island.

THE WOODBOX

29 Fair Street
Nantucket, Massachusetts 02554
(617) 228-0587
Innkeeper: Dexter Tutein
Rooms: 3 doubles, 6 suites
Rates: Doubles: $90; Suites: $110-140
Payment: Personal checks
Children: Welcome
Dogs: Welcome
Open: June to mid-October

Nantucket was first settled in 1659 by Thomas Macy, who had left his home in Salisbury, Massachusetts when he was harshly fined for harboring Quakers. When he first arrived, the island was inhabited with some 700 Indians. Subsequent settlers made their living by farming and hunting sperm whales. Then, in 1709, The Woodbox was built, giving it the distinction of being the oldest inn on the island.

Today, visitors will be pleased to find that the inn's interior has been carefully maintained, retaining much of its 1700's character. Guests usually enter the inn through the dining room and are immediately impressed with its feeling of antiquity. Look up, just slightly, and see the rough-hewn beamed ceilings. The original open hearth still looks as though it could be used for cooking. The architecture, coupled with period antiques, completes the desired effect. Wide-board floors slope and creak as guests walk up the tight twisting staircase to the bedrooms. Even the well worn red treads on the stairs seem to have a story.

Once on the second floor, guests will find a suite on the right and a double guest chamber on the left. A living room, two bedrooms, and a private bath complete the "pink suite," which is ideal for the traveling family. An eclectic assortment of furniture fills each room. Some pieces are ornate, in keeping with a more formal French style, while others are simply early American pieces. The double bedroom across the hall has a high canopy bed, more early American period furnishings, and a small fireplace. A modern bathroom with shower is only a step up from the bedroom. The inn has another antique guest house across the street, which is decorated in a similar fashion.

The additional benefit to staying at The Woodbox is that guests need only walk downstairs in the morning to enjoy one of the best breakfasts on the island. Dinner is also an event. The inn is famous for its popovers and other delectable creations. The half-dozen tables are simply set with brass candlesticks and fresh bouquets of flowers. The real treats are the entrees, which include beef Wellington, jumbo scampi, duck a l'orange, mustard veal, and the fresh fish of the day.

Whether one is planning a romantic weekend for two or a longer stay with the family, The Woodbox offers its visitors cozy guest rooms that are off the beaten track but still within walking distance to town.

FRISKY FRIVOLITIES:
* The Nantucket beaches are some of the prettiest you will find on the East Coast; however, check your dog regularly for ticks.
* Downtown Nantucket is filled with delightful shops, boutiques, and cobblestoned streets leading people through quaint residential neighborhoods.
* The streets around the inn are loaded with historical homes. Walk in any direction and take in the sights (the Historical Society has a map).

PHILLIPS HOUSE BED AND BREAKFAST

54 Fair Street
Nantucket, Massachusetts 02554
(617) 228-9217
Host: Mary Phillips
Rooms: 4 singles and doubles

Rates: $75
Payment: Personal checks
Children: Not appropriate for small children
Dogs: Welcome, but owners are advised the island has a flea and tick
    problem
Open: Open all year

The Phillips House is a charming gray-shingled Nantucket-style home located at the end of Fair Street, just a few minutes walk from the center of town. Guests could easily pass it by if they were not paying attention to the house numbers, as there is only a tiny sign by the driveway reading PHILLIPS.

Upon entering the foyer, guests will immediately be faced with the steep stairs leading to the second floor. Wedged in the staircase balusters are all sorts of reading materials on Nantucket and other local sights. The only guest room with a private bath (and the one most appropriate for people with a dog) is to the right of the front door.

This well lit, wallpapered room has an assortment of eclectic and well-worn country antiques. The bright blue painted headboard is the perfect backdrop for the handmade multi-colored quilt on the bed. A thin oriental rug covers the wide pine floors, and a fireplace completes the picture. The other rooms are located on the second floor. Guests may notice the little panes of glass at the top of each door have been painted white with finger-painted flowers.

One room has a narrow-beamed ceiling with a gigantic bow-front bureau in the corner and a fireplace against the far wall. A Vermont quilt, similar to the one in the downstairs room, covers the bed, and a wooden chest sits at the foot of the bed. A handstitched needlepoint alphabet sampler hangs on the wall. The two smaller guest chambers are decorated more simply than the others and share a bathroom. Shelves line the bathroom wall, one for each bedroom. On them guests will find a soap dish and two glasses, where they may store their toothbrushes. There is also space on the shelves for some antique jars for bicarbonate of soda, ammonia, toilet water, and tooth wash.

Each morning, Mary fixes a Continental breakfast for her guests. This is served in the charming downstairs dining room on the back side of the house. If guests prefer, they may also take their coffee and breakfast out to the small side yard and watch the world pass by on this quiet side street.

FRISKY FRIVOLITIES:
* Mary warns guests of the tick and flea problems on Nantucket. She prefers that rather than taking dogs to the beach, guests may opt to walk them downtown.
* Dogs who do not like boating may want to try some surf casting ... maybe the blues are running.
* After exploring the shops along the cobblestoned streets, you may wish to explore some of the island by foot and then bicycle to the more remote areas.

VERMONT

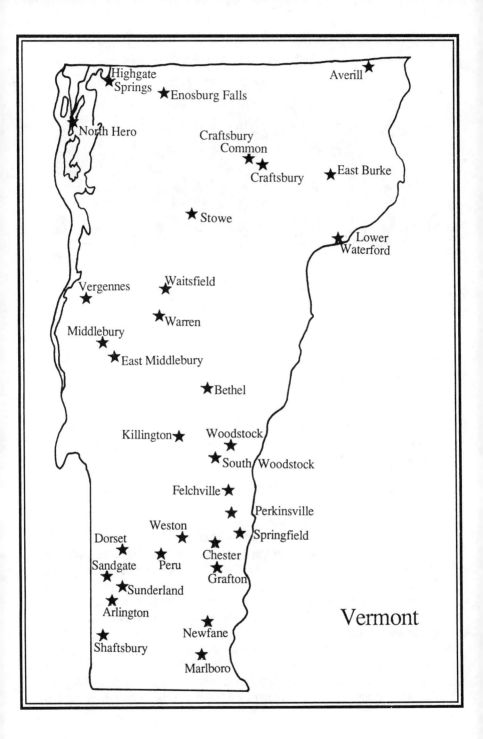

Highgate
Springs
Enosburg Falls
Averill

North Hero

Craftsbury
Common
Craftsbury
East Burke

Stowe

Lower
Waterford

Vergennes
Waitsfield

Warren

Middlebury

East Middlebury

Bethel

Killington
Woodstock

South Woodstock

Felchville

Perkinsville

Weston
Springfield

Dorset
Chester

Sandgate
Peru
Grafton

Sunderland

Arlington

Newfane
Vermont

Shaftsbury

Marlboro

WHETSTONE INN

Marlboro, Vermont 05344
(802) 254-2500
Innkeepers: Jean and Harry Boardman
Rooms: 10 doubles
Rates: $25-65
Payment: Personal checks
Children: Welcome (two years and older)
Dogs: Welcome
Open: All year

The Whetstone Inn lies in the diminutive town of Marlboro, which is comprised of a church, post office, and the inn. This Colonial-style home was originally built in 1785 as a tavern for the townspeople and passing stage coach passengers. The inn and the town remain relatively unchanged to this day.

Guests will proceed up a path, walk through the side door, and find themselves in a closet-sized entryway. The large living room lies to the left and is crammed with an eclectic assortment of furniture, comfortable couches, and bursting bookshelves. Collectibles are scattered throughout; among the more notable are the old slots originally used for the town's mail (when the inn served as the post office).

The majority of bedrooms are located on the second floor. As guests ascend the stairs, they cannot help but notice that the treads have been painted to resemble a carpeted runner. Beamed ceilings are overhead and wide pine floors are underfoot. The guest rooms are painted in cheery pastels or wallpapered in floral prints. The furnishings are antique, featuring captain's chests, rocking chairs, and old jugs that have been converted into lamps. Antique beds are draped with quilts. Views to the pond, white birch groves, and a forested hillside are framed by white lace or brightly patterned curtains.

After a peaceful night's sleep, guests will awaken to heavenly smells emanating from the kitchen. The country-style dining room is dominated by an enormous cooking fireplace. Hearty eaters will be treated to breakfast from an ever-changing menu. Fresh berries are available in the summer months, complemented by either eggs, bacon, and muffins, or pancakes and waffles covered with Vermont-made maple syrup. In the evening, dinners are served for a very reasonable price. Selections range from lamb and chicken to fish and veal. Guests will find their hosts to be casual and delightful and the experience to be memorable.

FRISKY FRIVOLITIES:
* The Molly Stark State Park is just a few miles down the road and is a great place for walking and exploring.
* There is a pond behind the inn for refreshing dips after picturesque walks down country roads.
* Cross-country skiing can be found on the property. The start of a trail is to the right of the side door, leading skiers to forested hills.

THE FOUR-IN-HAND

Marlboro, Vermont 05344
(802) 254-2894
Innkeepers: Peter and Sheila Kane
Rooms: 7 doubles, 1 suite
Rates: Doubles: $40-55; Suite: $75
Payment: MC, VISA
Children: Welcome in the suite
Dogs: Welcome with prior approval. Dogs must be leashed in the public areas.
Open: All year. Closed in April and the first two weeks of December

The Four-in-Hand is hidden in the foothills of the Green Mountains, an area that is not particularly well traveled but a nice surprise once discovered. The inn is rather unassuming from the outside, but once inside guests will find a cheery and casual atmosphere in both the restaurant and the guest rooms.

The bedrooms are adjacent to the restaurant, and are found on both the first and second floors. The first floor accommodations are most appropriate for people traveling with a dog as there is direct access to the outside. The rooms have a distinct country flavor. Handmade Vermont quilts, in an array of colors, set the theme for most of the chambers. The first floor suite is decorated in a vibrant green-and-white motif with a flowered border along the top of the wall. This is complemented by a painted bureau and armoire and a pair of arm chairs covered in chintz. Delicate, pale blue and white floral wallpaper sets the tone in another bedroom, and a third favors tinges of rose. Whichever bedroom guests choose, all are fresh and cheery and provide a private bath.

Once settled, guests will want to try the dining room fare, an interesting selection ranging from scallops of veal with wild mushrooms to the Chef's pasta of the day. Appetizers include smoked trout and escargot sauted with fresh herbs. Favorite dessert selections are creme brulee, sorbet, or terrine of chocolate. Afterwards, many choose to relax in the little nook just beyond the dining room that offers games, books, and a color television.

The Kanes are happy to direct guests to some very special and secret spots in the area where local artisans can be found creating everything from hand-blown glass pieces to intricately woven items. There are also antique stores and summer concerts given by renowned musicians. Guests are sure to leave with a feeling that they have experienced much of southern Vermont's unique flavor.

FRISKY FRIVOLITIES:
* There are a number of free cross-country ski trails that your hosts can direct you to, whether for a midnight ski venture or a mid-day picnic.
* The inn also has a secret (rumor has it) and beautiful lake for your sunning and swimming pleasure.
* Scenic Route 9 takes travelers through beautiful foliage regions, along picturesque mountain roads, and to historic Bennington.

THE MUNROE-HAWKINS HOUSE

Historic Route 7A
Shaftsbury, Vermont 05262
(802) 447-2286
Innkeeper: Ruth Ann Myers
Rooms: 6 doubles, 2 suites
Rates: Doubles: $40-50; Suites: $80 (weekly discount - last night free)
Payment: Personal checks

Children: Welcome
Dogs: Welcome with prior approval
Open: All year

The Munroe-Hawkins House lies on the historic road leading from Bennington to Burlington, Vermont. It is a house filled with a history that bears repeating. Joshua Monroe, a man who made his fortune selling wheat to France after the Napoleonic wars, designed and built this Georgian-style farmhouse in 1808. He made use of Ionic columns, triangular gables, and Palladian windows to achieve the desired affect. He lived in this house for decades. Two generations later, his granddaughter, Mary Hawkins, moved into the house. It is from these two family members that the inn's name is derived.

Ruth Ann Myers and her dog Caitlyn have been innkeeping for quite some time, and both will immediately make guests feel right at home. The six guest quarters vary in size and decor. The simple furnishings enhance the vaulted and rough-hewn beamed ceilings, handcarved dental moldings, and the original windows. Each bedroom has a working fireplace.

A full country breakfast is served in the cozy breakfast room, which is kept warm by a Vermont woodstove. For those wishing to take this meal in bed, special arrangements can be made ahead of time. Fresh fruit starts the morning with the option of pancakes (topped with locally made maple syrup) or eggs. These may be accompanied by bacon or sausage and homemade breads. Ruth is so kind and interesting that some will be tempted to stay and talk all day; however, this part of Vermont is well worth exploring, especially when the weather is accommodating.

One word of caution for dog owners: Ruth Anne is a little nervous about her guests' dogs and the nearby road. She recommends either leashing dogs or having them under voice command.

FRISKY FRIVOLITIES:

* The Green Mountains surround the inn, providing excellent hiking trails in the summer and cross-country skiing in the winter. The views of the Vermont hills are excellent from the Molly Stark trail.
* Bennington is just south of the Munroe-Hawkins House. Great walks can be had around the Bennington College campus or through the historic Battle Monument park. A self-guided tour of the town is also available at the Chamber of Commerce.
* Those who wish to plan a day trip may consider traveling south on scenic Route 7 through Williamstown to Lenox, the home of Tanglewood.

ARLINGTON INN

Historic Route 7A
Arlington, Vermont 05250
(802) 375-6532
Innkeepers: Paul and Madeline Kruzel
Rooms: 13 doubles
Rates: $48-125
Payment: MC, VISA
Children: Welcome
Dogs: Welcome with prior approval
Open: All year

A combination of Greek and Victorian elegance immediately comes to mind when thinking about the Arlington Inn. This Greek Revival mansion was built in 1848 by Martin Chester Deming, a railroad magnate and Vermont politician. Nothing about the home has changed since then, except that it is now an inn with cozy guest rooms instead of family bedrooms and a fabulous restaurant instead of an old-fashioned kitchen.

Dark mahogany and a sweeping staircase set the scene as guests initially enter the inn. A dictionary rests on top of a mahogany stand in the entryway, and a brass gaslight lamp lights the way. To the left is a sitting room filled with Sheraton-style antiques, an oriental rug or two, and an antique clock set amid other collectibles. A fireplace completes the scene. To the right of the foyer is a cozy dining room with another inviting fireplace and tables that have been beautifully set with white tablecloths and sparkling crystal. Beyond is the Tavern, a small intimate chamber, that is most conducive to relaxing with a drink before or after dinner.

Off the sitting room is a guest room with two double beds draped in rose comforters, a gigantic round table, a marble-topped armoire, and numerous personal touches. A special note should be made of the fan set in the intricate ceiling. Guests will soon learn that each of these distinctive rooms is named after a member of the original Deming family. Families might enjoy the suite where Mom and Dad can sleep comfortably in a double-bedded alcove set behind draped curtains, while the children rest in the twin beds in the main room. Oriental rugs are found throughout the room and a marble sink offers yet another taste of a bygone era. Antiques fill each bedroom, and hardwood floors are smooth under bare feet. Some chambers have gabled ceilings and are blessed with an abundance of afternoon sun, while others are painted a bright yellow to give guests the impression that the sun is always shining.

Of course, there is also the Carriage House, which offers a variety of accommodations. The suites are more spacious than the rooms in the main house. Some are decorated using only white wicker and have a French country motif, and others are more Victorian in style. Each room is elegant and uniquely appointed, making it difficult to ultimately select a favorite.

FRISKY FRIVOLITIES:
* The nearby Battenkill River offers canoeing and fishing for the outdoor enthusiast.
* The towns of Manchester and Bennington are within a short drive of the inn. Manchester is the home of Orvis, a great place to learn how to fly fish, shoot, or stock up on goodies for Bowser.
* In addition to the wonderful cross-country skiing available, many enjoy the hiking in the Green Mountains.

GREEN RIVER BED AND BREAKFAST

Box 370, Sandgate Road
Arlington, Vermont 05250
(802) 375-9481
Hosts: Betsy and Jim Gunn
Rooms: 2 doubles
Rates: $45

Payment: Personal checks
Children: Welcome
Dogs: Well-behaved dogs must get along with the Gunn's dog. If not, they
    will be asked to stay in the car or in the room.
Open: All year

The Green River Bed and Breakfast is located just off a country road in the heart of a scenic Vermont valley. The 1840's farmhouse has been recently refurbished with all the modern amenities that guests enjoy. The Gunns have created a home that maintains the country charm and elegance that travelers look for in a B&B. The pale blue/grey facade has also undergone a revitalization, with restored light blue shutters and naturally stained doors. Interesting woodworking around the doors contrasts with the simple Vermont-style farmhouse. A handmade wooden plaque outside the front door welcomes guests to this picturesque hillside location.

Inside, box-beamed ceilings and wide-pine floors can be found throughout the house. The newly remodeled kitchen and the adjacent family room draw guests' attention with a view of the valley through floor-to-ceiling windows. A woodstove in the corner keeps the house toasty. Warm weather often coaxes guests out to the new pressure-treated deck, which wraps around the back of the house. The slope below it drops off sharply; however, this only enhances the feeling of openness and space.

Guests may choose from two light and airy rooms. Both are decorated in a simple country theme aided by the use of stenciling (a pinecone pattern in one) around the windows. Some of the furnishings include a wide-pine chest with a painted checkerboard, beds with antique quilts draped over them, and dried flowers. Navy blue and white checked wool blankets keep guests warm on chilly nights. Throw rugs cover the honey-colored wide-pine floors. A unique Victorian bath is shared by both of the bedrooms.

Each morning, hearty appetites are treated to a delicious country breakfast that is served either on the deck (weather permitting) or in the dining area. The Gunns' chicken supplies the eggs, which are served in a variety of ways. Breakfast also includes fruit or juice, muffins, and coffee or tea. This area offers much to do, and the Gunns supply an intimate and cozy spot for unwinding after a day of hiking, skiing, or antiquing.

FRISKY FRIVOLITIES:
* The expansive valley below is an excellent area for burning off breakfast
    with your canine companion.
* Green River has a number of swimming holes for cooling off in on a hot
    summer's day.
* This is a wonderful region for peaceful cross-country skiing without the
    intrusion of other skiers.

86

THE INN AT SUNDERLAND

Route 7A
Sunderland, Vermont 05250
(802) 362-4213
Innkeepers: Tom and Peggy Wall
Rooms: 9 doubles
Rates: $65-85
Payment: AE, MC, VISA
Children: Special arrangements can be made for children
Dogs: Welcome with prior approval, but they are asked to sleep in the barn.
Open: All year

We were hesitant at first to include the Inn at Sunderland because dogs are not actually allowed in the inn. However, it should not be overlooked by those who are willing to part with their dog during the night. Guests are still able to be with their dog during the day and look after him up until they go to bed.

The Walls have done an exceptional job restoring this 1840's farmhouse so that it now gleams with natural beauty. Creaky wood floors lead guests to sun-filled sitting and dining areas packed with country antiques interspersed with more formal wingback chairs and Chinese rugs. The sitting room, in the front of the house, is a particularly nice spot to join other guests for hot cider and hors d'oeuvres. Of course, there is a fully stocked bar for those favoring stronger refreshments.

Guests may choose from either five rooms in the original inn, or from four in a new addition. The bedrooms are a bit snug, but are so charming that most will ignore the size and concentrate on the views from their rooms. Each is individually decorated with traditional floral wallpaper, complemented by wainscottings that have been painted in a variety of Williamsburg colors. Some guests may request a room with a fireplace or perhaps another with a four-poster bed. Nevertheless, you will always find thick towels, brass clocks, and fresh flowers. The Walls have also incorporated little bits of "pig-obilia" throughout the inn.

In the morning, it would be wise to come to breakfast with a hearty appetite. Although freshly baked breads are always available, guests are also treated to the inn's famous French toast, blueberry pancakes, and other delectable goodies. After breakfast, an invigorating stroll through the inn's seven acres with Bowser is a great way to begin the day. The Walls would be pleased to pack a picnic lunch for their guests' excursions throughout the Vermont countryside.

So, for those who are craving a bit of pampering and are comfortable with their dog spending the night in a country barn (with a few ponies for additional warmth), then the Inn at Sunderland is an ideal choice.

FRISKY FRIVOLITIES:
* Guests may want to visit Robert Todd Lincoln's Hildene, a scenic estate in Manchester, just up the road from the inn. There are rolling fields and woods and three trails. Telephone (802) 362-1788 for more information.
* Lake Shaftsbury offers a sandy beach which is a pleasant way to spend a portion of your afternoon. Should you wish to try your angling skills, the Battenkill River is within walking distance.
* Long Trail, part of the Appalachian Trail, runs through this area. This is a scenic way to get a little or a lot of exercise.

BARROWS HOUSE

Route 30
Dorset-in-the-Mountains, Vermont 05251
(802) 867-4455
Innkeepers: Charles and Marilyn Schubert
Rooms: 30 doubles, 4 suites
Rates: Doubles: $72-150; Suites: $175 (MAP)
Payment: Personal checks

Children: Welcome
Dogs: Welcome in guest rooms with outside access
Open: All year

Acres of green grass encircling traditional clapboard and shuttered homes is the setting for the Barrows House. The inn actually consists of eight buildings, each offering different types of accommodations, whether guests are traveling as couples, families, or with groups of friends. As the Schuberts prefer to place dogs in rooms with outside entrances, this description will focus on those particular guest rooms.

Each accommodation is as different as the cottage it occupies. There is a Vermont country feeling to the rooms; the simple furnishings usually consist of a pine bed and bureau, side chairs covered in faded flowered fabrics, and either braided rugs or well worn carpeting on the hardwood floors. Other rooms are more modern with sectional sofas and bright wallpapers. The Truffle House appears to have been recently redecorated with wall-to-wall carpeting, a four-poster bed, and some milk painted furniture. The Schubert Cottage, toward the back of the property, has a slate and brick fireplace, full kitchen, and two bedrooms on the first floor. A huge upstairs master bedroom has a private bath and adjacent study.

Many of the guests will enjoy the fragrant and brilliant flower beds while others seek out the myriad of activities available. Croquet, badminton, tennis, and swimming are some of the recreational outlets. What was once the stable is now a cross-country ski and bicycle shop that will rent skis in the winter and bicycles in the summer.

After a day of physical activity, the main inn is a wonderful place to unwind. A sauna will start the process and the crackling fireplace, in the front sitting room, will add the finishing touches. Try to stay awake for dinner though, as it is a tasty affair. The menu changes often but the emphasis is always on the freshest foods available. In the summertime, herbs and vegetables from local gardens are ever present. Homemade desserts top it all off. Guests may choose to eat dinner in one of the cozy dining rooms and perhaps have breakfast in the greenhouse as it is bathed with morning light. Afterwards, it is off to ski or to explore the beautiful Vermont countryside.

FRISKY FRIVOLITIES:
* The area is known for its downhill skiing and its more leisurely cross-country skiing. Ask the inn to pack a picnic lunch and head off for the day.
* The Green Mountain National Forest is close to the inn and offers hiking, fishing in streams, and exploring the woods.
* Dorset is a quaint Vermont village and is within easy strolling distance of the inn. Manchester is within driving distance and is also an interesting town for walking and window shopping.

OCTOBER PUMPKIN BED AND BREAKFAST

P.O. Box 226, Route 125
East Middlebury, Vermont 05740
(802) 388-9525
Hosts: Eileen and Charles Roeder
Rooms: 3 doubles
Rates: $45-55
Payment: Personal checks
Children: Welcome
Dogs: "Polite pets" always welcome
Open: All year

      The Roeders describe their home to perfection when they say it is an "architecturally significant nubbin of an 1850 Greek revival." The October Pumpkin is definitely small for a Greek revival; however, what it has lost in size it makes up for in charm. Its color, a deep pumpkin orange, fits in well with the off-white trim and rust shutters. Everything from the barn to the window boxes has been freshly repainted and restored to its original condition.

      The Roeders used to own a rambling inn just down the road in Brandon. Acres of property surrounded four barns and an in-ground swimming pool. However, once they sent their last child off to school, they felt it was time to move into something smaller and consequently opened a more intimate

90

B&B. The children were replaced by a puppy, who should now be on its way to being full grown.

When we arrived the finishing touches were just being completed. The fireplaced sitting room, painted a warm blue, lies to the left of the front door. This is a wonderful spot for relaxing at the end of an adventuresome day in the countryside. It offers peace and quiet allowing for conversation or reading. The stairs just off the sitting room lead to the three guest rooms. Take a moment to look at the enchanting doll house tucked into an alcove at the top of the stairs.

The bedrooms are moderately sized but are graced with steeply angled eves and gabled rooflines. Their colors vary from lavender to avocado green and each has whimsical stenciling. Antique or canopy beds can be found in each room with baskets of goodies placed at the ends. Country antiques are found throughout, with some of the more notable ones being a marble-topped dresser, a natural pine hutch, and a preponderance of wicker. The green guest room has a private bathroom, while the other two share a bath.

The country feeling of the inn is carried through to the dining room. In the morning, an ample breakfast is served. Guests are invited to help themselves to the various treats set out on the "groaning sideboard." In addition to a complimentary breakfast, the Roeders also will be happy to cook a delicious dinner for an extra charge of $10.95. The ambiance, the food, and, most importantly, the Roeders, combine to make this a most enjoyable B&B experience.

FRISKY FRIVOLITIES:
* The inn lies at the base of the Middlebury Gap, a favorite spot for foliage watchers and nature lovers alike.
* Whether one likes the tranquility of cross-country skiing or the beauty of hiking through the Green Mountains, the inn is centrally located to both.
* Lake Dunmore is nearby and offers some great boating and swimming.

THE MIDDLEBURY INN

Court House Square
Middlebury, Vermont 05753-0163
(802) 388-4961
Innkeepers: Jane and Frank Emanuel
Rooms: 77 doubles (dogs allowed in 20 bedrooms)
Rates: $54-90

Payment AE, MC, VISA, personal checks
Children: Welcome
Dogs: Welcome in the Emma Willard House or Governor Weeks House -
$5 fee
Open: All year

The Middlebury Inn's long history began in 1788, when Judge Gamaliel Painter deeded Simeon Dudley the lot that the inn would eventually occupy. Some six years later, Samuel Mattocks, Jr. built a tavern that ultimately burned in 1816. The rebuilding, refurbishing, and additions continued until the Middlebury Management Hotel Corporation purchased the property in 1927 and turned it into the Middlebury Inn. The Emanuels arrived in 1977 and were pleasantly surprised when the State of Vermont's Division for Historic Preservation provided matching funds for their restoration of the inn.

Of the six different houses and wings available to guests, dog owners may bring Bowser to either the Emma Willard House or the Governor Weeks House. These two houses are newer additions to the inn and have a more contemporary flair than the other accommodations. Although the exterior might be said to resemble a motel, the rooms' interiors do not reflect that feeling at all. Bedrooms in the Emma Willard House are decorated with Laura Ashley wallpaper with contrasting off-white trim. White Bates spreads adorn the beds. Modern amenities include coffee makers, color television, telephones, and air conditioning. The private, modern baths even have hair dryers. The guest quarters in the Governor Weeks House are similar in decor, but are a bit more spacious. Guests will definitely find these rooms to be comfortable and well appointed, and the outside entrances are ideal for pet owners.

Of course, guests in these accommodations are welcome to use all of the facilities at the main inn. Two elegant dining rooms serve hearty New England fare. Guests may want to visit in the spacious sitting areas or in the cozy bar. The main lobby contains sofas and a fireplace — a terrific place to sit and watch the world go by.

FRISKY FRIVOLITIES:
* Middlebury is a charming town and an easy one to explore on foot. There are a number of specialty shops catering to both college students and visitors.
* For winter fun there are many good cross-country ski trails nearby, and in the fall, the foliage is unbelievable throughout the area (especially in the Middlebury Gap).
* Middlebury College is within walking distance of the inn. The campus is great fun to meander through, particularly in the fall when the students are returning to school.

STRONG HOUSE INN

Route 22A
Vergennes, Vermont 05491
(802) 877-3337
Innkeepers: Laura and Liam Murphy
Rooms: 6 doubles
Rates: $45-60
Payment: AE, MC, VISA
Children: Welcome
Dogs: Welcome, but must stay in the garage
Open: December 25 to February 28 and June 1 to November 15

Vergennes bills itself as the smallest city in the United States. It is small indeed, charmingly set in the midst of Vermont's farm country, yet only a short drive to Middlebury, Burlington, and the shores of Lake Champlain. The Strong House Inn is a stately yellow 1834 Federal-style house perched on a hill overlooking the Green Mountains and the Adirondacks. Immediately surrounding the inn are acres and acres of rich farmlands.

The inn is simply elegant, as can be attested to by its placement on the National Register of Historic Places. A freestanding staircase with curly maple railings will lead guests to their beautifully decorated rooms. Some have elegant mahogany furniture, and others are filled with more simple oak or maple pieces. Wide pine floors have been painted warm beiges or blues and are covered with throw rugs. Nubbly spreads top four-poster beds. Yet another guest chamber has a fireplace and a rather unique "sleigh" bed. Most of the bathrooms are shared with the exception of one room with a private bath.

The public rooms are equally as elegant. The large dining room has nice views of the adjacent fields. An oriental rug covers the floor and there is even an old piano awaiting anyone who wishes to tickle the ivories. It is in this room where a full country breakfast is served each morning. Off the dining room is a living room painted a Williamsburg blue. It has a large fireplace, over which hangs a portrait of Samuel Strong, the original owner. The living room is a favorite place to spend the afternoons and evenings.

As a final note, we should mention that the Strong House Inn will not appeal to everyone traveling with a dog. If guests are not comfortable leaving their dog in the garage for the night, then perhaps another inn would be more suitable, as dogs are definitely not allowed in the house. But for those who feel that Bowser will be perfectly comfortable, then by all means come and enjoy a night or two with the Murphys.

FRISKY FRIVOLITIES:
* Otter Creek is quite close to the inn and flows directly into Lake Champlain. Many explore the creek and even test the waters with a little dip.
* Mt. Philo is within a short driving distance of the inn. There are hiking trails all over this mountain, where you can climb to the top or just half way up.
* Burlington is a fun city to explore, offering everything from beautiful views of the lake to terrific shopping. Visitors will also wish to take advantage of the wonderful parks and wide expanses on the University of Vermont campus.

MILLBROOK LODGE

RFD Box 62
Waitsfield, Vermont 05673
(802) 496-2405
Innkeepers: Joan and Thom Gorman
Rooms: 7 doubles
Rates: $44-75 (weekly rates: $195-330)
Payment: Most major credit cards
Children: Welcome ($30 per night)
Dogs: Welcome during the summer season
Open: All year except May

The 1850's Millbrook Lodge is a cape-style farmhouse that is situated about halfway between Waitsfield and Sugarbush. Arriving guests enter by way of the warming room, where in the winter, the Glenwood stove thaws frosty fingers and toes and dries boots and other snow gear. Passing through the living room, complete with rocking chairs and fireplace, guests will come upon the Willow Tree Room (the only downstairs bedroom). The stenciling in this room, as with all the others, is extensive. Thom and Joan stenciled each of the seven bedrooms differently, an incredibly time-intensive task. In this case, willow trees adorn the walls. Two antique maple beds are adorned with comforters. Joan has also found time to make many of the quilts found on the other beds.

The six upstairs guest rooms all have themes or stories behind them. The Henry Perkins Room is named for the founder of the inn, the Waterfall Room for its matching waterfall double bed and dresser, and the Wedding Ring Room for the double wedding ring quilt that lies on the antique rock maple bed. The stenciling is in great abundance and consists of everything from American folk art patterns to overflowing flower baskets to vines and berries. Many guests will sleep either under gabled eves or awaken to views of the Green Mountains. Antique furniture abounds.

The old dining room has been transformed into a cozy sitting area. A new addition created space for the gourmet country restaurant, which is decorated in French provincial fabrics. French doors open out into the garden. The Gormans enjoy this lifestyle, compared to the one they left in New York a little over eight years ago. However, it has not come about without a tremendous amount of effort and ingenuity. Deliveries of fresh fish and vegetables arrive regularly from Boston, as well as from Maine and Vermont. As a result, each night an innovative selection of dishes are offered to diners. Pasta, veal, shrimp, fish, and assorted Indian dishes are just a few.

FRISKY FRIVOLITIES:
* There is terrific hiking, canoeing, and windsurfing in the Mad River Valley.
* If Bowser has enjoyed exploring the Gorman's backyard and is searching for additional fun, the local country roads are quiet and very scenic.
* The charming country village of Waitsfield is just down the road. Bowser may enjoy hunting for antiques or good buys instead of his usual fare.

SOUTH VILLAGE

RR 1, Box 300
Warren, Vermont 05674
(800) 451-4574, (802) 583-2300
Reservations Manager: Jean Dean
Rooms: 66 condominiums and villas, 5 units available to people traveling
    with dogs

Rates: $100-170
Payment: AE, MC, VISA, personal checks
Children: Welcome (under 12 are free)
Dogs: Welcome in certain units with a $100 deposit
Open: All year

South Village is a beautifully landscaped complex, located only minutes from the lifts at Sugarbush. There are two types of accommodations available; the condominiums (offering one-level living) and the private mountainside Villas.

The guest quarters vary in size from two bedrooms with one-and-a-half bathrooms to four bedrooms with four-and-one-half baths. The natural rustic board exterior is just what guests would expect to find in ski country. Each unit is individually owned and thus varies in decor; however, most feature attractions such as brick fireplaces, cathedral ceilings, fully equipped kitchens, washers and dryers, and color cable televisions. Guests are provided with linens and towels, and at an additional charge, daily maid service is available.

Visitors to the area really come to experience the super recreational facilities and the spectacular surroundings. Guests not only enjoy easy access to the mountain and terrific skiing in the winter, but they also come to see the foliage in the fall. Scenic trails are favorites of hikers in the spring and summer months. This mountain and lake setting offers something for everyone. South Village provides guests with everything from golf, tennis, and squash to swimming, windsurfing, and therapeutic saunas. This is an ideal spot for a family vacation, offering a wide range of activities for even the most energetic child. The resort also provides babysitting services and permits children under 12 to stay for free with their parents.

FRISKY FRIVOLITIES:
* Mad River is great for fishing and Blueberry Lake is fun for windsurfing and swimming.
* Although Bowser would probably not enjoy a glider ride, even with the breathtaking views, he will surely like the hiking trails.
* Granville State Park covers over 1,200 acres along the eastern border of the Green Mountain National Forest. This is a beautiful setting for a picnic or for a cross-country skiing sojourn.

GREENHURST INN

Route 107
Bethel, Vermont 05032
(802) 234-9474
Innkeepers: Lyle and Barbara Wolf
Rooms: 12 doubles, 1 suite
Rates: Doubles: $40-65; Suite: $80
Payment: MC, VISA
Children: Welcome
Dogs: Welcome with prior approval
Open: All year

One need not travel to San Francisco to enjoy the pleasures of staying in a Victorian inn, because the Greenhurst Inn is located in New England, is just as magnificent, and is surrounded by lush Vermont countryside. Built in 1890 as a private home for a Philadelphia family, it was sold in the 1930s, only to reopen its doors a short time later as an inn. The present innkeepers, the Wolfs, have been busy restoring this Victorian mansion since 1981, and the results are gratifying both to the owners and guests.

High ceilings, detailed woodworking, and original brass fixtures combine to set Greenhurst's mood. To the left and right of the front door are spacious parlors, filled to capacity with antiques gathered at country auctions or borrowed from the Wolf's private collection. When we were visiting, Lyle was particularly excited about their most recent auction purchase, an intricately carved sofa and matching chairs. He said buying the set was a bargain, but reupholstering each piece was not. We all agreed that it was well worth the price.

The grand staircase leading to the guest rooms is lined with 90-year-old advertisements. One of Lyle's hobbies is to frame his collection of advertisements as well as his English prints. (He leaves the room decorating to his wife Barbara.) The first-floor landing is as grand as it is spacious, enhanced by Barbara's great grandmother's "crazy quilt." We could spend paragraphs describing it; however, let us just say that guests will want to take time to study its intricate workmanship and unique details.

Guest rooms are individually decorated, offering guests such features as a handmade quilt covering a high bed or a special antique piece of furniture. The physical space in each room is equally different. One used to be a doctor's operating room. He needed a lot of light, and so the windows in this room stand floor-to-ceiling. Other rooms have ornate fireplaces or rounded sitting nooks. Guests will always find bottles of Perrier on their bureaus and mints on their pillows. A decanter of sherry is also set out on the first-floor landing. In the morning, a Continental breakfast is served in the spacious dining room. Fresh fruits, muffins, and an assortment of preserves are always available. Coffee, tea, or hot chocolate will perk up even the sleepiest morning person.

FRISKY FRIVOLITIES:
* Local Silver Lake is a great spot for swimming and picnicking.
* Texas Falls are just off Route 125. The cascading water sets the scene for a walk along the nature trail or perhaps some fishing.
* The Long Trail Hiking Path can be picked up off Route 100. The Wolfs would be happy to supply directions.

POPLAR MANOR

RD 2, Route 107
Bethel, Vermont 05032
(802) 234-5426
Innkeepers: Bob and Carmen Jaynes
Rooms: 4 doubles; 1 suite
Rates: Doubles: $20-29, Suite: $32
Payment: Personal checks
Children: No small children accepted

Dogs: Welcome (cannot disturb other guests)
Open: All year

Opening and operating a successful B&B is not an easy task, but Bob and Carmen Jaynes have had a wonderful experience running the Poplar Manor during these last eight years. After living in New York, they moved to Bethel where they decided to open a small B&B. After a bit of searching, they settled on a big, old 1800's Colonial they felt would serve the purpose. Ever since then, Carmen and Bob have enjoyed a constant flow of guests.

The Jaynes' two Chesapeake Bay retrievers usually greet visitors at the front door and escort them into the living room filled with antiques the innkeepers brought with them from New York and also discovered while living in Vermont. Oriental rugs are scattered generously throughout the house over the well-worn wide pine floors. Beyond the living room is a dining room whose center of attention is a wonderful old country farmhouse table. This, in the morning, will be loaded with freshly baked breads (zucchini, squash, and/or cinnamon), orange juice, and coffee.

Of course, after the dogs escort guests into the house, they will be happy to accompany them upstairs to the bedrooms. Each room has a different flavor, yet each has a distinct Vermont country farmhouse feeling. Low open-beamed ceilings can be found in many variably sized rooms. For those requiring a little more space, there is one suite with a double bed covered in a Bates spread and a separate sitting area with a couch. Guests may also choose the room with a high bed or perhaps one with a handmade Vermont quilt. Bright blue and white quilts cover the twin beds in another room, the lavender trim contrasting nicely with the quilts and white walls. In all the rooms, sheer white tie-back curtains hang at the windows, creating a very airy effect. The only drawback, which might discourage some guests, is the one shared bath. This bathroom is quite modern though, even with its one concession to the past; a claw-footed bathtub. The Jaynes' told us that very few guests find sharing to be a nuisance.

The cozy bed chambers and entertaining hosts make a stay at the Poplar Manor a most interesting and enjoyable experience.

FRISKY FRIVOLITIES:
* The inn is located on a side road off Route 107. Locust Creek runs behind the inn and there is even a special swimming hole. It might be fun to take a walk along the side road and then go for a swim in the creek.
* This area is quite rural, and there are a number of hiking trails. Ask the Jaynes' for their recommendations.
* Many choose to wander further afield and explore the beautiful towns of Hanover (Dartmouth College) and Woodstock.

MOUNTAIN MEADOWS LODGE

Route 1, Box 3, Thundering Brook Road
Killington, Vermont 05751
(802) 775-1010
Hosts: Bill and Joanne Stevens
Rooms: 17 doubles
Rates: $42 per person double occupancy (MAP) (15% discounts apply for
    extended stays)
Payment: Personal checks
Children: Welcome
Dogs: Welcomed in the summer and fall
Open: November 15 to April 15, June 1 to October 15

    A casual friendly atmosphere is pervasive at the Mountain Meadows Lodge. This is the perfect spot from which to begin a sojourn on the Appalachian Trail or just enjoy the serenity of the Green Mountains. The Lodge was a working farm for well over 100 years. Today, the farmhouse, as well as the barn, serve as simple, clean, and inviting accommodations for visitors to the Killington area.

    Summer and fall are the months when guests and their canine companions are welcomed. This is a wonderful time of year in the Green Mountains, and many guests take advantage of the canoeing, fishing, and swimming on Kent Lake, conveniently located next to the Lodge. Guests also use the Lodge as a way station for overnight trips on the Appalachian Trail or as a base for day hikes. Each night they can then come home to hot showers and clean, comfortable beds.

    In the morning, those with hearty appetites gather in the rustic dining room for a filling country breakfast. There is a wide assortment of choices, which include cereal, eggs, pancakes, French toast, juice, and coffee. Many use this time to become better acquainted. The interaction between the guests and their hosts is informal but always quite lively. After a long day of enjoying this region's natural beauty, many gather in the living room to watch the reflection of the sunset on the lake through floor-to-ceiling windows. When the nights are cool, a roaring fire can be found in the enormous fieldstone fireplace.

    Dinner is an equally pleasant time to exchange tales of the previous day's excursions, while enjoying the Steven's home-style cooking. As with breakfast, the emphasis is on freshness and quantity. Afterwards, parents may enjoy lingering a bit to plan the following day's activities, while the children run off to explore the game room.

    The Mountain Meadows Lodge offers a relaxed atmosphere for a truly casual family vacation (with many diversions for the children).

FRISKY FRIVOLITIES:

* Kent Lake is next to the Lodge. Its water level lowers somewhat as the summer wears on, but early summer is a great time to fish, swim, and canoe on the lake.
* The Appalachian Trail emerges on one side of the lake, circles it and disappears into the woods on the other side. This is a terrific trail for both day hikes and overnight excursions. Bowser should either be leashed or under voice command.
* After visiting historic Woodstock village, one may want to take a picnic up one of the trails in Quechee Gorge or in one of the many other nearby parks.

KEDRON VALLEY INN

Route 106
South Woodstock, Vermont 05071
(802) 457-1473
Innkeepers: Max and Merrily Comins
Rooms: 29 doubles

Rates: $85-160 (MAP) (special rates for mid-week stays during non-holiday
    periods)
Payment: DC, MC, VISA
Children: Welcome
Dogs: Welcome as long as they do not disturb guests
Open: All year except two weeks in April

The Kedron Valley Inn is a must see and stay for anyone traveling to
the Woodstock area. This inn has been operational for over 150 years, but the
Comins have recently infused it with a new sense of life. They renovated all of
the guest rooms and brought in a gourmet chef, who has created imaginative
menus for the dining room.

The inn exudes a feeling of comfort and country elegance. The living
room, with its hand-crafted oak bar and crackling fireplace, is a wonderful spot
to while away an evening. The bedrooms are equally as welcoming. Antique
four-poster, canopy, or oak beds await guests. Most people will enjoy the
warmth of a fire from either a Franklin stove or fireplace. Wide-pine floors are
protected by braided and hooked rugs. The owners' collection of antique quilts
is displayed throughout the inn. Some of these quilts belonged to Merrily's
grandmother, others she has picked up in the South. The architectural features
of this historic building such as wainscotting, high ceilings, and wide-pine
floors lend themselves beautifully to the display of antique quilts. The Comins
have filled the two buildings with wonderful country antiques, many of which
were "in disguise" when they bought the inn. They found quite a few very nice
pieces that had been painted black. Merrily and Max stripped them down to find
beautiful natural pine.

The rates do include breakfast and dinner — two meals not to be
missed. The Comins have nicknamed their cuisine "Nouvelle Vermont" and it
certainly meets all those expectations. We felt the roast country duckling with
blueberry sauce was divine, but do not ignore the tender milk-fed Vermont veal
or fresh trout. They are also developing an extensive California wine list.
Breakfast in the morning is an equally delicious affair. Starting at 5:30 a.m., the
cooks are up preparing fresh muffins and other baked goodies. Choices also
include eggs (served any style), French toast, and blueberry pancakes. Fortu-
nately, there is plenty to do in the area and at the inn, so that any calories
consumed are quickly expended.

Favorite people activities include horseback riding and surrey rides in
the summer and sleigh rides in the winter. Antique shopping, a visit to a local
working dairy (there are even baby animals to pet), golf, and tennis are all
within a few minutes' drive of the inn.

FRISKY FRIVOLITIES:

* The inn has a large spring-fed pond with a sandy beach for sunning and swimming. A cool dip might be followed by a hike through the inn's 15 acres, or vice versa...
* In the wintertime, there are a number of spots for cross-country skiing (dogs are not allowed at the cross-country ski center) that are off the beaten track.
* The town of Woodstock is not too far up the road and well worth walking through. Afterwards, a little demonstration of either your canoeing or fly fishing prowess is sure to impress Bowser.

THREE CHURCH STREET

3 Church Street
Woodstock, Vermont 05091
(802) 457-1925
Innkeepers: Mrs. Eleanore C. Paine and family
Rooms: 11 doubles, 1 suite
Rates: Doubles: $52-68; Suite: $200
Payment: MC, VISA, personal checks
Children: Welcome
Dogs: Welcome
Open: All year except month of April

Three Church Street lies on the village green in the heart of charming Woodstock. Set across the street from a beautiful old stone church, this rambling brick Federal looks both regal and charming behind its white picket fence. The stately foyer enhances guests initial impression, due in part to the bust of Marquis de Lafayette that has been displayed in a niche for the last century. The living room is just off the central hall. It is elegantly appointed with a longcase clock, white couches, a piano, and a marble fireplace. The library, housing a television and comfortable sofas and chairs, is across the hall.

The beauty of Three Church Street lies in the fact that it feels more like a family home than a quaint New England inn. Guests will soon learn that Mrs. Paine has eight children, and when half of them left, she decided to turn the extra rooms into guest quarters. Now that most of her children are gone, the home has become a full-fledged inn. Two of the original residents are the chocolate lab and little terrier who enjoy welcoming new arrivals.

Of the bedrooms, our favorites are rooms 1 and 5 and the suite (9 and 10). The suite is ideal for dog owners as it has its own private entrance, features a sitting room with a wood stove, and has a bathroom the Paines claim is the smallest in New England. The remaining guest chambers are simply furnished with an eclectic collection of furniture acquired by the family over the years. Old-fashioned wallpapers are found in the hallways and bedrooms. There are antiques and tiny collectibles scattered throughout.

A complimentary breakfast is served each morning in the dining room overlooking the grounds. Chintz-covered tables are set with candles, and glass coffee cups are waiting to be filled with steaming coffee. Guests may choose from a number of breakfast items including eggs, waffles, pancakes, or homemade muffins and breads. Tennis and swimming are found on the premises for those who want to work off the effects of overindulgence.

FRISKY FRIVOLITIES:
* Although Woodstock is the site of the first ski tow, today great downhill skiing is found at nearby Killington. The cross-country skiing is also terrific.
* There are walking tours of Woodstock leaving from the green (June through the foliage season).
* Should one really want to be in the great outdoors, day hikes are plentiful on Mt. Tom, through Billings Park, and along the Appalachian and Long trails.

THE VILLAGE INN OF WOODSTOCK

41 Pleasant Street
Woodstock, Vermont 05091
(802) 457-1255
Innkeepers: Kevin and Anita Clark
Rooms: 9 doubles
Rates: $63-85
Payment: MC, VISA, personal checks
Children: Welcome
Dogs: Small dogs welcome
Open: All year

The Village Inn of Woodstock is a restored 1899 Victorian mansion, which is located within walking distance of Woodstock's village green, shops, and restaurants. The expansive grounds surrounding the inn are long gone; however, the building has been well maintained. In the process of restoring the inn, the Clarks have been able to preserve the original oak wainscottings, beveled-glass windows, and tin ceilings.

Guests will enjoy the casual atmosphere of the inn. The Clarks are sometimes unable to meet new arrivals and have been known to leave a key and a note directing guests to their rooms. The bed chambers are located on the second and third floors. Each is distinctively decorated, often with traditional floral wallpapers, simple country furnishings, and double or twin beds. One of the most requested rooms has a working fireplace. Three of the bathrooms are private and the others are shared. Many have the original fixtures.

Guests will find the common rooms to be particularly inviting. A working fireplace warms patrons in the dining room and adjacent bar. The mahogany bar, with its extensive assortment of wines and liqueurs, dominates this cozy room. This is also a favorite gathering spot after skiing or a day in the countryside. Dinner and breakfast are served to the inn's guests as well as to the public. Kevin is usually busy preparing the entrees and consistently offers a diverse and delicious fare. A complimentary full breakfast ranges from pancakes topped with locally-made maple syrup to homebaked breads and eggs served any style.

Guests will find the Clarks to be interesting and delightful hosts. They can offer suggestions for interesting day trips, special cross-country ski trails, or scenic walks.

FRISKY FRIVOLITIES:
* Guests will enjoy the short walk into the village, around the green, and by the historic Federal homes. There are three covered bridges in the immediate area.
* Silver Lake, in nearby Barnard, is a favorite place for swimming and picnicking.
* The hiking in this region is excellent. The trailheads for Mt. Tom can be found just outside the village on either River Street or Mountain Avenue. The Appalachian Trail also runs through this area.

THE INN AT WEATHERSFIELD

Route 106 (near Perkinsville)
Weathersfield, Vermont 05151
(802) 263-9217
Innkeepers: Mary Louise and Ron Thorburn
Rooms: 10 doubles, 2 suites
Rates: $65 per person double occupancy; $88 single occupancy (MAP and High English Tea)
Payment: AE, MC, VISA, personal checks
Children: Over eight years old welcome

Dogs: Very well-behaved dogs welcome with prior approval
Open: All year

The Inn at Weathersfield was originally built in 1795 as a four-room farmhouse on 237 acres. Over the years, additional rooms and a carriage house (now the dining room) were added in response to individual owners' needs. The inn has functioned as a tavern and stage coach stop, a hiding place for underground slaves during the Civil War, and a summer estate.

Today, the inn exudes a strong feeling of antiquity. An 18th-century beehive oven is still used to cook the inn's breads and muffins. Ten additional working fireplaces are found throughout the buildings. The five different common rooms reflect the same post and beam construction as is found in the attached farmhouse. Sloping and creaking wide-pine floors add character. The Thorburns have furnished the inn with an exquisite selection of period antiques. An antique grandmother's clock, an old-fashioned chess table, quilts, and an array of antique country pine and more formal mahogany furniture represent just a sampling. A sunny library is filled with a collection of over 4,000 books.

The guest rooms are found by ascending one of the three staircases. Most of the bedchambers are located in the original building; however, a few can be found in the new post and beam addition. Everything from the beds (some are canopied) to the bureaus are antique. Handmade quilts, electric bottom sheets, and fireplaces keep guests warm at night. Bowls of fruits and nuts are set out and mints adorn the pillows. The bathrooms are private and unique, some even have the original claw-footed bathtubs.

Each afternoon from 4:30 to 6:30, a formal High Tea is served at the inn. Complimentary wine or sherry is also available at this time. Tea is merely a prelude to the gourmet delights offered at dinnertime. The Nouvelle cuisine selections range from an appetizer of linguini with smoked scallops and salmon to filet of beef with bearnaise sauce, smoked trout, and filet of salmon with dijonaise. Sorbet is served between courses. While Mary Lou is busy running the inn, Ron stays involved with the dinner activities by assuming the role of wine steward and pianist. In addition to the wonderful music, the elegant ambiance and friendly staff combine to make this a memorable dining experience.

FRISKY FRIVOLITIES:
* Numerous paths and back roads are well suited for meandering or exercising Bowser.
* Stoughton Pond provides excellent swimming, fishing, and boating opportunities in the summer and skating in the winter.
* There is also a 400-acre recreation area, perfect for cross-country skiing. Fall and spring visitors will find apple pressing farms and maple sugaring houses to be favorites.

HAPGOOD COTTAGE BED AND BREAKFAST

Baileys Mills Road
Reading, Vermont 05062
(802) 484-5540
Host: Susan Singleton
Rooms: 3 doubles
Rates: $45-55
Payment: Personal checks
Children: Welcome
Dogs: Welcome with prior approval
Open: All year

The Hapgood Cottage is the epitome of a true New England farm-house. The home was built in the 1700s by David Hapgood, one of the many Hapgoods who settled Southern Vermont. Their influence was so great that even today visitors to the area will find a pond, a general store, and even a state forest bearing the family name. This particular B&B can be found a few miles off scenic Route 106. A winding rural dirt lane leads people past other farmhouses until they emerge at the Hapgood homestead, idyllically set amidst 250 acres of pasturelands.

Upon arriving, we found Susan on her way to the barn to check on the new lamb (Oscar), with her dog Maggie in tow. This is a small farm, and morning hours are spent tending to the cows, horses, and sheep. In between taking care of her guests, Susan spends the majority of her hours working the farm. Whether guests want to help or just tag along, it is great fun to learn about the intricacies of farm life.

The farmhouse is a cozy place to return to at night. A modern kitchen and family room have been added to the house, otherwise it is similar to the way it must have looked in the 1700s. A spacious and sunny living room runs the width of the house. Shiny hardwood floors reflect the light cast through the multi-paned windows. A Franklin stove keeps most of the house warm, and a navy blue couch (a favorite spot for Susan's cat) is a perfect place for guests to relax.

There are two bedrooms upstairs (sharing a bath) and a suite downstairs with a private bath and adjacent sun porch. The latter has a queen bed facing the fireplace and is furnished with assorted simple country antiques. The sun porch can either be used to sleep two more people on its foldout futon couch or provide extra space and privacy for those desiring it.

Guests who choose to get up early in the morning can help Susan with the chores and, in the process, work up a healthy appetite for breakfast. Others might feel more inclined to just roll out of bed and into the breakfast room where a hearty country breakfast awaits. Fresh fruit (in season) along with homebaked breads and a variety of egg dishes will definitely prepare guests for an active day in the Vermont countryside.

FRISKY FRIVOLITIES:

* Provided Bowser is not spooked by farm animals, there are extensive fields to explore.
* The dirt road that runs by the inn is not well traveled and is perfect for country walks. The trees overhanging the road provide shade in the summer months.
* This area is known for its cross-country skiing as well as horseback riding in the summer and sleigh rides in the winter. The Kedron Valley Stables, just up the road in South Woodstock, can arrange for equestrian activities.

HARTNESS HOUSE

30 Orchard Street
Springfield, Vermont 05156
(802) 885-2115
Innkeeper: Tom Spaulding
Rooms: 42 doubles, 2 suites

Rates: Doubles: $48-59; Suites: $69-75
Payment: AE, MC, VISA, personal checks
Children: Welcome (under 12 years old are free)
Dogs: Welcome
Open: All year

The Hartness House, built in 1904, is set on a hill above Springfield amidst 32 acres of woodlands and gardens. This stone and shingled inn has as interesting a history as the man it was built for — James Hartness. Hartness was not only responsible for patenting more than 120 machines, but he also built the now famous Turret Equatorial Telescope, one of the first American tracking telescopes. He also managed to find enough time to serve as Governor of Vermont from 1920-22. Mr. Hartness was an intense man, and in his search for complete quiet, he constructed a five-room office under the front lawn, connected to the house by an underground tunnel. Here he could work without any annoying disturbances. This home's interesting history combined with its fine restoration has earned it a position in the register of historic places by the Department of the Interior.

Upon entering this stately old house, guests will be struck with a sense of grandeur usually associated with the old-fashioned "summer cottages" of the well-to-do. Although the home is a bit dated, there is still a feeling of elegance enhanced by oriental works of art, antique furniture, an abundance of flowers and plants, and a dozen or so enormous oriental rugs. Three gigantic working fireplaces complete the effect. The guest rooms we recommend are all in the main building, as the newer rooms behind the inn are true motel units.

Guests will ascend a grand circular staircase that rises three floors. On each landing there is an inviting window seat. Many of the bedrooms have vaulted ceilings, period furnishings, and original fixtures such as crystal door handles. Beds are covered in Bates spreads, and lace curtains hang at the windows. Old-fashioned arm chairs provide comfortable resting places for watching television. Sewing baskets hold supplies for any last minute repairs.

The formal dining room is housed in a transformed stone portico, which originally served as the reception area for arriving carriages. The elegant surroundings are enhanced by the delicious menu and extensive selections of California and French wines. After dinner, guests can be found relaxing in several fireplaced sitting areas, perhaps listening to the piano and sipping a drink.

The inn still maintains the outdoor heated swimming pool, clay tennis court, and 600-power Turret Telescope for guests to use. The tunnel and five-room office are also available for exploration upon request.

FRISKY FRIVOLITIES:

* There are over 32 acres for Bowser to explore, accompanied by his master.
* There is an improvised skating rink just down the road from the inn and cross-country skiing through the woods.
* In the summertime, there are excellent hiking and fishing opportunities.

HUGGING BEAR INN

Main Street
Chester, Vermont 05143
(802) 875-2412
Innkeepers: Paul and Georgette Thomas
Rooms: 6 doubles
Rates: $45-70
Payment: Personal checks (MC or VISA may be used for deposit)
Children: Welcome
Dogs: Well-behaved dogs accepted with prior approval (one-time $5 fee)
Open: All year

Teddy bears do something intriguing to adults: they cause them to feel a little like children again. And, of course, children of all ages delight in these whimsical little creatures. Paul and Georgette Thomas have created a special retreat for the child in all of us, using teddy bears as the theme and an 1800's Victorian mansion as the backdrop. It seems that many people go away on a vacation to unwind so they are able to return to work refreshed and able to be more productive. The inn truly fosters that ideal.

The Hugging Bear Inn is difficult to miss on a drive through Chester. Teddy bears of all sizes peek out the bay windows at passing motorists, seemingly beckoning them to come inside. Guests will be happy they did so, as a special warmth pervades this house. Sophie, the family dog, may be lying peacefully in the living room, while tantalizing smells emanate from the kitchen. The Thomas' will immediately make guests feel at home. Before heading off to one of the cozy bedrooms (complete with a special bear), guests may want to take the time to explore the Thomas' downstairs shop, home to over 1,000 teddy bears. Georgette will even give informative tours describing the various bears' personalities.

In the morning, before heading off to explore this part of Vermont, guests will be filled with a full country breakfast. When we were visiting, some handmade napkins and placemats with teddy bears on them had just arrived, sent by a grateful guest. Afterwards, a stroll through the fields or a walk up the hill behind the inn will be just enough exercise to get the day off to an invigorating start.

FRISKY FRIVOLITIES:
* After warming up on the inn's hill, guests may want to test their hiking prowess on any of the nearby trails. The Thomases will divulge their favorite local spots.
* After exploring the town, many hasten off to try some cross-country skiing.
* During your travels along the scenic back country roads, take the time to visit the many antique shops, marvel at the spectacular fall foliage, and spend an afternoon in the picturesque town of Grafton.

THE STONE HEARTH INN

Route 11
Chester, Vermont 05143
(802) 875-2525
Innkeepers: Janet and Don Strohmeyer
Rooms: 10 doubles
Rates: $30-76
Payment: Most major credit cards

Children: Welcome
Dogs: Welcome only with prior approval
Open: All year

The Stone Hearth Inn is a fabulous old Vermont farmhouse built in 1810. Like so many other buildings of its era, it has been added onto year after year. The brick facade houses rooms rambling off in many directions. The upstairs consists of bedrooms and the downstairs of a living room, dining room, library, and front parlor with a pretty fieldstone hearth. Wide pine floors covered with braided rugs are found throughout the inn.

Great care has gone into selecting the wallpaper for the guest rooms. Colors in the rooms are vibrant and varied. Simple quilts cover the beds, usually picking up a bright pink, forest green, or pale blue color from the floral wallpapers. These rooms are structurally unique with exposed beamed ceilings in some and gabled beamed ceilings in others. One fascinating room has logs, bark and all, that form beams supporting the ceiling. The antique beds and furnishings further complement the country decor.

Guests who choose to come down early for dinner will find books to read in the library or can perhaps pick up a game of table tennis or pool in the game room, housed in the barn. After a hearty meal, it might be nice to relax in front of the fire before retiring for the night. Every morning, a full country breakfast is served consisting of eggs, French toast, pancakes or waffles, muffins, fresh fruit juice, and tea or coffee. With a comfortable night's sleep and a filling breakfast under their belts, guests should be prepared for a day's journey afield.

FRISKY FRIVOLITIES:

* The Williams River is just across the road and makes a wonderful spot for a swim or quick dip. Even if you do not want to get wet, Bowser will surely want to take the plunge.
* Chester is within driving distance of the inn. It is fun to walk the historic streets and peek in the shop windows.
* The bicycling is good in the summer and cross-country skiing is popular with winter guests. There are great ski areas nearby to try if you do not like to blaze your own trails.

THE DARLING FAMILY INN

Route 100
Weston, Vermont 05161
(802) 824-3223
Innkeepers: Joan and Chapin Darling
Rooms: 5 doubles, 2 cottages
Rates: Doubles: $55-65; Cottages: $58 for two
Payment: Personal checks
Children: Over eight years old in the inn, smaller tots in the cottages
Dogs: Welcome in the two cottages
Open: All year except Christmas

The Darling Family Inn was built over 150 years ago and is surrounded by acres of pasturelands. Today, the only major change is scenic Route 100 running by the inn; however, this does not present a problem as the inn is set well off the road behind protective trees. The main building is a typical Vermont-style farmhouse. It is a cozy, comfortable place filled with antiques. The downstairs sitting room has two couches, one of which is covered with a subtle partridge design. Wall-to-wall carpeting softens footsteps, and the original hardwood floors are visible in most of the other rooms. A small secretary and a harvest table fit perfectly into this inviting room warmed by a big wood stove. A grandfather clock ticks quietly in the hallway. The guest rooms in the main building are furnished in keeping with the rest of the inn, with country antiques from America and Europe.

Guests with dogs and young children are welcome in either of the two intimate housekeeping cottages on the hill. Tucked into a grassy, rock studded knoll, the cottages are surrounded by apple trees. Sheer white ruffled tie-back curtains frame the multi-paned windows which overlook the green pastures and grazing cows. The cottages are more simply furnished than the rooms at the inn, with country furniture and simple red cotton spreads covering the beds. A harvest table is provided for dining or playing one of the many board games available. Hardwood floors are found throughout. Each of the kitchenettes is fully equipped.

The inn is close to the famous Weston Priory, home to the singing monks. The nearby town of Weston is particularly quaint with much to offer visitors, and it is centrally located for people wanting to explore the countryside. Weston also has summer theatre and a terrific selection of antique and Vermont craft stores. There are many fine restaurants in the area; however, the Darlings will also be happy to cook a special candlelight dinner at the inn. Of course, those staying in the cottages also have the option of enjoying a quiet meal right at home.

FRISKY FRIVOLITIES:
* Guests can wander among the expansive grounds. There are cows grazing here and so you may want to leash Bowser so that he does not bother them.
* Cross-country skiing is available throughout the area in the wintertime.
* Many pick up a packed lunch from the inn and try the hiking or fishing nearby or visit the beautiful towns of Manchester and Woodstock.

JOHNNY SEESAW'S

Route 11 (on Bromley Mountain)
Peru, Vermont 05152
(802) 824-5533
Innkeepers: Nancy and Gary Okun
Rooms: 27 doubles, 3 suites
Rates: $40-125 per person/double occupancy (MAP)
Payment: MC, VISA, personal checks
Children: Welcome
Dogs: Welcome with prior approval
Open: June to October, December to April

Johnny Seesaw's has reaped the benefits of its picturesque location, 2000 feet up on Bromley Mountain, since 1927. This rustic-looking building sits well off the road leading to Bromley and Stratton mountains. Panoramic views of the Green Mountains and valleys can be had through the many windows.

As guests step through the main door, they enter a gigantic living room dominated by a raised circular fireplace. This, as it turns out, is a favorite gathering place after a day on the mountain. A more casual sitting alcove with soft furniture is just a few steps away. A painted scene of Vermont fills the entire back wall. Across the room is the dining room, where tables are set simply with blue tablecloths. Hearty meals are served here which include freshly baked breads and homemade soups, as well as beef and vegetarian specialties. Desserts are rich and gooey. Post-dinner and/or skiing activities include the game room for children, allowing adults to trade ski stories around the intimate bar or watch the evening glow on the mountains from the window seats.

The guest rooms are many and varied. During the ski season, the third floor in the main lodge is used as a dorm. There are also cottages sleeping four to ten people — great for families or groups of friends. Rooms in the lodge range from one to two bedrooms with private baths. The decor is simple but comfortable, with Bates bedspreads, sheer curtains, and maple furniture.

In the summertime, when life is slower and more relaxed, there is a tennis court and a marble-rimmed Olympic-size swimming pool. These are wonderful gathering places on warm summer afternoons. Visitors will find that any time of year is ideal for visiting Johnny Seesaw's, if not for the friendships to be formed then for the "Best Yankee Cuisine in New England" (according to Skiing Magazine).

FRISKY FRIVOLITIES:
* The Appalachian Trail runs just behind the lodge and supplies challenging day hikes and overnight sojourns.
* The logging trails running throughout the area make for terrific cross-country skiing.
* The Battenkill River is a short drive from the inn and home to many fish just waiting to be caught. For those wishing to brush up on their fly casting, then the world famous Orvis School of Fly Casting is just around the corner in Manchester.

THE OLD TAVERN AT GRAFTON

Grafton, Vermont 05146
(802) 843-2231
Manager: Richard C. Ernst
Rooms: 9 guest rooms in two separate houses
Rates: $45-245 (entire house may be rented)
Payment: Personal checks
Children: Under 8 years old welcome in only three of the rental houses
Dogs: Welcome in two recently renovated houses
Open: All year except April, Christmas Eve, and Christmas Day

The Old Tavern at Grafton dates back to 1801. Famous visitors to the inn have included Henry David Thoreau, Ralph Waldo Emerson, Nathaniel Hawthorne, Daniel Webster, and Rudyard Kipling. With a history such as this it is no wonder that in 1965 the Windham Foundation felt it was time to restore the tavern and most of the other town buildings, in an attempt to preserve the historical architecture and heritage.

The two restored historic buildings accepting dogs are the Tuttle House and the Phebe Frost House. The Tuttle House is located on a quiet street, just a two-minute walk from the Tavern. A suite, perfect for a family, takes up the entire first floor and has two private entrances. A nice deck is located just outside the back door. A large red couch faces the blue mantled fireplace in the living room. A rocking chair rests off to the side close to a pretty harvest table. Framed horse prints decorate the walls. A television, along with a very modern kitchen, are the only concessions to the present. The two bedrooms are tastefully decorated with white cotton textured spreads on the beds and delicate flower prints on the walls. Iron lamps rest on subtly colored braided rugs. The bath is shared.

The second floor also has its own private entrance and has three bedrooms; two share a bath and the other is private. Tiny blue-flowered paper covers the walls in one bedroom whereas another has been painted a more neutral color with a Williamsburg green chair rail adding accent. Horticultural prints are neatly framed and simple antiques fill each room. Fluffy towels on standing racks are provided for those sharing a bathroom.

The Phebe Frost House is just two houses down from Grafton's General Store. This house is larger with rooms that are more separate from one another. Wide-board floors have been completely restored. The shared living room is dominated by a fireplace around which are gathered chintz-covered arm chairs and a blue and white checked couch. The very spacious kitchen lies just beyond the living room. A long Windsor bench fills one wall looking out towards a brick fireplace. A gigantic circular table can accommodate all the house guests at once.

The rooms have been furnished with period antiques. A high double bed, Queen Anne side table, and an antique dresser with mirror fill one room. A pristine flowered paper complements the clean white lines of the Bates spreads in another. A bow-front dresser adds ornamentation. One room upstairs is particularly noteworthy as the bed is waist high and requires a slight hop to get into at night. The eaves in the top floor rooms also lend architectural interest. Guests will find the Old Tavern at Grafton has a warmth to it that allows people to feel right at home and eager to return year after year. It certainly lives up to its reputation as "New England's Most Elegant Little Inn."

FRISKY FRIVOLITIES:
* Grafton is made for walking. The side streets will lead you past antique homes and the main street will bring you to the country store and a few specialty shops.
* The Grafton Village Cheese Company manufactures a cheddar cheese from the milk of Vermont's dairy cows. This is a good walk from the inn. Bowser will enjoy the exercise and can wait outside, while you learn more about cheese.
* There is a natural swimming pond at the inn and hiking trails all around Grafton. Cross-country skiing is a favorite pastime in the winter.

THE HAYES HOUSE

Grafton, Vermont 05146
(802) 843-2461
Host: Margery H. Heindel
Rooms: 1 single, 3 doubles
Rates: Single: $25; Doubles: $40-50
Payment: Personal checks
Children: Welcome
Dogs: Welcome
Open: All year except April

The charming town of Grafton was established some 200 years ago, serving as a busy center for lumbering, sheep raising, and a number of other cottage industries. Unfortunately, the Civil War had a devastating effect on many of the Vermont towns. It was not until the Windham Foundation was formed in 1963 that the entire Grafton area began a strong resurgence. Today, the refurbished town proudly stands as it once did so many years ago.

The Hayes House projects a bit of this history. Built in 1803, it predates its next door neighbor, an antique covered bridge, by some 67 years.

Guests will find the house furnished with an eclectic array of antique and more contemporary furniture. They are guaranteed to find something in every nook and cranny, including two resident cats and two chocolate labs. It is a warm and comfortable place that guests soon refer to as their "home away from home."

The bedrooms are equally cozy with choices of twin and double beds bedecked with nubbly spreads. The room on the first floor is particularly delightful, with its waist-high four-poster bed (a giant leap or small stool is almost a requirement for gaining access to it), fireplace, and private bath. The bath adds a few touches of the whimsical, with a penguin-covered shower curtain and newspaper-clipping wallpaper. The special amenities are not ignored. Fresh flowers from the garden add a springtime flair, and a bowl of fruit and tasty cookies help fill your tummy.

Breakfast is a Continental meal with freshly baked muffins and breads being the early morning treat. This is served in a cozy downstairs beamed-ceiling dining room. There is also an extra refrigerator for guests who wish to store their own supplies. Further down the hallway, there are bookshelves offering guests a variety of selections for afternoon reading. Many take their reading materials out to the porch, where the meadow and the sounds of a babbling brook enhance this pastoral setting. In the wintertime, Margery has a steaming pot of homemade soup on the stove that guests may help themselves to after 2 p.m. The warmth and hospitality Margery shows to her guests during their stay lingers even after they have left.

FRISKY FRIVOLITIES:
* The village of Grafton is a two-minute walk from the Hayes House. Many of the antique homes have been restored, offering fascinating sightseeing.
* In the wintertime, many visit the area because of its terrific cross-country skiing. Take Bowser, a box lunch, and warm clothing for a day of skiing and picnicking.
* Should you wish a scenic drive, we recommend heading towards Manchester, where after enjoying the picturesque scenery, visitors will be delighted by this upscale Vermont town.

THE FOUR COLUMNS INN

230 West Street
Newfane, Vermont 05345
(802) 365-7713
Innkeepers: Sandy and Jacques Allembert
Rooms: 12 doubles
Rates: $65-105 (MAP)
Payment: MC, VISA, personal checks
Children: Eight years and older welcome
Dogs: Small, well-behaved dogs are welcome
Open: All year except a few weeks in April and November

The Four Columns Inn is a gracious white clapboard mansion built by General Pardon Kimball for his wife in 1830. In 1965, the mansion's barn was carefully renovated to restore it architecturally and preserve its original charm and beauty. Today, the two buildings house stately guest quarters and a renowned restaurant. The restaurant came into being when the chef from the neighboring Old Newfane Inn decided to branch out and open his own restaurant across the road.

Newfane is a delightful village offering picturesque surroundings and classic examples of Vermont construction. The Four Columns Inn adds to this setting with its graceful lines, charming decor, and hospitality. Specially selected country antiques are found throughout with unique bedsteads being the standout. Guests may find that their room contains a brass or canopy bed. One bed of particular interest is a four poster; the posts have been handcarved by a Newfane craftsman. The only modern concessions are air conditioning and private bathrooms.

Those who are staying at the inn are especially fortunate as they only need to walk to the converted barn to enjoy some of the finest food in this region. People come from near and far just to feast on the nouvelle cuisine. The herbs are fresh from the Allembert's garden, and the entrees are imaginative. A large brick fireplace, adorned with cooking utensils, is the focal point for the dining room. The shadows from the candlelight dance along the beamed ceilings and formally set tables. Wall coverings are reminiscent of the provinces in France. After-dinner drinks can be enjoyed in the tiny bar.

FRISKY FRIVOLITIES:
* The inn has over 150 acres that are filled with hiking and cross-country ski trails. In the summer, guests will enjoy the inn's various flower and herb gardens.
* Bowser may want a quick dip in the pond before a stroll through Newfane.
* There are a number of country roads within walking distance of the inn leading to secluded areas in and around Newfane.

NOTCH BROOK RESORT

Notch Brook Road
Stowe, Vermont 05672
(802) 253-4882
Manager: Ray Ostrander
Rooms: 50 townhouses (1 to 3 bedrooms)
Rates: $68-247
Payment: All major credit cards
Children: Welcome
Dogs: Welcome, any damage is the responsibility of the dog owner
Open: All year

The 15 year-old Notch Brook, a four-season resort, is located on a wooded hillside overlooking Mt. Mansfield. Each of the townhouses and apartments is privately owned and rented to the public through the resort management. Thus, the decor and furnishings vary depending upon the owner's personal taste. The basic floor plan may include a living room with fireplace, dining room, fully equipped kitchen, modern bathroom, and either a deck or terrace.

Over the last year, new draperies and wall-to-wall carpeting have been installed in each of the townhouses. The architectural lines are clean and simple, accented by the use of brick and lightly stained woods. Some of the furnishings in the accommodations utilize a Scandinavian design. The kitchens usually feature a pass-through window to the dining room. The living rooms are favorite gathering places at the end of a full day. From here guests may either enjoy the views of the mountains through the floor-to-ceiling windows or the warmth of the fireplace. Many of the bi- or multi-level townhouses have window seats, alcoves filled with bookshelves, and fold-out couch beds. The daily maid service is an added convenience for those who wish to omit that aspect of home living.

One of the best features to these townhouses is that they provide guests with many additional facilities and activities. Not only are there tennis courts and saunas, but the resort also offers an outdoor heated swimming pool and a hospitality room with a VCR and big screen television (first-run movies shown nightly). A shuttlebus service, from the resort to the Mt. Mansfield, runs daily between 8:30 and 9:15 a.m. and 3:30 and 4:30 p.m. A ski room, available for quick repairs, will keep guests' skis in tune during their visit. Each morning, a complimentary Continental breakfast is served between 7:30 and 9:30 a.m., giving guests an extra boost.

FRISKY FRIVOLITIES:
* The resort is located on a large piece of property, which will give Bowser ample opportunity to burn off steam.
* The local cross-country skiing is excellent, as is the hiking and nearby shopping (in the village).
* The maple sugar houses offer interesting tours of their facilities and an opportunity to purchase a variety of their maple products.

TOPNOTCH AT STOWE

Mount Mansfield Road, P.O. Box 1260
Stowe, Vermont 05672
(802) 253-8585
General Manager: Stephen Price
Rooms: 100 doubles, 15 townhouses with kitchens, 1 chalet with kitchen
Rates: Doubles: $70-160; Suites/Townhouses: $120-460 (tennis, ski, off-
    season packages available)
Payment: All major credit cards

Children: Welcome
Dogs: Welcome
Open: All year

Although Topnotch at Stowe is not exactly an intimate inn, it is a fine resort with all the personal service one would expect from a smaller inn. This is soon apparent as guests are attended to promptly and courteously at the front desk. The reception area resembles a wood-paneled library, and is tucked into a corner of the lobby.

The guest bedrooms are quite simple in design; however, unique handmade Vermont quilts can be found on each bed, antiques and reproduction furnishings are ever present, and there is a small library in each chamber. Many also feature large picture windows overlooking the gardens. A fragrant selection of imported soaps and gels can be found in each of the modern bathrooms. Other personal touches include ice (delivered to the room every afternoon), turned-down beds, and fine chocolates placed on fluffed pillows.

Guests will feel quite at home congregating in any of the cozy sitting areas scattered throughout the hotel. Hanging plants give one area the ambiance of a greenhouse, deep sofas make another feel like a den. There is a gigantic living room with picture windows overlooking Mt. Mansfield and a fireplace for warming guests' toes after an active day of skiing. The hotel also offers a myriad of activities for any who are yearning for some additional exercise.

It would be difficult to be bored during a vacation at Topnotch. Fourteen tennis courts (four indoor and ten outdoor) await racquet buffs. For those who would rather swing a club or mallet, there is both a putting green and croquet field. Swimming is also available in an outdoor heated pool. Guests craving indoor excitement will find an electronic game room, which also houses billiard and ping pong tables. Lastly, an invigorating workout may be had in the exercise room complete with stationary bicycles and a whirlpool.

Topnotch at Stowe is unparalleled in what it offers its guests. It is a terrific place to spend a week or just a few days. When booking accommodations, people should keep in mind that there are also privately owned townhouses available. These are a great bargain for a family or a group of friends traveling together. They offer a kitchen and a variety of bedrooms providing additional privacy, as well as full use of the hotel's facilities.

FRISKY FRIVOLITIES:
* Hiking trails are in great supply all around Mt. Mansfield. There is also terrific cross-country skiing and outdoor skating.
* There are a number of local fishing streams. You can fish, while Bowser explores from the banks.
* Drop the kids off at the Alpine slide and take Bowser up Mt. Mansfield's auto road. The views from the top can stretch as far as 70 miles.

122

THE 1860 HOUSE

Box 276, One School Street
Stowe, Vermont 05672
(802) 253-7351
Hosts: Richard M. Hubbard and Rose Marie Matulionis
Rooms: 5 doubles
Rates: $50-100 (weekly rates available)
Payment: Personal checks
Children: Welcome
Dogs: Welcome with prior approval
Open: All year

The 1860 House is located in the center of Stowe village opposite the Library Art Center. This charming B&B is listed in the National Register of Historic Places. The interior of the house has been nicely refurbished, mostly in keeping with the prevailing ambiance of the 1800s. The inviting den acts as the nucleus, drawing guests together for conversation, games, and relaxation. A sectional sofa, matching arm chairs, and a woodstove are the focal points for the room. Built-in bookshelves, filled to capacity, line one wall. Antiques can be found in every corner, including an antique writing/game table and an upright piano. Huge beams support the archways.

Two of the three upstairs bedrooms have private bathrooms, one of

123

which is reported to be the smallest bath in Stowe (a converted closet). The adjacent bedroom has natural light streaming in through a skylight, onto a bright green and blue Vermont quilt. Simple antique furnishings set on wide pine floors are the norm for each room. Thoughtful touches include baskets of fresh fruit and splits of wine. A particularly appropriate guest bedroom for those traveling with a dog is downstairs, below the den. A private back entrance leads through a storage room (perfect for damp dogs, skis, and boots) to a long rectangular bed chamber. An extremely high queen-size bed rests at the end of the room. There are pretty views of the terraced garden. A great way to relax at night is either in the sauna, jacuzzi, or steam room, which is available to guests.

In the morning, a light breakfast of orange juice, coffee/tea, freshly baked muffins or breads, and cereal is served in the formal dining room. A filling meal will give guests the energy to see all that Stowe has to offer.

FRISKY FRIVOLITIES:
* The back yard has a peaceful, enclosed sitting area for a well-behaved Bowser and his master.
* Hiking trails abound throughout the area. Your hosts will provide their favorite ideas.
* The streets in and around Stowe are great for walking. The stores on the side avenues are quaint and the homes are interesting.

TEN ACRES LODGE

P.O. Box 3220, RR 1, Luce Hill Road
Stowe, Vermont 05672
(802) 253-7638
Innkeepers: Dave and Libby Helprin
Rooms: 14 doubles, 2 cottages
Rates: Doubles: $55-140; Cottages: $140-200
Payment: Major credit cards, personal checks
Children: Welcome
Dogs: Well-mannered dogs welcome in cottages only
Open: All year with exception of two weeks in April

The Ten Acres Lodge prides itself on providing charming guest rooms, personal service, and tantalizing New England cuisine. It succeeds in all respects. The main inn is furnished with country antiques. A fieldstone fireplace is shared by the living room and a cozy library, which is well stocked with classic books. There is also a comfy, cushioned window seat underneath a bay window. From this vantage point it is easy to be distracted from reading by the enchanting views of the meadows. The living room lies between the dark, paneled bar and the intimate dining room. Deep sofas around the fireplace provide a perfect setting for sipping either afternoon tea or an after-dinner drink.

Guests traveling with a dog are welcome in the cottages. These are a two-minute walk from the inn and accommodate between four and six people. They are most appropriate for either two to three couples or a family. Each has been recently renovated and reflects a Vermont country theme. The Red Cottage is the largest with three bedrooms, one of which has its own private bath. Wide pine floors covered with throw rugs are found throughout. White Bates spreads cover the beds and the walls have been papered with Laura Ashley-style country prints. Many an evening could be spent in the living room in front of the fireplace. Duck decoys rest on the mantle and duck prints grace the walls.

The Grey Cottage has much the same feeling, with hardwood floors, braided rugs, and cut and pierced lamp shades. The only significant difference is that this cottage has a newly remodeled kitchen. A small fireplace will warm toes on chilly evenings. Guests are also provided with a television and telephone. A pool and tennis court lie between the cottages and the inn for everyone's enjoyment.

Dinner at the inn is an elegant affair and it is suggested that when guests book their rooms, they should also make dinner reservations. The specialties include swordfish, lamb, and veal served with a variety of delicious sauces. Homemade breads, soups, and pastries are fine accompaniments. Many people come back year after year to partake in the gastronomical delights and fine wines. The inn also serves a delicious breakfast to its guests.

FRISKY FRIVOLITIES:
* Cross-country skiing is available just outside the door and across the street.
* The inn is located on the edge of Stowe, lending a country feeling to it.
  In the summertime, hiking trails are within a five-minute drive of the inn.
* Long walks along rural back roads can be found by stepping out the cottage door and heading in either direction.

GREEN MOUNTAIN INN

Main Street, Box 220
Stowe, Vermont 05672
(802) 253-7301
Innkeeper: Lewis Kiesler
Rooms: 58 doubles
Rates: Doubles: $58-115; MAP an additional $26 per person (package rates
  available)
Payment: AE, MC, VISA, personal checks
Children: Welcome
Dogs: Well-mannered dogs welcome
Open: All year

Some people come to Stowe to get away from it all. Others like to be
in the thick of things, close to the restaurants and stores. The Green Mountain
Inn is particularly appropriate for the latter group. Built in 1833, the inn is listed
on the National Register of Historic Places. The main building went through
major renovations during its 150th birthday in 1983. What has emerged is a
delightful combination of the old and the new.

Guest rooms have been furnished in keeping with a Colonial feeling.
Hardwood floors creak and slope, wainscottings are painted in the traditional
Williamsburg blues and reds, and walls are papered in complementary tiny
prints. Canopied pencil post beds are draped with equally simple textured white
spreads. The innkeeper even had reproduction 18th-century furniture crafted
for the rooms. The bathrooms are a bit on the small side, but are very clean.
Guests who are looking for accommodations with character should ask for a
room in the main building; however, if ease of access or an outside entrance is
important, then the annex quarters are more appropriate.

Around every corner guests will find a cozy nook for reading or
relaxing. There is a living room on the first floor with dark green Chippendale-
style sofas pulled up before a crackling fireplace. These formal furnishings
combine nicely with the more traditional New England pieces. There is even
a small chess board set up on a leather-topped table for those who wish to
partake in a quick game.

The energetic will enjoy the fitness center, housed in an old barn to the
rear of the property. This is a fully equipped spa with everything from steam
rooms and saunas to rowing and bicycling equipment. There are also squash
and racquetball courts, should one tire of skiing and hiking. Guests are
encouraged to make full use of these facilities. In fact, there are even special Spa
packages.

The two fine restaurants found on the premises should not be missed. One first floor dining room is a bit more elegant than the one on the garden level. The former is known for its New England meat and potatoes, while the "Whip" restaurant serves a lighter fare which includes quiche, hearty sandwiches, and fish. For those who want to know, the menu boards even supply the calorie count for each dish. This restaurant overlooks the patio and running stream through a wall of French doors. The adjacent mahogany bar is a favorite gathering place after skiing.

FRISKY FRIVOLITIES:
* Guests will want to take advantage of the window shopping available in town and at the ski resorts.
* Take Bowser down to Ben and Jerry's ice cream factory and store. He can romp through the adjacent meadow while you eat your ice cream.
* Many choose to visit the Stowe area in the summer, when windsurfing, canoeing, nature walks, and tennis are the preferred sports.

ONE AKER FARM BED AND BREAKFAST

East Craftsbury Road
Craftsbury Common, Vermont 05827
(802) 755-6705
Hosts: Dale and Ed Leary
Rooms: 2 doubles
Rates: $25-30
Payment: Personal checks
Children: Welcome
Dogs: Welcome
Open: All year

Craftsbury was discovered by Colonel Ebenezer Crafts in 1788. His son, Samuel, became the head of the town and eventually the governor of Vermont. The nucleus of Craftsbury is a charming village of quaint New England homes and churches located around a grassy green. One Aker Farm, built around 1830, could be termed a more recent addition to this area.

Surrounded by other dairy farms, One Aker Farm was a working farm until 1973. Now it is comprised of the original farmhouse and barn encircled by an acre of land. Horses, chickens, and sheep give it a pastoral feeling. A simple lifestyle amid picturesque surroundings were just what Ed Leary was searching for when he left Duxbury, Massachusetts. He had grown up in this charming coastal town, and after serving as the town's conservation officer, Ed and his wife Dale decided it was time to move to Vermont. Craftsbury seemed to offer all that they had been searching for in terms of lifestyle and setting. They have opened their home in order to share this special spot with guests from all parts of the country.

The 150-year-old farmhouse has two upstairs rooms for guests with either a double or twin beds available. They are simply decorated, each with a homey feeling. Although both share a single bathroom, this does not seem to bother most guests. After a good night's sleep nestled under soft sheets and thick blankets, guests are treated to an old-fashioned country breakfast.

Vermont-made maple syrup tops light pancakes made with eggs gathered from the farm's chickens. Of course, the eggs can also be scrambled or poached and served with toast and muffins. Coffee and tea are also offered. There are many activities in the immediate area to help guests work off a One Aker Farm breakfast. They might even want to help with the chores or perhaps go out and visit with the farm's animals.

FRISKY FRIVOLITIES:
* Craftsbury Common is hilly, which makes for invigorating walking excursions. The roads around the farm are a little flatter and are more fun for those wanting to meander.
* The Northeast Kingdom offers guests many nearby fishing spots, as well as wonderful country roads for walking, jogging, or bicycling.
* Cross-country skiing is one of the major attractions of the area. There are both groomed and ungroomed trails for the novice and the expert skiers.

THE INN ON THE COMMON

Main Street
Craftsbury Common, Vermont 05827
(802) 586-9619
Innkeepers: Michael and Penny Schmitt
Rooms: 18 doubles
Rates: $95-195 single occupancy (MAP); $80-105 per person double occupancy (MAP)
Payment: MC, VISA, personal checks
Children: Welcome
Dogs: Well-behaved dogs accepted with prior approval ($10 fee per pet per visit)
Open: All year

128

Country elegance and sophistication combine in northern Vermont to create one of the most unique spots in all of New England, the Inn on the Common. Everything about the inn is close to perfection. Bright, bold, and beautiful fabrics have been chosen for both the guest rooms and the sitting areas. The gardens have been landscaped with an incredible array of perennials, and the views of the surrounding countryside should not be missed.

Three buildings make up the Inn on the Common. From the outside, they are like so many of the antique Colonials found throughout New England — beautiful but not terribly unique. Step through the door though, and guests are immediately struck by the exceptional elegance. The sitting room has an eye-catching bold black, pink, and red chintz sofa with matching balloon shades at the windows. Pink and white striped papers adorn the walls. Antiques are found throughout. If guests have a little extra time before they check in, then all the better, as there is an interesting array of books in the built-in bookshelves.

The guest rooms are equally elegant. Handmade Vermont quilts cover every bed whether they be brass, pine, or a combination of brass and porcelain. The quilts also set the tone for the colors selected for each of the rooms. Whether it be seafoam green contrasting with pink or vibrant blue, or green and red flowers against a stark white background, guests are sure to enjoy the warmth and interesting color combinations. Most bedrooms come with private baths; however, those guests with shared baths are in some ways fortunate as there are thick terry-cloth robes provided for their use.

After settling in their rooms, many like to come downstairs before dinner to get acquainted. Meals are wonderful affairs, as much for the beautifully prepared food as for the view through the picture windows of the English gardens. For those feeling a bit sated, post-dinner activities could include a walk through the 15 acres, a proper game of croquet, a refreshing dip in the pool, or for the more energetic, a game of tennis on the clay court.

The Inn on the Common is not the sort of place for a one-night stay. The accommodations and the surrounding area deserve at least a few days for exploration and appreciation. Guests are welcome to make use of the Craftsbury Sports Common. This is located on Big Hosmer Lake and offers swimming, sailing, horseback riding, canoeing, fishing, and even sculling. In the wintertime, activities shift to downhill skiing, snowshoeing, skating, and cross-country skiing. For those planning a trip to Vermont, a visit to Craftsbury is well worth one's consideration.

FRISKY FRIVOLITIES:

* There are many nature trails in the area for hiking and walking. Ask the innkeepers for their seasonal favorites.
* The lake is a perfect place for all sorts of water activities that you and Bowser

can partake in. If you do not want to canoe, swimming and retrieving are certainly viable options.

* Many enjoy touring scenic Route 100, which leads them to maple sugaring houses, Ben & Jerry's ice cream factory, and an assortment of charming towns and villages.

BERKSON FARMS

Junction Routes 108 and 105
Enosburg Falls, Vermont 05450
(802) 933-2522
Innkeepers: Dick and Joanne Keesler
Rooms: 4 doubles
Rates: $25-45
Payment: Personal checks
Children: Always welcome
Dogs: Welcome
Open: All year

Northern Vermont is a part of New England that remains largely unexplored. The people who do take the time to drive up near the Canadian border will be rewarded with the sight of seemingly endless emerald green pastures and rolling hills dotted with beautiful farms. Berkson Farms is no exception. Guests of the Keeslers will find a working dairy farm, complete with cows, sheep, lambs, geese, ducks, rabbits, and chickens. There is enough to both entertain and educate children and adults alike.

Guests are welcome to come and relax; however, the real fun involves actually working the farm with the Keeslers. Choose a different job each day, including collecting eggs, *helping* to milk the cows, or bringing in the hay. In the spring, collect the buckets of sap from the maple trees or plant the garden.

Guests sleep soundly at night in one of the four bedrooms. An eclectic collection of New England country antiques can be found throughout the house. One bedroom has a headboard that fills most of the wall behind it and a rocking chair set strategically to take advantage of the views. Hardwood floors are covered with braided rugs and antique bureaus await guests' clothing. Only one bedroom has a private bath, while the rest share facilities.

Each morning, well rested workers (guests) are rewarded for their previous day's efforts with a full country breakfast. It is always plentiful, hearty, and homecooked. Many a leisurely morning has been spent around the huge circular table exchanging stories, while the woodstove warms the brisk morning air. The dining room is particularly inviting with its rose-colored wallpaper and old-fashioned mahogany sideboard. There is also a sitting room looking out over the 600 acres of land belonging to the farm.

FRISKY FRIVOLITIES:
* The farm has cross-country ski trails on the property. Just put on your skis and go.
* In the summertime, there are secret swimming holes fed by sparkling creeks. Ask the Keeslers for directions to these special spots.
* To visit many of Vermont's maple sugar houses, call (802) 828-2418 for information and an extensive map. The same back roads leading to the sugar houses may also be enjoyed during fall foliage season.

TYLER PLACE ON LAKE CHAMPLAIN

Box 100, Route 7
Highgate Springs, Vermont 05460
(802) 868-3301
Hosts: The Tyler Family
Rooms: 20 doubles and suites; 30 cottages
Rates: $62-90 (AP and includes most recreational activities; off-season rates
    available)
Payment: Personal checks

Children: Always welcome (children's rates available)

Dogs: "Gentle, well-behaved" dogs are welcome in cottages. Dogs must always be leashed, kept away from the pool, guest swimming, and boating areas.

Open: Mid-May to mid-October

The Tyler Place is a 165-acre resort located right on the shores of Lake Champlain, and it caters to the entire family. Children ranging in age from 3 to 18 years will find a myriad of group activities available to them. The children are placed together according to their age bracket. Those families who are considering bringing tiny tots should not despair, as there are also the Junior Midget (1 to 3 years old) and Pre-Midget (1 month to 3 years old) programs. Finally, there are also parent's helpers and baby sitters available. The programs have been designed to keep everyone happy and give the adults a little extra time to enjoy some tennis, windsurfing, sailing, water-skiing, fishing, golf, or badminton.

After a very active day, most guests will return to their cottages. Some of these are rustic in design, resembling deluxe summer-camp cabins, while others are more quaint with white shingles and red shutters. Many are grouped on the lake or tucked into the rocks overlooking the water. They range in size from three to six rooms and all of them have working fireplaces. Some have kitchenettes and one small bedroom, while others are geared more for families offering a living room, full-size kitchen, and assorted bedrooms. They are simply furnished with white wicker, floral papers, and area rugs covering hardwood floors. Guests will find the mood in all to be bright and cheerful.

Dining at the inn is a very casual affair. Breakfasts are served buffet style and light lunches are featured. The food is simple yet tasty. Some evenings the men might want to wear a jacket for the candlelit dinners; however, for the most part jeans and sweaters are the standard dress. The Tyler Place also features theme nights, such as Monte Carlo or the South Sea Islands. Guests are encouraged to call in advance for the theme during the week of their visit. Movies, videos, and guitar sing-alongs are some of the quieter evening activities.

Guests will not complain of boredom during their stay at The Tyler Place, as there is something offered for anyone who enjoys the outdoors, the scenery of Vermont, or lakeside activities. Those who prefer a quieter vacation experience should think about visiting during the off-summer months when it is not quite so busy.

FRISKY FRIVOLITIES:

* Water-loving dogs will enjoy swimming in the lake as long as they are exercised away from the main water sport areas.

* The resort has 165 acres to explore with a leashed dog. There are hills and flatlands as well as trails along the shore.
* Bicycling is terrific in this area as the roads are flat and the countryside scenic. Only dogs who are used to running alongside a bicycle should accompany their masters.

SHORE ACRES INN AND RESTAURANT

RR 1, Box 3
North Hero Island, Vermont 05474
(802) 372-8722, 372-5853
Managers: Mike and Susan Tranby
Rooms: 18 doubles
Rates: $40-70
Payment: MC, VISA, personal checks
Children: Welcome
Dogs: Welcome
Open: Lakeside units open May 1 to October 31, B&B open all year

The Shore Acres Inn is perfectly situated to take advantage of the panoramic views of Lake Champlain and the Green Mountains. This rural setting, coupled with expansive grounds and over a half mile of private shoreline, provides guests all the solitude and tranquility they could expect.

There are a number of accommodations available to guests. The B&B rooms are just opposite the farmhouse. These newly renovated guest quarters have clean lines accented by Scandinavian furniture. White and blue striped comforters cover comfortable beds with simple light pine frames. Navy blue fabric with white dots covers the armchairs. The bathrooms were not overlooked during the renovations and are also quite modern. Air conditioning, clock radios, and color television are additional amenities. All of the B&B rooms have terrific views of the lake from both the windows and from the new pressure-treated semi-private decks. At the end of a long day, there is nothing quite as refreshing as a lake breeze.

Further down the road, on the lakefront, are the guest quarters that resemble a motel in structure only. The new managers have spent an extraordinary amount of time updating the bedrooms and bathrooms. They have the same simple, airy feeling found in the B&B rooms. During our visit, the final coats of paint were being applied, new furniture was arriving, and pretty country curtains were being hung at the windows. The beds with maple headboards are covered with white Bates spreads. Guests may lounge comfortably on some of the more classic furniture. What makes these accommodations truly unique are their 180-degree views of and accessibility to the lake.

There are a number of activities to keep people busy during the day. Of course, swimming in the lake is a favorite pastime, as are windsurfing and fishing. There are also lawn games, an informal 300-yard driving range, and horseback riding. Hearty appetites will definitely be sated at the newly remodeled restaurant. The chefs at Shore Acres are proud of their new menu, which emphasizes hearty homemade meals using the freshest local vegetables, fruit, fish, and Vermont-raised lamb. The Tranby's are wonderful hosts, who will also go out of their way to accommodate their guests' needs. For those who enjoy the water and a very casual way of life, this resort is an especially appropriate choice.

FRISKY FRIVOLITIES:
* There are acres and acres for Bowser to romp on and an enormous lake to swim in.
* Those who have not explored Burlington may wish to take a short drive and see how a recent transformation has improved this city on the lake.
* After taking a ride on the Lake Champlain Ferries, a wonderful trip may be had by driving to historic Montreal.

RABBIT HILL INN

Pucker Street
Lower Waterford, Vermont 05848
(802) 748-5168
Innkeepers: Sharon and Bill Risso
Rooms: 19 doubles
Rates: $55-75 per person double occupancy (MAP)
Payment: Personal checks preferred; MC, VISA accepted
Children: Not appropriate for small children
Dogs: Well-behaved dogs welcomed with prior approval
Open: All year with exception of first three weeks in November and the
    month of April

The Rabbit Hill Inn has been a part of the Vermont countryside and history for well over a century, serving travelers for the majority of its lifetime. One of the three buildings standing today was originally used as a tavern and general store. The main building was later constructed and used as a shop for manufacturing sleighs, wagons, and wheels. It was subsequently enlarged to service the tradesmen traveling the busy route between Portland and the interior of New England. The final addition came in 1855, when O.D. Hurlburt bought the inn and built a rather unique ballroom (due to its bent-wood construction creating a springy floor).

Today, the inn retains all of its original charm and beauty, catering to guests from all over the country as well as the local New England visitor. Antiques can be found throughout the inn. Five of the spacious bedrooms have working fireplaces. One in particular has two loveseats arranged next to the fireplace with an antique organ off to the side. Other rooms have high canopy beds or perhaps antique four-poster beds blanketed by handmade Vermont quilts. Braided rugs cover the hardwood floors. Views of the mountains can be seen through paned windows in almost every bedroom. Guests might be tempted to spend more of their vacation in the room if the public areas were not so inviting.

One sitting room has a gigantic woodstove, that many like to gather around while waiting for dinner. Meals at the inn are special events, served in an interesting and creative manner. Afterwards, guests might want to pick out something from the book nook or perhaps go for a stroll along the one main street in the village. The church, dating back to 1859, is just across the street and the lending library is only a few steps away. The library is probably one of the few places that still permits people to check out books on the honor system. Lower Waterford still remains a testament to the old way of life in a true New England village.

FRISKY FRIVOLITIES:

* In the wintertime, cross-country skiing is the favorite pastime, as trails run from the inn down by the Connecticut River. The surrounding woodlands are accessible to those who want to blaze their own path.
* Hiking along the inn's trails in the summertime is a terrific way to get in shape for the more challenging climbs that can be found in the local White Mountains.
* If sailing is more appealing, then the waters above Moore Dam would be most appropriate. Those who prefer to paddle will find the Connecticut River to be an inviting place to start a canoe trip.

THE OLD CUTTER INN

Burke Mountain Access Road
East Burke, Vermont 05832
(802) 626-5152
Innkeepers: Marti and Fritz Walther
Rooms: 9 singles and doubles, 1 suite
Rates: Singles and Doubles: $20-36; Suite: $72
Payment: MC, VISA, personal checks
Children: Welcome
Dogs: Welcome
Open: All year except April and November

The Old Cutter Inn was originally a farmhouse, built in 1845. Located at the end of a winding road, near the Burke ski resort, this red-shingled inn has a wonderful view of the mountains, valleys, and lakes below. The low-ceilinged farmhouse contains a restaurant and rustic tavern with circular wood tables. Both the restaurant and tavern draw many of the locals who, after a long day of skiing, like to pull up in front of the crackling fireplace to exchange stories. They also come for the delicious and hearty meals. Fritz's dinner specialties are veal Cordon Bleu, fresh rainbow trout, and coq-au-vin.

The less well-known guest rooms are tucked into the second floor of the farmhouse or can be found in the building across the way. They are all very simply decorated with Colonial wallpaper reflecting either a patriotic theme or a floral design. Some bedrooms feature charming eaves with tiny windows tucked into them, while others have low ceilings giving the room a cozy feeling. Well worn hardwood floors are covered with braided rugs. Guests may choose from bedrooms with either shared or private baths. For those desiring more privacy, rooms are available in the separate building next to the farmhouse.

In addition to the great alpine and Nordic skiing, many of the inn's guests opt to visit in the summertime to take advantage of the bicycling and walking to be found along these Vermont country roads. The inn offers special packages for both bicyclers and skiers. Lunch supplies for hikers or skiers can be found at Bailey's Country Store. This newly remodeled store features all sorts of gourmet goodies and hearty sandwiches, as well as an assortment of sweets and an excellent selection of wines. The staples of life can also be found alongside decorative Vermont quilts and sweaters. Bailey's is not to be missed as it is a most unusual country store.

FRISKY FRIVOLITIES:
* Walking these beautiful country roads is a terrific way to see the old farm-houses, grazing livestock, and Vermont greenery.
* There is wonderful cross-country skiing in the area. Dashney Farm offers lessons for the novice and the expert.
* The hiking trails are plentiful throughout the area and the fishing is terrific in the many lakes. Combine the two for a day of activity and relaxation.

QUIMBY COUNTRY

P.O. Box F
Averill, Vermont 05901
(802) 822-5533
Innkeeper: June LaRou
Cottages: 20
Rates: $55-65 for adults daily; $25-$45 for children 3-15 years old
Payment: Personal checks
Children: Welcome
Dogs: Very welcome, but they should be kept on a leash around the cottages
      and lodge areas
Open: May through September

Quimby Country is the ultimate family vacation spot for those who enjoy the beauty and serenity of northern Vermont. Visitors will not be disappointed in their selection of Quimby Country. Over 700 untouched acres surround the 1800's lodge and cottages that are nestled along the edge of Forest Lake. New guests will be welcomed by the old-timers who will, in turn, introduce them to the other families who have also been coming here for years.

It will not be long before guests are settled into the cottages and feeling a part of the Quimby "way of life." Simple, well-worn maple furnishings, parchment paper lampshades, and Franklin stoves can be found in each cottage. Some are even equipped with kitchenettes for those who prefer to cook rather than take advantage of the three meals served each day in the main lodge. Of course, the fishing for salmon and smallmouth bass is excellent and fishermen can always catch their dinners. Many choose to have breakfast brought directly to their cottage.

There is a 70-person guest limit at Quimby Country, which ensures a personal touch and a casual atmosphere. The counselors plan activities with children over the age of five, and baby-sitters are available for the younger tykes. This leaves parents free to canoe, sail, windsurf, or play tennis. After a busy day, many like to gather at the lodge in front of the fieldstone fireplace to catch up on the day's events.

Quimby Country is a wonderfully rustic spot that works well primarily because of the people who come back year after year and the close family ties this creates. It also has much to do with the attitude of the management, which is reflected in a statement contained in their brochure: "We believe ....vacations should bring you three measures of happiness and benefits: full enjoyment in anticipation, deep pleasure in daily realization, and glowing memories to last always."

FRISKY FRIVOLITIES:
* There are more acres to wander through than most people could cover in a week. The inn will pack a picnic lunch and you supply the rest.
* Bowser and the family should go down to the lake for a paddle, dip, or just some sun.
* Many have true water dogs. If yours fits the bill, try a tippy canoe ride or a sail across the lake for an afternoon of fun.

NEW HAMPSHIRE

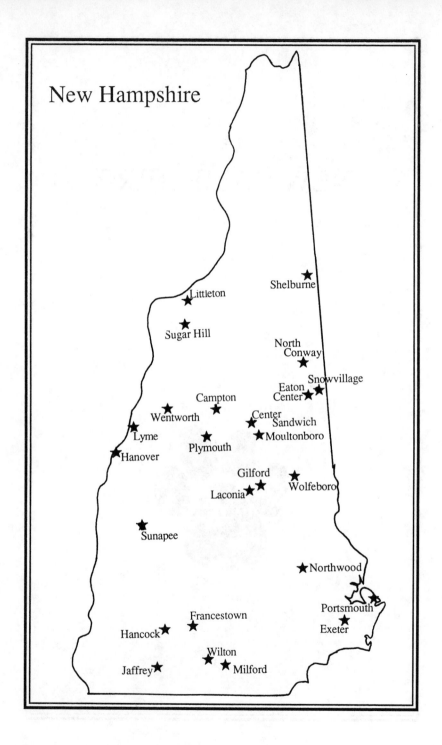

New Hampshire

Littleton

Shelburne

Sugar Hill

North
Conway

Snowvillage
Eaton
Center

Campton

Center
Sandwich

Wentworth

Moultonboro

Lyme

Plymouth

Hanover

Gilford

Wolfeboro

Laconia

Sunapee

Northwood

Portsmouth

Francestown

Hancock

Exeter

Wilton

Jaffrey

Milford

PHILBROOK FARM INN

North Road
Shelburne, New Hampshire 03581
(603) 466-3831
Innkeepers: Nancy Philbrook, Constance and Larry Leger
Rooms: 20 doubles, 6 cottages
Rates: Doubles: $34-55; Cottages: $250 per week (MAP) (AP available for
    weekly stays)
Payment: Personal checks
Children: Welcome
Dogs: Allowed in the cottages, summer months only
Open: May 1 to October 31, December 26 to March 31

    The Philbrook Farm Inn has been an institution in this part of New
Hampshire since 1861. Through the years, the innkeepers have carefully
maintained the farmhouse and cottages, paying special attention to preserving
their charm and character. Perhaps this is one of the reasons guests return year
after year. First-time visitors will find this portion of the White Mountains to
be beautiful, and the simplicity of the accommodations and lifestyle are
refreshing.
    Guests traveling with a dog are welcome in the cottages during the
summer. These are slightly newer than the rambling farmhouse and are

occasionally updated. The cottages' exteriors are white shingled with forest green trim. Some have screened-in porches and are located next to babbling brooks. Others are set into the hillside, offering privacy and expansive views of the valley below. The cottages vary in size and in number of bedrooms and bathrooms. Kitchens can be found in all but one accommodation, and dining rooms are added conveniences in others. The decor is simple but comfortable with hardwood floors covered by hand-braided throw rugs, overstuffed couches, and both wicker and bent-wood rocking chairs. Fireplaces or woodstoves keep guests warm on cool nights. Walls are brightly painted or papered with flower prints.

Meals are served inside the rambling farmhouse. The dining room is spacious with golden wood-paneled walls and a number of pine tables surrounded by Windsor chairs. One entree is served for dinner and it is always well received. Lamb, pork, or beef roasts are the specialties of the inn, and are complemented by freshly picked vegetables from the garden. Even the desserts and pastries are all made fresh daily. They do not have a bar; however, guests are invited to bring their own libations.

Afterwards, many people gravitate to the cavernous living room. Here guests will find puzzles, games, and an extensive library of books on New Hampshire. If Nancy has the time, she might share her rug braiding technique (an art her mother and grandmother have passed down to her). Guests will be intrigued with the old paintings, photographs, and interesting artifacts that can be found tucked into every corner of the inn. Philbrook Farm has been an integral part of this region for over 125 years and will hopefully remain open to guests for years to come.

FRISKY FRIVOLITIES:
* There are over 1,000 acres of trails and pastures for guests to wander upon.
* Should Bowser tire of you playing badminton or horseshoes, you may wish to take him for a dip in one of the naturally formed swimming holes made by the mountain stream.
* Hikers can gain access to a fork of the Appalachian Trail relatively easily. The trailhead is a short drive from the inn.

THE OLD RED INN AND COTTAGES

P.O. Box 467
North Conway, New Hampshire 03860
(603) 356-2642
Innkeepers: Don and Winnie White
Rooms: 8 doubles, 10 cottages (5 with kitchenettes)

Rates: Doubles: $48-72; Cottages: $48-86
Payment: AE, MC, VISA
Children: Welcome
Dogs: Welcome in cottages
Open: All year except April

North Conway is known as much for its outlets as it is for the Mt. Washington Valley International Tennis Classic and the Summer Arts Jubilee Program of Performing Arts. The Old Red Inn and Cottages is a perfect base for taking advantage of all the activities this region has to offer. Guests traveling with a dog are welcomed in the Old Red Inn's cottages. There are an assortment of accommodations to suit most people. All of the two-bedroom cottages have screened-in porches and the option of either a kitchenette or living room. Smaller families may prefer one-bedroom cottages with an optional kitchenette. Each accommodation is extremely clean and cozy with wood-paneled walls. The furnishings are attractively simple with comfortable armchairs, couches, and quilted spreads covering maple bedsteads. The modern amenities have not been overlooked, as each cottage does have color television and well-equipped bathrooms. One particularly noteworthy aspect is the view from the cottages of the beautiful, formal flower and herb gardens.

In the morning, guests will want to take advantage of the Continental breakfast served in the restored and antique-filled inn, which was built in 1810. On cold days, guests will be warmed by the gigantic woodstove in the parlor. Breakfast includes fresh muffins and breads, which many guests smother with homemade herb jelly or maple butter (from the inn's own maple trees). Rich hot chocolate and coffee or a selection of teas will further warm one's bones.

The Whites are very helpful in assisting guests with planning their day's activities. They will steer them in the direction of bargains or toward fun hiking trails and lake-side activities.

FRISKY FRIVOLITIES:
* The Saco River runs through the area and offers several swimming areas for the brave. Of course, fishing is also an option.
* In the wintertime, cross-country skiing and ice skating are within walking distance of the inn. Pack a picnic lunch and explore this picturesque region. There are also many other cross-country skiing trails within driving distance of the inn.
* Those who are in the mood to drive should take the Route 112 from Conway to Lincoln. There are a number of scenic overlooks that include Rocky Gorge and Swift River Valley. There are also a number of hikes. One hike takes only 15 minutes from the road and leads to Sabbaday Falls.

THE 1785 INN

P.O. Box 9, Main Street
North Conway, New Hampshire 03860
(603) 356-9025
Innkeepers: Becky and Charlie Mallar
Rooms: 14 doubles
Rates: $40-80 (MAP available for $25)
Payment: Major credit cards
Children: Welcome - $10 extra
Dogs: Welcome
Open: All year

The 1785 Inn lies in the midst of the scenic Mount Washington Valley region. The house was originally built by Captain Elijah Dinsmore on a parcel of land that New Hampshire had given him for distinguished service in the Rangers. Ten years later, he discovered that this area had growth potential and secured a license to open a "publik house." By the time the 10th New Hampshire turnpike opened in 1803, the inn needed to be expanded. The logical way was to raise the roof and add a second floor. Although a three-story wing has been added since that time, the inn has retained much of its character with exposed hand-hewn beams and a center chimney.

The approach to the inn is along a semi-circular driveway, where overflowing window boxes, large flower gardens, and wine cask planters are a welcoming sight. A rustic wood-paneled pub is the first impression one has of the inside of the inn. Overstuffed couches are set on oriental rugs, and a woodstove is kept well stoked to keep patrons warm. The bar is particularly unique because its top is made out of the vertical sections of a tree.

The dining rooms and two cozy living rooms are located just off the pub. The beamed-ceiling dining rooms are relatively small; however, they are nicely appointed and have views of the mountains through shuttered windows. Bay windows are filled with plants. The living room is just as comfortable with its beige ell-shaped couch, an old chest used as a coffee table, and two rocking chairs all facing the fireplace. A second sitting room with yet another fireplace is even more casual and is equipped with a television set and VCR.

The guest bedrooms are each decorated differently with furnishings varying from brass, four-poster, and antique bedsteads to white wicker and country antiques. Some of the rooms that do have wall-to-wall carpeting still have the creaky and sloping original wood floors underneath them. Cheery wallpapers are nicely contrasted with authentic trim colors. The third-floor rooms are the only ones to have air conditioning. Even with the addition of these modern conveniences, the Mallars have tried to maintain much of the inn's original ambiance.

FRISKY FRIVOLITIES:
* Main Street is packed with all sorts of outlet or factory stores, where even discriminating Bowser can find a good buy.
* In addition to the beautiful scenery, the Mt. Washington Valley offers great cross-country skiing, ice skating, hiking, and miles of fun back roads to enjoy.
* Pinkham Notch is within a short drive of North Conway and offers great hiking trails and access to the Crystal Cascades and Glen Ellis Falls.

SNOWVILLAGE INN

Snowville, New Hampshire 03849
(603) 447-2818
Innkeepers: Trudy, Frank, and Peter Cutrone
Rooms: 15 singles and doubles
Rates: $55-94 per person (MAP), B&B rates available
Payment: AE, MC, VISA

Children: Welcome
Dogs: Welcome in the Library rooms
Open: All year except April and May

The Snowvillage Inn is located 1,000 feet up Ross Mountain, and is graced with panoramic views of the Presidential Range. During the summer months, the flower gardens are ablaze with color, and can be found nestled against the meandering stone walls. The main inn is located at the top of the circular drive, and the annex (referred to as the Library) is just beyond, set into the hillside. The buildings are painted red with contrasting white trim.

Before guests have a chance to wander too far up the front path, the inn's dogs and assorted cats will probably poke their heads out to check on the new arrivals. The main building seems friendly and inviting. One of the most comfortable places is the living room with its beamed ceilings and hardwood floors. Overstuffed sofas flank the brick fireplace, and a plethora of collectibles adds character to the room. Guests find this a favorite place for relaxing in front of a crackling fire, exchanging stories with others, or reading a good book in one of the comfortable rocking chairs.

A short walk brings you to the Library's guest rooms. The boxed beams, rustic wood walls, and low ceilings add simplicity to this charming building. The cathedral-ceilinged central common room has braided rugs covering hardwood floors and walls of built-in bookshelves. A handmade patchwork quilt is draped over the couch. A refrigerator and coffee maker are provided as an added convenience.

The bedrooms are found on both the first and second floors. The second floor chambers are located just off a balcony that looks down onto the common room. The somewhat rustic decor is enhanced by the honey-colored knotty pine walls and alcoves. Oriental rugs grace the hardwood floors and floral fabrics complement the fluffy comforters on the beds. Rattan furniture has been painted cheery blues and whites. Sunshine streams in through the small-paned windows. There are also pleasant views of the woods and rock walls through these same windows.

The grounds are picturesque and provide many diversions. A tennis court lies at the base of the hill; its backdrop is the beautiful mountains and dense foliage. There are extensive lawns for walking and seemingly endless hiking trails for roaming. The latter are used in the winter as cross-country ski trails. The innkeepers have devised clever names for them, such as Cake Walk, Wiz Bank, Snapper, and Gracie's Glen (these range from beginner to more advanced). There are also porches to relax upon, and white wooden chairs, scattered about the property, in which guests can recline.

* Crystal Lake is a favorite of guests and townspeople alike for its swimming and sunning opportunities.
* If Bowser is not in the mood to shop at the hundreds of factory outlet stores in North Conway, then try a more natural experience in the White Mountains National Park.
* There are extensive grounds for Bowser, as well as long trails to wander along.

ROCKHOUSE MOUNTAIN FARM

Eaton Center, New Hampshire 03832
(603) 447-2880
Innkeepers: The Edge Family
Rooms: 15 doubles; 3 bunk rooms
Rates: $42-65 per person (MAP)
Payment: Personal checks
Children: Welcome
Dogs: Welcome with prior approval
Open: June 15 to November 1

 The Rockhouse Mountain Farm has been in operation since 1946. Two generations of the Edge Family have dedicated themselves to quality innkeeping and have, as a result, created a relaxed environment that generations of families return to year after year. Located on the side of Rockhouse Mountain, the traditional New England farmhouse is surrounded by 400 acres of fields and woods. Guests in this remote part of New Hampshire will discover wildlife thriving in an unspoiled and picturesque setting. The farm has a more domesticated form of wildlife in the form of horses, cows, pigs, chickens, peacocks, Moscovey ducks, and pheasants.
 Guests will soon discover that the Edges' secret to success lies in their focus on simplicity rather than modern amenities and frilly furnishings. They feel this type of existence allows families to focus on each other. To quote an excerpt from their 1976 newsletter, "We have tried to create an inn for families, because we believe that the family, which was the basis of society, business, and religion in 1776, is, and should be, the basis of our lives today."
 The sprawling grounds, water activities on Crystal Lake, and farm chores provide enough diversion for guests of all ages. Children will enjoy the

sailing, fishing, and informal canoe trips. Parents are welcome to also partake in their children's activities or spend their time more leisurely. After a full day, the immaculate and comfortably furnished guest rooms are inviting. The only sounds you might hear are the night owls calling and the breezes rustling the branches of the trees.

A full country breakfast is served each morning in the farmhouse. This repast is a very casual affair with guests coming and going as they please. The aroma of fresh blueberry pancakes draw even "non-breakfast" eaters out of their rooms. The dinners are a bit more formal with generous quantities of homemade meat dishes, breads, fresh garden vegetables, and pies rounding out the menu. The honey is fresh from the farm's beehives, and the raspberries and asparagus come from the gardens. Adults and children eat in separate dining rooms, allowing each to dine at his or her own pace. Afterwards, guests should take some time to wander around the farmhouse and check on the collection of antiques, many of which were brought from Wales. The Edge family also has a fine collection of paintings; some of these are registered with the Tate Gallery in London.

FRISKY FRIVOLITIES:
*
The grounds are extensive and meant for exploring. Take Bowser on a sunrise or sunset romp.
* The lake is crystal clear and comfortable for swimming. The fishing is not bad either.
* Walks along old logging roads and even through an ancient Indian cave are favorite activities for hikers.

ISAAC SPRINGFIELD HOUSE

R.F.D. 1, Route 28 South
Wolfeboro, New Hampshire 03894
(603) 569-3529
Innkeepers: Rose LeBlanc and Andrew Terragni
Rooms: 4 doubles
Rates: $50-55
Payment: Personal checks
Children: Welcome
Dogs: Welcome as long as they are quiet and clean
Open: All year

The Isaac Springfield House is a yellow clapboard home, originally built by Isaac Springfield in 1871. Opening to guests just three years ago, the house is a relatively new addition to the New Hampshire B&B circuit. Since that time, Rose and Andrew have slowly been refurbishing the guest rooms and exterior of the house. The day we arrived, the final repairs were just being completed on the wrap-around veranda, while the last coats of paint were being applied to the railing.

Guest rooms are located on the second floor and are accessible by two staircases. Darkly stained hardwood floors contrast with the cream-colored wallpapers and bright blue accents. In one bedroom, a brass bed is covered with a fluffy, floral comforter. In another, a handmade quilt (compliments of Andrew's mother) is the centerpiece for a bed framed by carved finials. Rocking chairs are well placed to take advantage of sunshine streaming in from the many windows. Pottery lamps are within easy reach of the bed. There are two shared bathrooms. The larger of the two has an oversized combination bath/shower.

Each morning, guests are treated to a full, hearty breakfast. Rose does not offer any meat products with the meal; however, you will find her pancakes, eggs, cereal, muffins, and fruit to be quite filling. The views of assorted dogwood trees, overflowing planters, and brilliant flowerbeds are equally as satisfying. After breakfast, you might want to relax on the spacious front porch and read the morning paper. Equally inviting is the new pressure-treated deck overlooking the attractively landscaped back yard. The Isaac Springfield House is a welcoming B&B, offering guests comfortable and cozy bedroom accommodations, friendly hosts, and an opportunity to explore the beautiful Lake Winnipesaukee region.

FRISKY FRIVOLITIES:
* Lake Winnipesaukee offers visitors everything from terrific swimming to great fishing.
* After hiking the trails in the White Mountains, many stop in bustling North Conway.
* You may also wish to take advantage of the magnificent fall foliage along the Kancamagus Highway (Route 112), one of New Hampshire's most scenic and least spoiled drives.

TIN WHISTLE INN

1047 Union Avenue
Laconia, New Hampshire 03246
(603) 528-4185
Innkeeper: Maureen Blazok
Rooms: 4 doubles
Rates: $50-70
Payment: Major credit cards
Children: Over 10 years old welcome
Dogs: With prior approval
Open: All year except the month of November

The Tin Whistle Inn is a dark shingled Victorian home that rests on a hill overlooking Route 3 and the Paugus Bay. A gently rising walkway lined with flower beds leads guests to the veranda and even more vibrant flowers flowing out of window boxes and planters. The rocking chairs and the view from this spot tend to draw guests to this pleasant location.

There are two comfortable common rooms available to guests. The living room is inviting, with light streaming in through the leaded glass windows flanking the brick fireplace. A bright blue floral sofa, unique double rocking chair, and several armchairs are indeed welcoming after a day in the country. Double French doors lead to the charming rose-wallpapered dining room, where tables are set with burgundy tablecloths.

Upstairs, guests will find the four bedrooms. The "Honeymoon Room" is particularly interesting. This hardwood-floored guest chamber is decorated in a red and white floral wallpaper. A rocking chair, period furnishings, and an antique brass bedstead surround a wonderful working crimson claw-footed bathtub in the corner. The remaining bedrooms also have antique headboards, country furnishings, and a variety of floral and striped wallpapers.

Each morning, guests will enjoy a hearty Continental breakfast in the dining room. The views through the small picture window are pleasant. This repast features juice, fresh fruit, and an assortment of muffins or breads. Those who want something more substantial will be treated to either French toast or pancakes. A breakfast casserole is also a specialty of the house.

FRISKY FRIVOLITIES:
* Lake Winnipesaukee is just down the road, offering visitors a range of water sport activities.
* Located a short drive north is the White Mountains National Park.
* In addition to the inumerable summer activities, this region also offers excellent fall foliage, great cross-country skiing, and ice skating.

THE CARTWAY HOUSE

Old Lake Shore Road
Gilford, New Hampshire 03246
(603) 528-1172
Innkeeper: Gretchen Shortway
Rooms: 4 singles, 6 doubles
Rates: $42-52
Payment: MC, VISA, personal checks
Children: "Very welcome" (under 12 years old free)
Dogs: Only with prior approval
Open: All year

The Cartway House is a yellow clapboard farmhouse perched atop a hill and blessed with views of the distant mountains and lakes. The house was built in 1771, but when Gretchen Shortway discovered it a few years ago, there was major work to be done. After receiving estimates of what the refurbishing costs would run, she decided to undertake the work herself. She did everything from pouring concrete footings and laying pressure-treated sills to adding a small cafe and landscaping the overgrown backyard. In addition to tackling the restoration of the farmhouse, Gretchen also chose to raise her son rather than return to an office job. With the added responsibilities of raising a child, Gretchen started a wallpapering business to earn enough money to pay the bills.

Today, the inn is a charming representation of what a lot of drive and determination can lead to. Guests enter the inn from the back, a particularly lovely stroll past flower beds, a hot tub, and a flagstone patio. Upon entering the newly remodeled kitchen, guests might be tempted to sit down at the long wooden kitchen table inlaid with tiles, sip a cup of coffee, and stay awhile. This is a sunny spot with light flowing in through a wall of long, narrow windows. The entire house is equally as welcoming. Guests will find that the interesting use of contrasting colors and country wallpapers are effective in bringing life to the walls and rooms.

The bedrooms are located upstairs. The first set of rooms are what Gretchen calls the "ski rooms." These are attractively decorated with charming wallpapers and area rugs over the hardwood floors. Sleeping accommodations include a variety of double and bunk beds. Further down the hall are the larger chambers. Beamed ceilings set the tone in some of the rooms, and the wallpapers vary from flowers to stripes (and sometimes a combination of the two). Hand-painted hardwood floors support double beds covered in either handmade quilts or Bates spreads. Dried wreaths hang on the walls. Guests are invited to make themselves comfortable in the large, rough-hewn beamed ceiling room at the end of the hall. Here you will find a television, refrigerator, sink, and coffee maker.

Each morning, Gretchen prepares a hearty breakfast that includes eggs and bacon, homemade muffins, fresh fruit, and pancakes with real maple syrup. Afterwards, guests may want to relax on the front porch in a comfortably cushioned ladder-back chair and take in the views of the distant mountains. Overflowing window boxes and small gardens are pervasive. The stenciled yellow wheelbarrow in the front yard adds whimsy.

Whatever reason you find for passing through the New Hampshire lakes region, a stop at the Cartway House will give you all the comforts of a tastefully decorated inn, coupled with the hospitality and warmth of an innkeeper who truly enjoys her job.

FRISKY FRIVOLITIES:
* The backyard and surrounding woods are great areas for walking Bowser. The hilly streets also provide more challenging excursions.
* The inn is located only a few miles from Route 3, thus giving visitors access to Lake Winnipesaukee, Squam Lake, and Lake Waukewam.
* Many enjoy the town of Meredith for its shops, antiques, and restaurants. Those who prefer more formal amusements will want to visit Weir's Beach for miniature golf, slip and slide rides, etc.

KONA MANSION INN

P.O. Box 458
Center Harbor, New Hampshire 03226
(603) 253-4900

Innkeepers: The Crowleys
Rooms: 10 doubles, 6 cottages
Rates: Doubles: $45-140; Cottages: $350-650 (weekly)
Payment: MC, VISA, personal checks
Children: Welcome
Dogs: Welcome in the cottages with prior approval
Open: May to October

The Kona Mansion was built in 1900, when Herbert Dumaresq purchased many of the surrounding local farms and formed the 1,500-acre Kona Farm estate overlooking the expansive Lake Winnipesaukee. Herbert and his wife Julia Jordon (the daughter of Eden Jordon of The Jordon Marsh Co.) wanted to ensure that their home would not only be stately but also one that would far outlast their lifetime. This goal was accomplished by using a combination of sturdy fieldstone and enormous timbers to build their home. In addition to the eight fireplaces that kept the house warm, the walls were insulated by using seaweed from the ocean. Today, the estate has been reduced to 130 acres; however, this is still more than enough land for golf, tennis, walking, lawn games, and lake swimming.

From the main road, guests will take a secluded 2.5-mile drive out Moultonboro Neck to the Kona Mansion. A tree-lined driveway brings guests to the crest of a hill, where views of the expansive grounds suddenly appear. Most will think they have stumbled upon a country club, as a golf course and tennis courts flank the mansion. The main house is English Tudor in style, bedecked with ivy climbing up from the stone foundation. The interior of the inn is reminiscent of days gone by with its spacious and airy guest rooms. Window seats and alcoves add definition to these rattan and antique furnished chambers. Views are of either the lake or the golf course.

Those who wish to be closer to the lake, or who are traveling with a dog, will want to stay in the more rustic yellow housekeeping cottages at the base of the hill. These are not overly spacious but do offer comfortable accommodations with direct views of the water and the islands. The cottages are just 100 feet from a small private sandy beach and next to the ivy-covered Polynesian-style boat house, with its two indoor boat slips. There is also a nice grass lawn for guests and their dogs to fully enjoy.

Besides the wonderful activities available to guests, many come to the inn to take advantage of its privacy and hospitable treatment. The mansion's original formal dining room, living room, and library have been converted to accommodate three intimate dining rooms. The Valhalla dining room has interesting ceiling detail, a blue tile fireplace, and light blue walls serving to enhance the charm of this rather small room. Another dining room features a glassed-in porch that overlooks the golf course and the road leading to the lake.

FRISKY FRIVOLITIES:

* In addition to the spacious grounds and trails the inn has to offer, the road leading to the inn is terrific for scenic walks.
* Besides Lake Winnipesaukee, there is Squam Lake and Weir's Beach (amusement activities) available within a short drive.
* This region is surrounded by the White Mountains with their many scenic hiking trails and picnic spots.

THE CORNER HOUSE INN

Box 204
Center Sandwich, New Hampshire 03227
(603) 284-6219
Innkeepers: Jane Kroeger and Don Brown
Rooms: 4 doubles
Rates: $50-60
Payment: AE, MC, VISA
Children: Well-behaved children welcome
Dogs: Accepted with prior approval
Open: All year except a few weeks in April and November

The Corner House Inn lies at the corner of two rural routes intersecting a picturesque village. The inn was originally built in 1849, and boasts that it "has been in continuous operation for over 100 years." Although the main function of this old establishment is more dining than lodging, it still provides four charming bedrooms for overnight guests.

Bordered by an antique shop and a museum, the white clapboard inn is adorned with overflowing planters set next to old stone hitching posts and a brick courtyard with black iron benches. A parlor is the receiving area for both the dining and guest rooms. The walls of this cozy chamber are papered with tiny crimson and white polka dots. The hardwood floors are adorned with an oriental rug. A brick fireplace is the centerpiece for the room; a small hutch, overstuffed sofas and chairs, and an old checker-board table provide added character.

A hallway directs guests past a spinning wheel to the staircase leading to the quaintly decorated guest chambers. The same Victorian furnishings and small print wallpapers are found here as are prevalent in the downstairs rooms. You will find brass or antique bedsteads adorned with nubbly bedspreads or quilts. A little handmade teddy bear might be hidden among the pillows. The white wicker, country antiques, Queen Anne mirrors, and assorted plants further complement the bright and cheery bedroom decor. Three of the guest rooms share baths, and the fourth has a private bath.

Mornings start with a hearty full breakfast that may include anything from overstuffed omelets to delicious pancakes with locally made maple syrup. Jane and Don also offer guests freshly squeezed orange juice, coffee, and an assortment of teas. Lunch and dinner are served to the public in the four dining rooms. Guests dine on lobster and scallop pie, sellfish saute, or brandied peach duckling as a ceiling fan silently turns overhead. Hanging quilts and blue-green wainscottings add ornamentation.

FRISKY FRIVOLITIES:
* This rural area is filled with back roads that wend their way past antique barns, sprawling farms, and classic-style New England homes tucked behind white fences.
* Center Sandwich has one of the largest populations of artists in the entire state. Guests should take time to visit the craft shops, antique stores, art galleries, and various art fairs held throughout the year.
* There is a wonderful cross-country ski trail selection in these parts, ranging from five nearby ski resorts to simply heading off into the woods to blaze your own trail.

NORTHWAY HOUSE

RFD 1, U.S. Route 3 North
Plymouth, New Hampshire 03264
(603) 536-2838
Hosts: Micheline and Norman McWilliams
Rooms: 3 doubles
Rates: $22-36
Payment: Personal checks
Children: Small children welcome, under 5 years old free
Dogs: Welcome
Open: All year

Ever since the mid-1700s, this region of the White Mountain National Forest has been quite popular with hikers, fisherman, and recreational outdoorsmen. The Northway House is located along rural Route 3 in the Pemigewasset River Valley. This white clapboard and black-shuttered B&B is tucked just off the road behind spruce and white birch trees. As guests approach the house, they will find that the two bird feeders along the front walkway are buzzing with hummingbird activity. The front porch is bedecked with pretty planters and potted mums.

The B&B only has three guest rooms, but each is quite homey. Colonial papers brighten the walls and double and single beds (roll-away beds are available) are adorned with white Bates spreads or comforters. The furnishings are equally as simple. The one shared bathroom is located at the top of the landing. It is a cheery yellow and offers a combination shower/bath and thick towels for drying off afterwards. Much of the charm of this B&B actually lies with the friendly hosts. Guests are made to feel as if they are visiting longtime friends and are encouraged to use the McWilliams' home as their own. As a result, the atmosphere is conducive to relaxation.

Those who enjoy being outside will find a white rail fence leading to the private backyard. In the summertime, guests will discover a vegetable garden and a flower-lined rock wall beside the expansive lawn. During the cooler autumn and winter months, the living room, with its crackling fireplace, is the perfect place for reading a good book or magazine. Guests frequently congregate here to get to know each other or the McWilliams.

Each morning, weather permitting, guests are invited to take their hearty English breakfast on the patio. On more inclement days, the dining room and cozy kitchen serve as backups. Once sated, most are ready to head out and visit the picturesque New Hampshire countryside.

FRISKY FRIVOLITIES:
* The Northway House is close to both Squam Lake and Lake Winnepesaukee. The fishing, swimming, and walking around these lakes is always pleasant.
* Four ski resorts are located nearby, along with several terrific cross-country ski trails for those who prefer fewer people and a quieter setting.
* Waterville Valley is close to the Northway House. In the summertime, this area hosts an art festival, as well as offering hiking, fishing, and lake swimming.

THE MOUNTAIN-FARE INN

P.O. Box 553
Campton, New Hampshire 03223
(603) 726-4283
Innkeepers: Susan and Nicholas Preston
Rooms: 9 doubles
Rates: $28-32 per person
Payment: Personal checks
Children: Welcome
Dogs: Welcome with prior approval
Open: All year

     The Mountain Fare Inn is a handsome white farmhouse set in a residential neighborhood. A semi-circular driveway leads to the house. Evergreen bushes line the front rock wall and, in the summertime, the large front porch is filled with beautiful flowering window boxes and wine casks. Several hanging plants complete the effect. In the winter, the white porch and sign posts are wrapped with evergreens and wreaths are hung from the doors.

     The house is primarily geared for skiers, as it is located only a short distance from Franconia Notch and Waterville Valley. However, hikers and foliage fans love this scenic area as well. The inn is inviting any time of the year, especially the cozy living room. This is a comfortable place where guests enjoy relaxing on the sofa and watching television or the crackling fire in the red woodstove. Reading is also a pleasant way to while away the afternoon, as soft music plays in the background. The dining room is large enough to accommodate several long tables and a piano. Throw rugs cover hardwood floors and dried wreaths hang on the walls. The views from this room are of the back deck and yard. Meals are served family style. This presentation allows the Prestons to serve up to 28 people (guests can bring their friends) at a time. Dinner prices range from $8-12. The breakfasts are just as hearty and feature blueberry pancakes, fruit, eggs, coffee cake, and juice.

Guest bedrooms vary in size and decor, from a single bedroom to a more spacious chamber that sleeps six in both bunk and double beds. Most of the beds have simple carved wood headboards and are covered with yellow cotton coverlets, Bates spreads, or brightly colored blankets. Large braided throw rugs cover hardwood floors, and furnishings include rocking chairs, oak bureaus, and couches.

Chairs on the back deck have views of the spacious, recently landscaped yard. There is ample room for a volleyball net, wooden swing-set, and a picnic table. In the wintertime, novices may also wish to try some easy cross-country skiing here before they attempt one of the more challenging local areas.

FRISKY FRIVOLITIES:
* Whether you have come to hike, canoe, or fish, Crickets, a nearby gourmet shop, will supply all the ingredients needed for an excellent picnic lunch.
* The Prestons allow guests to barbecue in the back yard. This is a good way to top off an active day in the White Mountains or on Squam Lake or Lake Winnipesaukee.
* The cross-country skiing in this region is excellent. Ask the Prestons to recommend their favorite spots.

THE HILLTOP INN

Main Street
Sugar Hill, New Hampshire 03585
(603) 823-5695
Innkeepers: Meri and Mike Hern
Rooms: 4 doubles, 1 suite, 1 apartment
Rates: Doubles: $35-45; Suite: $45-65; Apartment: $100
Payment: MC, VISA
Children: Welcome; the inn can provide crib and toys

Dogs: Welcome. The Herns have dogs and cats, so guests' dogs must be
well behaved and good around other animals.

Open: All year

The town of Sugar Hill is located in the heart of the White Mountains
and offers visitors everything from spectacular fall foliage to glider rides and
skiing. The Hilltop Inn has been a part of this region since 1895. From the
outside this Victorian home has clean, simple lines, a simplicity that is carried
through to the interior. What attracts most guests to this inn, besides the
outdoors, is the warm, hospitable, and easy-going nature of the Herns. Not only
do they have enough energy for innkeeping, but they are also full-time caterers.
On the day we arrived they were preparing food for a party of 75.

Guests enter the building through the back door and after pausing in
a small vestibule, are welcomed into the large country kitchen. The centerpiece
of this room is an enormous Garland stove from which a hearty homemade
country breakfast is provided, including freshly baked muffins. This meal can
be taken in the dining room, but more frequently guests like to eat on the
expansive deck overlooking the New Hampshire hills. The evenings on the
deck can be equally as pleasant. Wine and cheese are served as the sun sets on
the horizon.

The spacious common rooms are furnished with a number of antiques. The bedrooms share the same open feeling and are simply decorated,
good-sized, and neat. Guests will find the Herns radiate a sense of family and
hospitality that is difficult to find in these changing times. This quality, terrific
homecooking, and comfortable accommodations attract visitors from all parts
of the country.

FRISKY FRIVOLITIES:
* You will enjoy the terrific canoeing, fishing, and swimming in the area, and
  Bowser will too.
* Those who wish more rigorous exercise should try hiking in the White
  Mountains National Park.
* Sugar Hill is a superb walking town because of its hills, foliage, and views.
  Many of the houses were built in the 1800s and are well maintained.

EDENCROFT MANOR

R.F.D. No. 1, Route 135
Littleton, New Hampshire 03561
(603) 444-6776
Innkeepers: Barry and Ellie Bliss, Bill and Laurie Walsh

Rooms: 6 doubles
Rates: $35-60
Payment: AE, MC, VISA
Children: Welcome
Dogs: Welcome
Open: All year except two weeks in March

The Edencroft Manor is a great place to know about if you are traveling in and around St. Johnsbury, Vermont or perhaps elsewhere in Vermont or New Hampshire. The inn is a two-minute drive from Interstate 93. It provides guests with the coziness and warmth of an inn, as opposed to some of the more basic highway motel accommodations.

Six comfortable bedrooms await weary travelers. Most have private baths; two share a large hall bath. Each guest chamber is named after a color and is decorated around that theme. Yellow bedspreads and curtains predominate in one room, warm brown and tan quilts in another. Guests will find each room to be spacious, clean, and comfortable. Simple country antiques add a charming touch. The Brown Room, with a fireplace, is a favorite and should be reserved in advance.

The inn also has a common room downstairs, where children will find games and toys (the innkeepers have children of their own) and adults will discover a small library. Guests do not have to travel far for meals as the Edencroft does serve dinner to guests as well as to the public in the adjoining dining rooms, complete with fireplaces. The dinner menu is quite extensive and offers a number of variations on veal, beef, seafood, and pasta. After dinner, drinks and cordials are served in the living room in front of yet another fireplace.

Breakfast is served to guests only, after 8:30 a.m. A typical hearty repast will include a choice of home fries and eggs or perhaps French toast. Breakfast costs an extra $3.50, but is quite substantial and a true bargain. Well-sated guests will then be ready to explore this very interesting portion of New England.

FRISKY FRIVOLITIES:

* Hiking trails are located both adjacent to the inn and throughout the region. Pack a picnic and head off for the day.
* In the winter, there is good cross-country skiing from the inn.
* Moore Lake is also nearby. Here you can rent canoes, as well as swim and sun.

HOBSON HOUSE

Town Common
Wentworth, New Hampshire 03282
(603) 764-9460
Innkeepers: Cay and Bob Thayer
Rooms: 4 doubles
Rates: $30-55
Payment: Personal checks
Children: Welcome
Dogs: Welcome
Open: June 1 to mid-April

The tiny village of Wentworth dates back to 1766. Today, the town common remains much the same as it was over 200 years ago. The Hobson House is a favorite among those touring the area by car as well as by bicycle (a special area in the parking lot has been set aside for bicycles). This part of New Hampshire is popular among cyclists who find the hills and back country roads to be challenging. A brick walk leads past benches set amid flower gardens to the front door. Undoubtedly, either Hobson (an Irish setter) or Spencer (the basset hound) will hear the approaching footsteps and be on hand to greet newcomers as they love "entertaining" visiting dogs.

A cozy cafe and breakfast and living rooms make up the first floor rooms. The woodstove in the living room makes it particularly inviting. Sheraton-style antiques, a comfortable rocking chair, and a well-worn couch complete the effect. A center chimney separates this room from the breakfast area. The focal points for this chamber are a large dining room table, grandfather clock, and a mahogany sideboard complete with a silver tea service. Each morning, the Thayers serve a full breakfast here. Choices range from Belgian waffles and pancakes to overstuffed omelets and fresh fruits.

The front stairs lead to the bedrooms. These are decorated with a variety of old-fashioned floral wallpapers in pale pinks and yellows. Braided cloth or straw rugs cover the hardwood floors. White wicker chairs and headboards are mixed in with more formal Sheraton-style armoires and bedside tables. These are simple accommodations without the modern distractions of televisions or telephones. The two shared baths are good sized and have old-fashioned touches such as a claw-footed bathtubs and standing porcelain sinks.

The inn also has a restaurant called Hobson's Choice. Pink and white checked tablecloths cover the handful of tables. A casual bar is well stocked with an assortment of wines. Dinners in the cafe are delicious with the emphasis on hearty, well-cooked country meals. After a delightful dinner, many choose to take a walk around the common and enjoy the breezes from the surrounding hills.

FRISKY FRIVOLITIES:
* There are nice back roads for walking or bicycling if Bowser is adept at this.
* Hanover, the home of Dartmouth College, is just a short drive away. There, you can enjoy the ambiance of this college town as well as the campus.
* Those who prefer the water may enjoy the activities available on the Connecticut River. An age-old question, that has yet to be resolved, is whether New Hampshire or Vermont has the best fall foliage.....maybe you will be able to decide.

THE HANOVER INN

P.O. Box 151
Hanover, New Hampshire 03775
(603) 643-4300
Manager: Matt Marshall
Rooms: 98 doubles, 6 suites

Rates: Doubles: $83-104; Suites: $140-170 (MAP available for $25 extra
(Seasonal and honeymoon packages available)
Payment: All major credit cards
Children: Welcome
Dogs: Welcome
Open: All year

The Hanover Inn is owned by and located just across the street from Dartmouth College. Visiting parents and alumnae have been enjoying the inn for years, as much for the amenities as for the chance to catch up with their children and old schoolmates. The inn is quite large, but the public and guest rooms exude a feeling of coziness and tradition that is in keeping with its Ivy League surroundings.

The bedrooms vary in their traditional Colonial decor. Canopied pencil post beds covered in eiderdown comforters can be found in some rooms. These guest quarters tend to have the more formal flower-covered wing chairs and upholstered Chippendale-style side chairs pulled up to mahogany writing tables. A butler's tray table might stand in front of a hunter green sofa, and often Queen Anne-style dressing tables complete the effect. Old-fashioned floral papers cover the walls, with colors ranging from subtle tans to china blues. Other bedrooms are more simple, with white Bates spreads covering beds with maple headboards and handmade shades adorning the bedside table lamps.

In keeping with tradition, the inn serves high tea in the afternoons in the library with a fireplace, also known as the Hayward Lounge. This chamber is filled with period furniture including a secretary, wing chairs, and brass sconces serving as accents. The elegant main dining room serves traditional New England fare. In the warm summer months, a favorite gathering spot is the Terrace for drinks and a lighter menu.

The college's athletic facilities are available to all guests whether their game is squash or tennis. Dartmouth's performing arts center is located next door. It hosts art exhibits, films, and concerts during the school year.

FRISKY FRIVOLITIES:
* The Connecticut River runs close to the inn. Safe swimming areas can be found along the river for you and Bowser. Fishing is also a favorite pastime.
* The Dartmouth Campus is a wonderful area for meandering with Bowser. The buildings are historically interesting and your companion will find the grounds to be prime for frolicking.
* Many head over to the charming town of Woodstock, Vermont and try the cross-country skiing on the way.

LOCH LYME LODGE AND COTTAGES

Route 10
Lyme, New Hampshire 03768
(603) 795-2141
Lodgekeepers: Paul and Judy Barker
Cottages: 25
Rates: $43 (MAP); $26.50 (EP) per person (weekly rates available)
Payment: Personal checks
Children: Welcome
Dogs: Well-behaved dogs are allowed (cottages only) but are prohibited
    from the beach area.
Open: Memorial Day to early September

A casual, relaxed, and inexpensive summer family vacation is not always, contrary to popular belief, easy to achieve. The Loch Lyme Cottages is a rustic spot that both children and adults are sure to enjoy. Close to Dartmouth College, hiking, fishing, and the lakes of New Hampshire, the cottages offer a myriad of choices for the active family.

One word of caution - do not expect to find modern conveniences such as telephones, air conditioning, and color television. What you will discover are one-to four-bedroom rustic cottages set on a hillside overlooking Post Pond. Each has well-worn hardwood floors, a living room with a fireplace (wood is supplied), and separate bedrooms. The cottages are kept very clean with either daily or bi-weekly maid service and are well stocked with linens and fresh towels. Evenings can be spent on the porch or taking advantage of the many available activities.

Meals are very casual with the emphasis on good New England cooking and the use of fresh vegetables from the garden. Guests are offered a choice of meal plans. Some may opt to take breakfast and dinner at the lodge, while others find they prefer the B&B plan. Of course, those who are staying in cottages with a kitchenette can cook all of their meals, or if they prefer, occasionally join other guests in the dining room.

One of the best features about the lodge is that there are a myriad of ways to work up an appetite. The lake is a two-minute walk from most of the cabins. There is a sandy beach for the little tykes and a deep water float for those who wish to swim and sun. Canoes and boats are available for those wanting to take advantage of the water without getting wet. Badminton, croquet, and volleyball are just a few of the sports available to guests, as well as tennis on one of two clay courts. For those who prefer to just relax, both the cottages and grounds give you plenty of solitude to do just that. There is also a small lending

164

library offering a variety of good books. Loch Lyme Cottages is not pretentious; it is a good bargain for families or groups of friends who wish to enjoy a casual and activity-filled vacation.

FRISKY FRIVOLITIES:
* A picnic area is located on the hill behind the cottages. Ask the chef to pack a box lunch the night before and wander up the hill for a special treat.
* Dogs are not allowed on the beach; however, there are a number of trails along the lake and through the hills. Many people like to fish from shore and let Bowser do some swimming.
* The back roads are perfect for walking or bicycling. Hanover (home of Dartmouth College) is a small town offering pleasant walks and interesting shops.

DEXTER'S INN & TENNIS CLUB

Sunapee, New Hampshire 03782
(603) 763-5571
Innkeeper: Michael Durfor
Rooms: 17 doubles and singles
Rates: Singles: $65-95; Doubles: $105-140 (MAP)
Payment: MC, VISA, personal checks

Children: Welcome
Dogs: Welcome in the annex ($5 per night)
Open: May 1 to October 31

Dexter's Inn is located atop a 1,400 foot New Hampshire hill with picturesque views of the distant mountains and lakes. The house was originally built in 1803 by Adam Reddington, who was well known for his carved bowls that held ship's compasses. In 1930, Samuel Crowther, a famous economist and financial adviser to Herbert Hoover, purchased the ramshackle house. He completely refurbished the home and, in the process, also restored the stone walls, gardens, and overgrown lawns. In 1948, the Simpsons bought the house and made it an inn, and since then have offered guests an all-around resort experience.

A long road leads to the yellow clapboard and black shuttered inn. A tiny, stone-walled parking area is well placed for checking in and unloading the car. The interior of the inn is spacious, particularly the living room with its sofas and chairs set around a grand piano. The floor-to-ceiling bookshelves are filled with an extensive collection of books. You may select one and curl up in front of the fireplace. Adjacent to the living room is a screened-in porch with white wicker furniture contrasted with a vibrant orange and white design painted on the ceiling.

Guests with dogs are welcome in the annex, which is actually a converted horse barn. Much of the original barn is still visible with its exposed rough-hewn beams and wallboards. The Norman Arluck Room (recreation area) appears to have been the old tack room. This cavernous chamber is large enough to easily hold a bumper pool table, a ping-pong table, and two televisions. Woodstoves keep the common rooms warm on cold winter days. An eclectic collection of wall hangings include a mounted deer's head, snowshoes, and wagon wheels.

Bedrooms are found either Up The Hill (on the second floor), along the side wing, or in the original barn on the ground level. Each room is nicely decorated and comfortably furnished. Traditional Bates spreads rest on queen or twin beds, and walls are papered with a variety of floral prints. One room is particularly appropriate for guests with dogs, as it has a second private entrance which opens onto a small patio encircled by a rock wall. A large back yard lies just beyond the patio.

The ground's keepers have been busy at Dexter's Inn. The flower beds are brilliant with color, and stone walls are thick with ivy. Mature shade trees provide a respite from the summer sun. From the inn's back patio, the expansive grounds can be truly appreciated. Sweeping views are of the two tennis courts, a large pool surrounded by hedges, and the lawns and gardens.

The inn also offers a number of activities. Croquet, horseshoes, and shuffleboard are just a few of the lawn games. There are also numerous meadow trails for afternoon walks. Horseback riding and sailing on Lake Sunapee are available within a short driving distance from the inn. Summer theater and antique shops might appeal to others.

FRISKY FRIVOLITIES:
* The many paths through the woods and meadows are great walking for Bowser as well as his owners.
* Other than Lake Sunapee, there are a number of lakes and streams in the region that provide excellent fishing opportunities.
* The roads around the inn are quiet and appropriate for long walks.

THE JOHN HANCOCK INN

Main Street
Hancock, New Hampshire 03449
(603) 525-3318
Innkeepers: Glynn and Pat Wells
Rooms: 10 doubles
Rates: $52-60
Payment: MC, VISA, personal checks
Children: Welcome
Dogs: Welcome with prior approval and a $2 charge
Open: All year, except Christmas day and 10 days in both the spring and fall

The John Hancock Inn is located along the tree-lined Main Street in the picturesque village of Hancock. Built in 1789, the home originally fronted a stagecoach route. Today, the inn claims to be the oldest continually run hostelry in New Hampshire. Step inside and the inn has a most unique flavor.

The guest rooms are located on different levels, each of which has a private landing that houses a small sitting area. Here guests will find a television as well as antique checker sets, an assortment of books and magazines, and charming decorative pieces such as antique milk churns, writing desks, and wooden trunks. The 1700's theme is carried through to the bedrooms, with lace curtains, period furnishings, and painted hardwood floors covered with braided throw rugs. Decorative wainscottings and stenciling add charm. Beds range from king-size to four poster and canopy. Windsor chairs, along with wicker and rocking chairs, are scattered throughout. Some side tables are made of mahogany and others are simple country tables stained with milk paint. Dishes containing mints add the final touch.

There are three dining rooms at the inn where guests are served delicious meals. Entrees include trout, roasted chicken, prime rib, duck a l'orange, and veal. The Carriage Room Lounge is another favorite among guests and locals alike. Its atmosphere is also reminiscent of the 1700s, enhanced by the tables constructed out of old bellows, seats taken from old buggies, and wall boards removed from an old horse barn.

For those who prefer to lounge outside, there is a lush lawn behind the inn surrounded by tall trees. It is a private place where people feel as comfortable stretching out on the grass as they do visiting around the tables and chairs clustered atop wooden platforms. Those who prefer a different type of activity will want to sit on the front porch and watch the comings and goings along Main Street.

FRISKY FRIVOLITIES:
* This region of New Hampshire offers everything from hiking and swimming to cross-country skiing and fishing.
* Many opt to borrow a bicycle from the inn and explore the picturesque back roads, visit the nearby antique shops, or just enjoy the fall foliage.
* Hancock is an interesting town for walking, with its mix of quiet residential streets and a cute downtown area.

WOODBOUND INN

Jaffrey, New Hampshire 03452
(603) 532-8341
General Manager: Martha Jones
Rooms: 33 doubles, 13 cottages
Rates: $86-140 (MAP); B&B: $50-70
Payment: AE, MC, VISA, personal checks
Children: Welcome (under 2 years old free; $26-48 for children 3-12)
Dogs: Welcome in cottages
Open: All year

A vacation resort since 1892, the Woodbound Inn is set alongside the Contoocook Lake and encompasses over 200 acres of landscaped lawns and woodlands. Nominated by *Better Homes and Gardens* as one of the country's best family resorts, the inn offers sailing, canoeing, golf, croquet, volleyball, and tennis, as well as fishing in its wonderful trout pond. In the winter, guests may take advantage of the terrific cross-country skiing, sleigh rides, ice skating, downhill skiing, and tobogganing. The Woodbound Inn offers just about every family activity imaginable, and what it does not have on the premises is usually found nearby.

Driving up the long tree-lined road, guests will come to the rambling white clapboard inn. After registering, a walk or short drive past the horseshoe pit, clay tennis court, putting green, and the nine-hole golf course will bring guests to the lakeside cottages. Situated under large pines, the dark wood cottages (one is even topped with a hunting dog weathervane) have great views of the water. They vary in size, accommodating from two to eight people, and feature large living rooms with either a stone fireplace or wood-burning Franklin stove. The decor is rustically simple, with knotty pine wainscotting and hardwood floors adding authenticity. A picture window provides fine views of the lake. French doors lead onto a screened-in porch or large deck. Striped or sheer white curtains hang at the windows. The bathrooms are also quite simple in design but large enough to easily accommodate the needs of a family. The greatest draw to these cottages is their proximity to the lake. Guests can enjoy peaceful walks, take a refreshing dip, or just admire the reflection of the mountains off the lake from their wooden, cushioned lounge chairs.

The main inn is very homey and inviting. Guests are usually found congregating on the wrap-around screened-in porch in the green cushioned presidential rockers. On inclement days guests gravitate to the common rooms. The innkeeper's dog, Angel, can usually be found in the sitting room in front of the blazing fire beside one of the comfortable wing-back chairs. Brass standing lamps light this cozy retreat filled with antique collectibles. An old rifle hangs on the mantle and an antique radio sits off in a corner.

The dining room, highlighted by beamed ceilings and French-blue wallpaper, is an inviting place for meals. The chef is always experimenting and offers diners a combination of traditional New England and nouvelle cuisine. Thus, the dinner entrees vary and may include lobster, roast leg of lamb, veal scallopini, turkey, and various fresh fish dishes. The inn not only uses locally grown vegetables but also serves homebaked pastries and breads. Regulars do not need much of an excuse to return year after year; however, newcomers will find that the hospitality, scenery, and plethora of activities to be inviting.

FRISKY FRIVOLITIES:
* The lake is quite invigorating, as are the miles of hiking trails that lead all over the property.
* Cross-country skiing is a favorite activity at the inn and on the surrounding trails.
* Many dogs love to frolic on the ice. Take Bowser ice skating and let him show you his tricks.

THE BENJAMIN PRESCOTT INN

Route 124 East
Jaffrey, New Hampshire 03452
(603) 532-6637
Innkeeper: Richard L. Rettig
Rooms: 8 doubles, 2 suites
Rates: $50-100 (weekend packages available)
Payment: MC, personal checks
Children: Older children preferred in some suites
Dogs: Welcome with a $5 charge
Open: All year

      Ten years ago, areas like Peterborough and Jaffrey had not been thought of as viable year-round towns because many felt they were not within a commutable distance to Boston. However, these regions along the southern border of New Hampshire have finally been discovered and as a result have become quite popular. Richard anticipated this region's growth potential and completely renovated the inn to accommodate the eventual influx of visitors. The inn now has new wiring and plumbing that has been carefully installed around the original post and beam construction. Extensive carpentry has recreated the detail work. The inn now boasts of modern conveniences but has held on to its charm and architectural integrity.
      The Benjamin Prescott is located two miles outside of Jaffrey. The

yellow clapboard inn with black shutters rests just back from the road. The natural setting is enhanced by various planters and flower gardens along the front of the house. As guests step inside the foyer, they will be able to see the salmon-colored dining room/common room.

The bedrooms can be found on all three levels of the house. Each chamber is named after a member of Benjamin Prescott's family. For instance, Rachel's room is beautifully furnished with an oriental rug, four-poster bed, and handmade quilts. Other guest quarters feature brass beds, Windsor chairs, and antique trunks. Country wallpapers and/or quilts highlight the walls. Some of the most interesting rooms are in the converted attic. The John Adams Suite is entered by way of pocket doors. A ceiling fan, hanging from the cathedral ceiling, slowly moves the air. The king-size bed is flanked by two queen-bedded alcoves. Two additional features are the wet bar and a small deck overlooking the inn's 100 acres.

After a peaceful night's rest, guests will be served a complete country breakfast. This could include pancakes, French toast (with locally produced maple syrup); a choice of eggs, omelets, bacon or sausage; pumpkin or lemon breads; fruit; and juice. After breakfast, the screened-in porch is a favorite place for reading the morning paper. Guests have been tempted to spend the day on the porch or in the sitting room, but will find the region has a lot to offer in terms of history and activities. One will leave the Benjamin Prescott Inn with fond memories of its historic charm, the quaintly decorated guest chambers, and Richard's many thoughtful touches.

FRISKY FRIVOLITIES:
* In addition to the wonderful back country roads, the towns of Peterborough and Jaffrey also give visitors a true flavor for this area.
* Many enjoy a leisurely stroll up Witt Hill Road, lined with stone walls, where guests have a beautiful view of the mountains and surrounding pastures.
* Mt. Monadnock is covered with trails for climbing and hiking. Cross-country skiing is also a favorite pastime in the winter.

THE INN AT CROTCHED MOUNTAIN

Mountain Road
Francestown, New Hampshire 03043
(603) 588-6840
Innkeepers: John and Rose Perry
Rooms: 6 singles, 8 doubles
Rates: $50-95 per person (MAP), B&B rates $15 less per person

Payment: Personal checks
Children: Welcome
Dogs: Welcome with a $2 charge
Open: Mid-May to end of October, Thanksgiving to the end of the ski
   season

The Inn at Crotched Mountain is located on the north side of Crotched Mountain, with a picturesque view of the Piscataquog Valley. Originally built in 1822, the farmhouse had a secret tunnel connecting the cellar and the Boston Post Road. Slaves were hidden here during their journey along the Underground Railroad. In the 1920s, the farm gained fame for its prize-winning sheep, championship horses, and Angora goats. After a devastating fire in the mid-1930s, the farm was rebuilt; some 40 years later the Perrys purchased the home.

Today, the ivy covered brick inn is still in the business of taking in weary travelers and offering them a safe, comfortable place to stay. There are a number of inviting common rooms. The living room is a cheery place with its twin fireplaces, period furnishings, and bold floral print sofas and matching side chairs. An antique sewing machine table has been converted into a side table and a harvest table holds a vase of fragrant flowers. Bright oriental rugs cover the gray painted hardwood floors. More privacy can be found in a small sitting room across the way from the living and dining rooms. This rustic chamber has beamed cathedral ceilings, a deer's head mounted on the wall, and assorted antique carpentry tools hung on plaques above the fireplace.

Most of the guest rooms are simply furnished but have wonderful views of the mountains. Many offer fireplaces, perhaps a private entrance (great for guests with dogs), and others have private bathrooms. Whether it is summer or the winter, some of the primary draws to this cozy inn are the panoramic views, numerous outdoor activities, and the delicious food.

The casual dining room has a brick fireplace which enhances the intimate mood. Rose and John were both trained in hotel and restaurant management and are adept at creating delicious entrees. Diners may choose from baked stuffed jumbo shrimp, chicken boursin in puff pastry, filet mignon, roast Long Island duck, Indonesian fish, or one of "the chefs' seasonal selections."

There is much to do for the active guest. The inn has two clay tennis courts and a 60-foot swimming pool on the premises. Excellent hiking, fishing, and good skiing are available in and around Crotched Mountain. Whether one chooses to sit by the stone wall alongside the pool, take a refreshing morning walk, or just watch the logs crackle in the fireplace, the Inn at Crotched Mountain provides it.

* There are cross-country trails that begin from the inn, as well as plenty of acreage for guests to roam on.
* Many enjoy scenic walks or drives along the country roads in and around Jaffrey, Peterborough, and Hancock.
* Others frequent this region for the maple sugaring season, fall foliage, or for the opportunity to be out in a natural setting.

THE RAM IN THE THICKET

Milford, New Hampshire 03055
(603) 654-6440
Innkeeper: Dr. Andrew and Priscilla Tempelman
Rooms: 9 doubles, 2 suites
Rates: Doubles: $45-55; Suites: $100
Payment: MC, VISA
Children: Welcome
Dogs: With prior approval
Open: All year

The Ram in the Thicket derives its name from the biblical story of Isaac and Abraham. As the story goes, the Lord sent Abraham a ram that had been caught in a thicket to replace a son, who had died. The Tempelmans' felt they had a similar analogy when they left behind their former lifestyle in the Midwest and started fresh in this lovely, rural section of New Hampshire. Andrew and Priscilla purchased this Victorian-style home in 1977. Their long-time dream of owning an inn and settling in New England had finally come to fruition.

The inn is set on top of a hill amidst a natural abundance of greenery. Cobblestones line gravel paths that are bordered by flower gardens. After extensive renovations of the old mansion and conversion of the old music room and library into four charming dining rooms, the new owners have opened their doors to the public. The common rooms, intimate bar, and dining rooms are on the first floor. Sheraton-style antiques are quite at home amid these pleasant surroundings.

The guest chambers are more informal and can be found on the second floor. Many of the bedroom walls are painted in soft tones and stenciled; the remaining walls are covered in floral papers. One room boasts a four-poster bed and others have canopy or white iron and brass bedsteads. The built-in features, including fireplaces, floor-to-ceiling bookshelves, and decorative wainscottings, are particularly appealing. Handmade quilts, white wicker mirrors, and brightly cushioned rocking chairs add an open, airy feeling to many of these chambers. Most of the guest rooms share bathrooms; several of these have claw-footed tubs.

The dining rooms are each somewhat different in decor. A particularly memorable one has an oriental rug covering the hardwood floor and blue tablecloths which complement the balloon curtains. The constantly changing menu offers a variety of delicious entrees. These range from veal Monterey and Pork Nagoya to Indonesian Sate and Zuni lamb succotash. If it is a pleasant evening, guests may wish to have dinner on the screened-in summer porch and watch the setting sun.

FRISKY FRIVOLITIES:
* In addition to the great hiking, there is terrific cross-country skiing nearby.
* The area is interesting any season of the year. Hiking and swimming around and in the nearby mountain lakes are always favorites.
* Southern New Hampshire is an excellent area for bicycling. Take Bowser along some quiet back roads close to the inn.

STEPPING STONES

Box 208, RR 1
Bennington Battle Trail
Wilton Center, New Hampshire 03086
(603) 654-9048
Host: Ann Carlsmith
Rooms: 2 doubles
Rates: $25-35
Payment: Personal checks
Children: Welcome (crib: $10)
Dogs: Welcome if "under control"
Open: All year

The historical town of Wilton Center lies at the end of a winding road lined with mature trees, meandering stone walls, and beautiful 200-year-old houses. At the crest of the hill you come upon the charming village. The first Unitarian Church settlement of 1763 is found on one side of the road, and just beyond are Andy's Summer Playhouse (children's theater) and a rambling auction barn. Just as the road begins a turn to the right, guests will see a small sign for Bennington Battle Trail and Stepping Stones.

The B&B is surrounded by a tiered garden of colorful perennials and dense woods. A stone walkway leads to the summer porch decorated with dried wreaths Ann has made. Dustin, the resident dog (golden retriever/collie mix), is often on hand to greet new arrivals and welcome them into his home. The breakfast room and kitchen have recently been renovated, and now skylights and wall-to-wall windows brighten these charming rooms. Hanging plants and vases of flowers add color to the modern country kitchen. In the wintertime, a Resolute woodstove supplements the heat created by the passive solar system.

Guests will notice one loom resting in the corner of a back hallway and yet another in an adjacent room. Ann spends most of her free time during the quieter months weaving colorful throw rugs and coverlets. The summer months she devotes to B&B guests and her beautiful gardens.

The two upstairs bed chambers are decorated in cheery yellows and greens. Each is filled with interesting yet traditionally simple pieces of furniture. A tiny wooden crib is tucked into a corner in one room. The walls in the other are adorned with interesting prints of plants and herbs (particularly appropriate given Ann's interest in gardening). Both guest chambers have views of the backyard and woods. The beds are covered in down comforters and handwoven rugs grace the floors. A modern bathroom, located at the beginning of the hallway, is shared.

Breakfast is "complimentary, full, and bountiful." It is served in the sunny breakfast room and includes everything from overstuffed omelets and croissants to Belgian waffles and French toast with real maple syrup or homemade preserves. A light breakfast of fresh fruit, juice, and muffins is also offered. Afternoon tea is available, giving one time to meet the other guests and savor the relaxed and warm ambiance at Stepping Stones.

FRISKY FRIVOLITIES:
* The B&B lies just down the road from a beautiful reservoir, providing excellent walks for Bowser.
* The country roads surrounding Wilton Center are scenic. Guests should also take the time to explore the charming town on foot.
* The Monadnock region offers visitors a complete selection of activities ranging from cross-country skiing to hiking and fishing.

LAKE SHORE FARM

Jenness Pond Road
Northwood, New Hampshire 03261
(603) 942-5921
Host: Eloise Ring
Rooms: 32 doubles
Rates: $35-45
Payment: Personal checks
Children: Welcome
Dogs: Welcome
Open: All year except Christmas

The Lake Shore Farm is a wonderful resort, appropriate for the entire family. Ever since 1926, this rambling farmhouse on Jenness Pond has been providing guests with an informal, interesting environment, where people of all ages will find something to keep them entertained and amused.

Arriving guests will be surprised at the size of the farmhouse, with its annexes and additions surrounded by expansive grounds. Guests who try to check in at a front desk will search in vain as the heart of the operation is in the kitchen. Eloise keeps all of her reservation's paperwork on a desk in the back of the kitchen. This gives her the flexibility of overseeing meals and attending to pressing concerns at the same time. Nevertheless, staff members are always passing by, and will escort new arrivals to their rooms.

Most of the spacious guest quarters are simply furnished with maple headboards, beds covered with bold floral spreads, and well-worn furniture.

The windows, framed by sheer curtains, have views of the water or the sprawling grounds. The whole effect is homey and quite comfortable. Guests will be pleased that they have private bathrooms. They will also soon discover that very little time is actually spent in the rooms, as there are lots of outdoor activities to be enjoyed.

One may choose to take a walk by the duck pond and tennis courts, or maybe pick some blueberries on the way down to the swimming beach and wooded grove. Red wooden lawn chairs are found along the way for those who prefer to stop a moment and enjoy the serenity of the setting sun or watch a badminton or baseball game. Those who prefer a milder form of recreation will be able to choose from horseshoes, chip n' putt, and croquet. Canoeing or fishing for bass and pickerel are favorite water sports. If the weather should be less than favorable, then guests often find ping pong, pool, or the assortment of board games more to their liking. A crackling fire is always blazing in the downstairs fireplace on cool New England days. The wonderful part about this setting is that everyone is quite at ease, allowing family members and friends to spend some quality time together.

The meals are all served in a family-style setting. The various small dining rooms each hold a handful of long tables covered with checkered tablecloths. A freshly baked loaf of bread and several pitchers of either juice, water, or milk are placed on each table. The industrial-size kitchen produces delicious home cooking, satisfying even the heartiest appetites. Each week there is a cookout that is followed by a dance or some other activity geared for "children of all ages, six to ninety-six."

The Lake Shore Farm offers simple accommodations, a myriad of activities for young and old, and a chance to enjoy the natural serenity of this pretty New Hampshire setting.

FRISKY FRIVOLITIES:
* There are ample grounds for Bowser to romp on, with both a duck pond and the larger Jenness Pond to cool off in.
* If you are craving a short excursion, then a trip to nearby Portsmouth will offer terrific shops and galleries, as well as historic Strawberry Banke to explore.
* Those who wish to capture a more complete flavor of New Hampshire may want to spend the day hiking through this region.

MEADOW FARM BED AND BREAKFAST

Jenness Pond Road
Northwood, New Hampshire 03261
(603) 942-8619
Hosts: Janet and Douglas Briggs
Rooms: 3 doubles
Rates: $30-40
Payment: Personal checks
Children: Welcome, over three years old preferable
Dogs: Welcome with prior approval
Open: All year

The Meadow Farm Bed and Breakfast is located on a meandering back road that encircles a large pond. This 1700's four-chimney New England Colonial is set amid 50 acres of woods and meadows. The grayish-brown home and adjacent barn rest in a truly idyllic setting.

As guests arrive, they will be greeted by the two resident dogs; a very friendly doberman and a Jack Russell terrier (Rainee and Nifty). First impressions reveal a home whose architectural heritage is still intact. The wide-board floors, hand-hewn beams, beehive oven, and original wood paneling are features that are difficult to find in today's buildings. The views out to the horse pastures take one back to the 18th century.

Two cozy sitting rooms do have modern concessions which include comfortable furnishings and a television. The keeping room has been transformed into the breakfast room, where hearty full meals are served each morning. Janet's specialty is a Bismarck -- a delightful pancake creation that must be tasted to be fully appreciated. Other selections vary and are dependant upon the whim of the cook, but may include fresh fruits, eggs, waffles, blueberry pancakes (with locally made maple syrup), bacon or sausage, homemade breads and muffins, and freshly brewed coffee.

The guest chambers also maintain an 18th-century look, including original wood paneling, wide-board floors, and hand-hewn beams. Doug and Janet have repainted most of the house using authentic colors and adding stenciling for a touch of country whimsy. Furnishings consist of four-poster beds, mahogany bureaus, and dressers. Although the windows do not provide views of Jenness Pond, they do look out upon the sprawling pastures.

In addition to the wonderful walking paths and roads, guests will surely want to take advantage of the sailing and canoeing available on the pond. There is also a pony for the little ones. The B&B also has access to nearby tennis courts, for those who wish to utilize them. Most who come to this part of New Hampshire are either on their way to one of the nearby cities or just want to escape the trappings of a rigorous work week.

FRISKY FRIVOLITIES:
* There are ample grounds for Bowser to romp on, as well as a tranquil pond in which he can cool off.
* Portsmouth, Concord, and Newburyport are all within a short drive of the B&B. Visitors will find everything from historic walks to wonderful shops and restaurants.
* There is terrific cross-country skiing right on the property and also nearby.

THE EXETER INN

90 Front Street
Exeter, New Hampshire 03883
(800)782-8444, (603) 772-5901
Innkeeper: J.H. Hodgins
Rooms: 8 singles, 38 doubles, 2 suites
Rates: Singles: $50-65; Doubles: $60-80; Suites: $115-135
Payment: Most major credit cards

Children: Welcome
Dogs: Welcome, but "must not be left alone"
Open: All year

The Exeter Inn was made possible by a generous gift from Mrs. William Boyce Thompson and her daughter, who gave the inn to Phillip's Exeter Academy to accommodate visiting families and "young ladies who came to visit Academy students." The brick Georgian-style inn was built in 1932. Architecturally, the inn has remained much the same; however, over the years it has been tastefully updated to include some of the modern amenities guests appreciate.

Old rock hitching posts still flank the inn, leading guests to a burgundy awning which extends over the steps to the front door. There is an elegance about the inn that you feel immediately upon entering. The public rooms are sumptuous and filled with period and reproduction antiques. In one room, a flecked, deep burgundy carpet sets the tone for the furnishings. The centerpiece is a three-pedestal dining room table surrounded by eight Chippendale-style chairs. This is accented by an antique secretary, side tables with brass lamps, and leather chairs facing the two marble fireplaces.

Guests will either ascend the deep red, carpeted stairs or ride the elevator to their floor. The bedrooms vary in size and decor but include beds covered in Bates spreads, antique bureaus, and old-fashioned writing desks complete with ink wells. The colors are fairly neutral, utilizing striped or floral wallpapers and complementing trim. Sheer draperies are at the windows. The modern amenities have not been overlooked, as each room has individual climate control, color television, telephone, and tiled bathrooms. A fruit basket is also placed in each chamber.

During their stay, guests should make a point of sampling the meals in the dining room. Crisp white tableclothed tables are set with china, sparkling glassware, and flatware. Light streams in through the rounded windows. Guests will enjoy a varied selection of entrees. The courteous service, elegant decor, and comfortable guest rooms are just a few reasons you may wish to visit the Exeter Inn. The predominant one is surely to see the Phillip's Exeter Academy and the historic town of Exeter.

FRISKY FRIVOLITIES:
* The streets in and around the inn are excellent for walking with Bowser. The inn is also located just a few blocks from Exeter's historic downtown.
* The Hampton Beaches and Portsmouth are within easy driving distance of the inn.
* The Phillip's Exeter Academy is also a terrific place for walking. The school was founded 200 years ago and visitors will find it has maintained its sense of history.

SHEAFE STREET INN

3 Sheafe Street
Portsmouth, New Hampshire 03801
(603) 436-9104
Innkeeper: Kevin Finnigan
Rooms: 5 doubles
Rates: $45-50
Payment: AE, MC, VISA, personal checks
Children: Welcome
Dogs: Welcome
Open: All year

The Sheafe Street Inn is a small, center staircase Federal built in 1815. Located on a back street in historic Portsmouth, it has been beautifully maintained and preserved over the years. Kevin Finnigan has also added his own charming touches to bring the inn to life.

The only first floor bedroom has a four-poster bed with a burgundy comforter and floral dust ruffle. An oriental rug is laid before a charming fireplace. An antique bureau provides ample space for storing clothes, and a circular bedside table holds assorted reading materials. The mood of this chamber is further enhanced by pretty dried beach lavender and soft light coming from both the original paned windows and brass chandelier. The bathroom is private. Most of the other guest rooms can be reached by ascending a twisting staircase to the second and third floors.

One upstairs bedroom has a rocking chair and queen-size bed set on a soft blue carpet and hardwood floors. Bedside tables with small potted plants on them are placed to either side of the bedstead. A beautiful dressing table with inlaid wood adds further appeal. A third room uses a small quilt, hung on an exposed brick wall, as its centerpiece. A cozy rocking chair, bedside tables, a library stepping stool, and an old desk rest upon the oriental rug. A handsome double bed is adorned with a forest green quilt. The remaining guest rooms include such amenities as a window seat, a wicker-backed rocking chair, a comfortable sofa, and views of the water.

Each morning, Kevin serves a complimentary breakfast of fresh fruit, pastries, and coffee/tea in the tiny breakfast room. If guests are not completely sated (or are later in the mood for a light snack), then just around the corner they will find a terrific bakery offering an assortment of sweets, quiches, and breads.

FRISKY FRIVOLITIES:
* Bowser will surely want to take a walk in Prescott Park. This is a lovely area set between the river and the Strawbery Banke museum.

* Historic Strawberry Banke offers interesting architecture, lovely gardens, and fun shops and outdoor restaurants.
* New Hampshire is filled with all sorts of crafts, artwork displays, galleries, etc. that are worth a visit. For a detailed description and map, contact the League Foundation.

THE INN AT CHRISTIAN SHORE

335 Maplewood and 5 Northwest Street
Portsmouth, New Hampshire 03801
(603) 431-6770
Innkeepers: Charles Litchfield, Louis Sochia, and Tomas Towey
Rooms: 5 doubles, 1 single
Rates: $30-60
Payment: Personal checks
Children: Not appropriate for small children
Dogs: Welcome with prior approval
Open: All year

The Inn at Christian Shore is an 1800's Federal on the edge of Portsmouth, a once-famous shipbuilding town that today is a beautifully preserved city of marked historical interest. The inn, set two blocks from the river, is a perfect place to use as a base for exploring Portsmouth.

The three hosts are delightful and will be happy to share tidbits of information on the area as they escort guests to the bedrooms. The rooms are each furnished with period antiques accented by walls papered in subtle floral or striped patterns. One of the chambers boasts a canopied bed covered in a navy fabric with tiny pineapples. Another of the upstairs bedrooms has very low ceilings and is colored in deep maroons with blue accents. A mahogany writing table sits in the corner. The half bath in this room is of particular note, as it requires most guests to duck before entering. Once inside though, there is plenty of headroom. Other guest quarters offer canopy beds with Bates spreads, televisions, air conditioning, and wall-to-wall carpeting. Around every corner guests will discover interesting antiques such as a barometer or perhaps an impressive grandfather clock.

Breakfast at the inn is delicious and could be one of the many reasons people return year after year. The enormous fireplace warms those sitting at both the long tavern table or one of the smaller tables for two. This hearty repast usually consists of steak and eggs, tenderloin of pork, omelets, or something as simple as cereal, depending on one's preference and appetite.

After a most filling meal, many wish to try their hand at the organ, which lies tucked in the corner of the breakfast room. Others retire to the sitting room, a particularly cozy place furnished with period antiques, wing-back chairs, and a most inviting sofa. Some have been tempted to stay and visit all day, but guests should try to get out and explore Portsmouth.

FRISKY FRIVOLITIES:
* Downtown historic Portsmouth (Strawberry Banke) is a long but pleasant walk from the inn.
* The area immediately around the inn offers some quiet streets lined with antique homes.
* Many also wish to explore the nearby towns along the Maine coast. Kennebunkport and York are just two of the many options.

MAINE

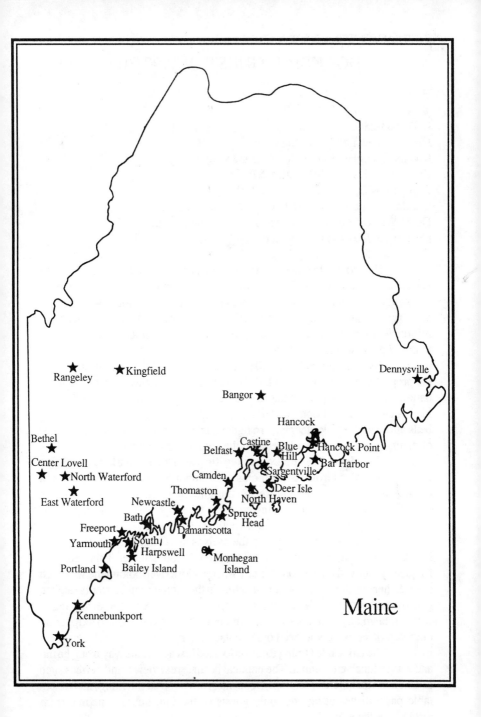

Rangeley

★Kingfield

Dennysville

Bangor ★

Hancock

Bethel

Belfast

Castine

Blue
Hill

Hancock Point

Center Lovell

★ ★North Waterford

Camden

Sargentville

Bar Harbor

East Waterford

Thomaston

Deer Isle

Newcastle

North Haven

Bath

Spruce
Head

Freeport

Damariscotta

Yarmouth

South
Harpswell

Portland

Bailey Island

Monhegan
Island

Kennebunkport

York

Maine

DOCKSIDE GUEST QUARTERS

Harris Island Road
York, Maine 03909
(207) 363-2868
Hosts: Harriet and David Lusty
Rooms: 2 singles, 14 doubles, 6 cottage suites
Rates: Doubles: $41-70; Suites: $79-98
Payment: MC, VISA (for bills under $75), personal checks
Children: Welcome in first-floor guest rooms (Crib $7)
Dogs: Welcome in four cottages only (one dog per building)
Open: Late May to mid-October

The Dockside Guest Quarters is located on a small island across the harbor from the town of York. In 1953, David Lusty purchased the 1880's home, garage, and barn. By the following year, the Maine house was ready to accept guests and visiting yachtsmen. Over the years, the Maine house has been refurbished and four cottages (with suites and efficiency units) have been added to the original accommodations.

The four simply furnished cottages accepting dogs are scattered about the property, and all boast wonderful harbor and ocean views. The accommodations in the gray pine cottages feature a living room, private bathroom, kitchenette, twin bedroom, and a deck, complete with captain's chairs. Sofa beds allow for flexible sleeping arrangements. Skylights let in ample amounts of natural light. The overall theme in the cottages is nautical.

The Maine House also has terrific views of the harbor, expansive lawns, and gardens from its bedrooms and rambling porches. A collection of marine paraphernalia is also present in this guest house in the form of sailboat models, nautical prints, and sailing books. A telescope is set up, giving guests an opportunity to study the harbor activity at close range.

Each morning, guests help themselves to a Continental buffet breakfast that is elegantly displayed on the dining room table. This repast is frequently enjoyed on the porch or down at the kiosk overlooking the water. Of course, there is always the option of eating in the dining room. After breakfast, guests may want to walk about the seven acres or relax in one of the many wooden lawn chairs overlooking the harbor. Should you wish to skipper an outboard or sailboat, you need only contact the marina.

The Dockside Dining Room is located just across the way from the inn and serves lunch and dinner. The nautical decor, great views, and entrees such as chicken Rockefeller, scallops Dockside, roast stuffed duckling, and delectable pasta dishes attract not only guests of the inn, but also people from throughout the area.

FRISKY FRIVOLITIES:
* There are five local sandy beaches for swimming and sunning.
* York offers a cliff walk that runs along the rugged cliffs above the Atlantic ocean. A few minutes from the inn, there is a foot path leading along York River.
* There is a self-guided walking tour of the York/York Harbor areas. The Chamber of Commerce provides maps.

COVESIDE COTTAGES

P.O. Box 631, South Main Street
Kennebunkport, Maine 04046
(207) 967-5424
Hosts: Sandra and Michael Severance
Rooms: 15 cottages
Rates: $260-620 per week
Payment: Personal checks
Children: Welcome
Dogs: Welcome, $25 damage deposit may be collected
Open: May to October

The Coveside Cottages are white shingled one-and two-bedroom accommodations situated on a picturesque tidal cove. The cottages are set around a semi-circular driveway amid cedar, walnut, and apple trees. The grounds are nicely landscaped; some space has even been left for a wooden jungle gym. These simply furnished units are ideal for those who need a base for exploring southern Maine and do not want the intimacy of an inn or B&B.

The pine-paneled cottages have fully equipped kitchenettes, private baths, and small living rooms. The accommodations are not spacious, but they are extremely clean, tastefully decorated, and even have views of the water. White wicker and rattan furniture are complemented by attractive periwinkle blue and yellow floral curtains. Bates spreads cover simple maple bedsteads. Brass lamps provide light for reading or game playing on quiet Maine evenings. The cottages do not come equipped with televisions, but they may be requested for an additional $15 a week.

Set just off a lane on two acres, the Coveside Cottages offer a good deal of privacy; yet they are also within walking distance of Kennebunkport and the ocean. Dories are available for exploring the harbor and the water is comfortable for swimming.

FRISKY FRIVOLITIES:

* In addition to the shops in town, there are a number of interesting lanes and streets to meander along. Kennebunkport is rich in history, including captains' mansions, impressive Colonial architecture, and beautiful waterfront properties.
* Portland, a 45-minute drive, is a city that has recently undergone quite a revival. The waterfront, parks, and old town are excellent areas for walking and shopping.
* An interesting long walk starts at the cottages, takes guests over the hill past The Colony hotel, and along the ocean.

THE CAPTAIN JEFFERDS INN

Box 691, Pearl Street
Kennebunkport, Maine 04046
(207) 967-2311
Innkeeper: ~~Warren Fitzsimmons~~   Jane
Rooms: 12 doubles, 1 suite, 3 efficiency apartments rented by the month or
     the season
Rates: Doubles: $45-85; Apartments: $525-800
Payment: Personal checks
Children: Over 12 welcome
Dogs: Well-behaved dogs welcome with prior approval
Open: All year except November, open on weekends only

Fine craftsmanship is a luxury few can afford to build into their homes today. This makes it particularly fun to visit the old sea captains' homes, where no expense was spared and the finish work was exquisite. The Captain Jefferds Inn, a 180-year-old Federal mansion owned by a merchant sea captain, is a perfect example of this architecture. It was carefully refurbished and restored by Warren Fitzsimmons and his partner Don in 1981. They took the remainder of the inventory from their New York antique business and used it to furnish the inn. They also have an extensive collection of folk art, Majolica pottery, and Staffordshire china. The impressive furnishings are coupled with bright decorative colors to create a unique ambiance that entice guests back year after year.

Each of the bedrooms has a different color scheme and floral motif. Laura Ashley wallpaper and matching bed linens add a touch of the English countryside. Simple Americana antiques combine with more formal English antiques, including the waist-high beds, and serve to tie the room together. Most of the bathrooms are private, and some still contain the fixtures from years ago. Although they are a bit dated, these facilities still provide every convenience you would expect to find in a modern bathroom.

Every morning, guests are called to either the first or second breakfast seating by the sounding of a tinkling bell. This delicious morning repast ranges from eggs Benedict and quiche to blueberry crepes and New England "flannel" (a combination of corned beef hash and a poached egg). Afterwards, guests may want to form their plans for the day in the living room, an inviting chamber filled with bright chintz-covered sofas, English antiques, and an elegant Steinway piano. After a busy day, guests return for tea or lemonade. This is often served on the outdoor brick patio.

FRISKY FRIVOLITIES:
* The inn is just around the corner from town. Walk down the street and turn right for a window shopping expedition, and turn left to head out toward the water and sandy beaches.
* A drive back through Kennebunkport will lead to Parson's Beach, and an afternoon of sunning, swimming, and picnicking.
* A short drive will bring you to either Portland or Portsmouth, both of which are thriving towns/cities that offer a myriad of shops, cafes, and parks as well as interesting historical houses.

THE SEASIDE

Gooch's Beach
Kennebunkport, Maine 04046-0613
(207) 967-4461 or 967-4282
Hosts: Sandra and Michael Severance
Rooms: 1-4 bedroom cottages
Rates: $315-730 per week
Payment: Personal checks
Children: Welcome
Dogs: Welcome in cottages only, $25 damage deposit required
Open: May to October

The Seaside inn was originally built in 1756; more recently a motor lodge and cottages have been added. The cottages are perfectly suited for a family or group of friends who are looking for a self-sufficient vacation experience without all the frills of a country inn. Located on 20 acres of sprawling land that abuts over 3,000 feet of sandy beaches, these cottages have views of either the ocean or a tidal river. There is also ample space for walking with Bowser.

Each of the cottages is furnished a bit differently in a traditional Maine style. Single beds with maple headboards and white Bates spreads are the norm for most of the cozy bedrooms. Cots and cribs are also available at a slight additional charge. Some cottages offer single-level living, and others have bedrooms upstairs and a living room and kitchen down. One interesting cottage has a circular staircase leading up to the bedrooms.

The living rooms are open and have comfortable couches, 18th-century reproductions, and rattan chairs adorned with bright cushions. The kitchens are well equipped with pots and pans, dishes, and flatware. There is usually a dining area for family meals. A color television is also in residence, just in case people run out of things to do. Electric heat will keep the cottage comfortable on chilly Maine days.

The cottages are usually rented by the month, although weekly rentals are available. Long-and short-term guests will appreciate the laundry facilities. When the beach becomes dull, children will enjoy and make use of the playground. Shuffleboard and croquet are two of the other favorite pastimes for all ages.

FRISKY FRIVOLITIES:
* After sunbathing and a refreshing swim, you may want to take a bicycle ride with Bowser running along at your side.

190

* A long walk will take you into town. A shorter walk runs along the shore - - either on the beach or on the sidewalk.
* Parson's Beach is within driving distance of the cottages. This is a favorite spot as it is usually relatively uncrowded and pleasant for walking.

THE INN ON SOUTH STREET

South Street
Kennebunkport, Maine 04046
(207) 967-5151 or 967-4639
Innkeeper: Eva Downs
Rooms: 3 doubles
Rates: $60-85
Payment: MC, VISA, personal checks
Children: Over 10 years old welcome
Dogs: Welcome only with prior approval
Open: All year except January

The Federal-style Inn on South Street was built by Ivory Goodwin in the early 1820s. The home is listed in the National Register of Historic Places and has been beautifully preserved. French doors lead out to balconies and picture windows have views of the water. The stateliness of the house is enhanced by the decor. Hardwood floors are covered with vibrant rag rugs, English and oriental antiques occupy the rooms, and walls are painted in soft colors and stenciled. The second floor has a sitting room for guests' use, appointed with oriental collectibles. The French doors open to a balcony which is a peaceful place for reading.

The three guest chambers are decorated differently but share an airiness and spaciousness. One bedroom has bright, bold floral wallpaper and another is done in delicate wildflowers. White wicker, lacy curtains, Bates spreads, and brass beds with throw pillows are featured. Two rooms offer either a day bed or an old-fashioned sleigh bed, now used as a couch. The bathrooms are private and modern. One chamber has a spacious step-up bathroom and the other has a corner closet that has been converted into an intimate white tiled bathroom with a skylight.

Every morning, guests are invited to the breakfast room for early bird coffee at 7:00 a.m., or a more casual full English breakfast a few hours later. This delicious repast is served on a large oval table and includes fresh fruit, homemade muffins and breads, eggs, souffles, and other treats (guests' plates are usually adorned with freshly picked wildflowers). The views of the water from the breakfast table are particularly appealing.

FRISKY FRIVOLITIES:
* There is a park just down South Street that is perfect for walking Bowser (and is on the way to downtown Kennebunkport).
* For an energetic morning constitution, a walk along the water out by The Colony hotel and Vice President George Bush's house is worthwhile.
* Cape Porpoise is a short drive from Kennebunkport. This is a quieter community offering beaches (Goose Rocks Beach) and a working fishing port.

THE COLONY

Ocean Ave, Box 511
Kennebunkport, Maine 04046
(207) 967-3331
Manager: John S. Banta
Rooms: 139 hotel rooms
Rates: $89-255 (AP)
Payment: AE, MC, VISA
Children: Welcome

Dogs: Welcome ($15 per day)
Open: Mid-June to mid-September

The Colony has been a tradition in Kennebunkport ever since the Boughton family took over operations in 1948. Set on a small peninsula overlooking the ocean, this massive old hotel combines a casual summer atmosphere with the elegance only a few hotels in New England still possess.

The resort is actually composed of the main hotel, the Galland House, and the motor inn (across the street). Rooms in the hotel are most desirable, as many have water views and exude an old world charm. It is apparent that this hotel was built during the days when it was fashionable (and affordable) to "summer" on the coast of Maine. The Colony reflects these grand times. The lobby is cavernous; its windows overlook the veranda, terraced gardens, and glistening ocean. Just off the lobby, guests will find a viewing room with a large screen television, a card room, a game room, and a library.

The Colony's spaciousness is also reflected in the guest rooms, due more to the high ceilings than to the actual size of the chamber. The "ocean view" rooms are most desirable. Each is traditionally decorated with Bates bedspreads, brass bedside table lamps, and antique dressing tables with mirrors. Each chamber is unique and has a different configuration. The tiled bathrooms can either be private or connecting. The original porcelain fixtures are both functional and add a sense of timelessness to the rooms.

There are many recreational activities available at The Colony. A heated salt water swimming pool is built high above the water; the decks boast incredible views of the ocean. Guests also have access to the course at the Arundel Golf Club. For those who just want to practice a bit, there is always the hotel's putting green. The hotel also hosts social events such as bridge parties and arranges for lecturers and entertainment.

Rates are based on the American Plan, which includes breakfast, lunch, and dinner. The first two meals of the day are rather informal; however, at night guests are asked to dress more formally. It is a solid tradition, that like the hotel, lives on despite the changing times.

FRISKY FRIVOLITIES:
* The ocean is only a few hundred feet away. Steps from the inn lead to a path that skirts the shore for a mile or so.
* Ogunquit has a wonderful mile-long foot path (Marginal Way) that follows the spectacular coastline. Afterwards you may enjoy exploring this artists' colony.
* Ferry Beach is just north of Kennebunkport. It offers panoramic views, white sand beaches, and interesting nature trails through the forests.

HOMEWOOD INN

Drinkwater Point, P.O. Box 196
Yarmouth, Maine 04096
(207) 846-3351
Innkeepers: Fred and Colleen Webster, Doris and Ted Gillette
Rooms: 15 buildings housing guest accommodations
Rates: Doubles: $40-85; Suites and cottages: $90-214
Payment: AE, MC, VISA, personal checks
Children: Welcome (cribs free and baby-sitter available)
Dogs: Small pets welcome with prior permission from the manager; not to
     be left alone in the cottages.
Open: Mid-June to mid-October, cottage winter leases available

     Set at the end of a series of forked roads, the Homewood Inn has a
beautiful view of Casco Bay and the Calendar Islands. The resort is only a short
drive from Portland, but guests feel far removed from hectic city life.

     After checking in at the main cottage, you will then be led down a
series of country paths to the cape-style shingled cottages dotting the shoreline.
A variety of accommodations are available; some are single housekeeping
cottages, others are double cottages with private entrances. Those who prefer
to rent rooms rather than an entire cottage may want to request a suite in the
Maine House. Built in 1742, this historic building has four spacious rooms
furnished with antiques.

     Guests will find the cottages to be homey and comfortably furnished
with white Bates spreads on the beds, and a selection of 19th-century American
antiques interspersed with reproductions. Tab Colonial patterned curtains
frame windows looking out to the bay. The tiled bathrooms are immaculate and
the towels fresh. A number of extra blankets coupled with the warmth from the
fieldstone fireplaces and woodstoves keeps the cold at bay on brisk Maine
nights. Living rooms have invitingly soft sofas and chairs.

     Some like to relax on vacations but others need activities to keep them
occupied. Tennis courts and a swimming pool should keep even the most
energetic busy. If not, then croquet and shuffleboard are other available outdoor
activities. Of course, Maine is known for its sailing waters; boats may be rented
at the local marina. Pool and ping-pong account for some of the rainy day
pastimes. The resort is self-contained, so guests do not have to worry about
anyone straying too far.

     All three meals are served at the inn's main lodge, a charming old
building with paneled wood walls and well-worn hardwood floors. A fieldstone
fireplace warms diners and the faint smell of a crackling fire adds a homey

touch. Emphasis is on fresh seafood. On Monday nights, the inn hosts a hearty Maine clam and lobster bake, which is eaten outside at rustic wood tables.

Guests are sure to enjoy their vacation at the inn. For years, this family run resort certainly has done a terrific job at making everyone feel a part of the family.

FRISKY FRIVOLITIES:
* Wolf Neck Woods State Park is 15 minutes from the inn and is a great place for hiking. Ask the inn to pack a picnic lunch and spend the day there.
* While walking Bowser in the meadows, take the time to notice the extensive bird population. Bring or borrow a pair of binoculars for some excellent bird watching.
* Yarmouth is a charming town, only a few minutes' drive from the inn. There are stores for shopping and quiet streets for walking.

THE ISAAC RANDALL HOUSE

Independence Drive
Freeport, Maine 04032
(207) 865-9295
Innkeepers: Glynrose and Jim Friedlander
Rooms: 8 doubles
Rates: $40-65
Payment: Personal checks
Children: Welcome in certain guest rooms
Dogs: Welcome
Open: All year with a few breaks in the winter

This Federal-style farmhouse was built in 1823 as a wedding present to Isaac Randall and his new wife Betsy Cummings. Mr. Randall, a direct descendent of Myles Standish and Priscilla Mullins, was an affluent farmer with over 60 acres of land. The Randalls raised eight children in the fifty years they lived in this house. In the years since then, the farmhouse has been used as a way station for the Underground Railroad, a dairy farm, a dance hall, and as an apartment house.

Today, the inn consists of the original farmhouse with its additions and a large barn. Guests park in front of the barn, which, if Jim has his way, will eventually be transformed into an intimate French restaurant. The inn's entry way leads visitors into the enormous country kitchen with beamed ceilings and an abundance of copper pots. A pretty hand-painted rug is ornamentation for the hardwood floors.

The bedrooms can be found both upstairs and down. They are painted in a variety of warm pastel blues, roses, and lavenders. The cheery decor is enhanced with an array of bright quilts. A favorite room of the Freidlanders is the rose room off the parlor. This has been decorated with an eclectic combination of Victorian furniture, including a huge floor-to-ceiling gilt mirror.

Our favorite bedroom is on the ground level and has a private entrance. The decor and the furnishings are completely different from the other more traditional guest quarters. The general mood is that of Santa Fe, New Mexico. The white walls contrast with natural wood trim and exposed beams. The bed and throw pillows are done in a rust French provincial print. A unique touch is a steer's skull on the wall. The Friedlanders, who would someday like to move to New Mexico, enjoy the western ambiance this cozy chamber exudes. The spacious bathroom features a copper bathtub.

A kitchenette and adjacent parlor are available to guests. The kitchenette gives guests the flexibility of preparing and storing their own snacks or lunches. The parlor is decorated with an oriental rug, colorful country quilts, and a standing copper coffee maker (that Jim found and spent many hours refurbishing) resting near an antique chest. A television, chess table, and assorted board games are also provided for guests.

Each morning, guests will enjoy the friendly conversation around the kitchen table. A delicious complimentary breakfast may feature eggs, Maine blueberry pancakes, French toast, muffins, or some other "Glynrose concoction." Guests will definitely find it difficult to leave because the Friedlanders are such warm and interesting people. However, most people take with them fond memories of this special B&B experience.

FRISKY FRIVOLITIES:
* There is ample room for Bowser to play on the inn's five acres and a spring-fed pond for him to cool off in afterwards.

* The town of Freeport, a short distance away, is filled with all sorts of terrific shops and is the home of L.L. Bean (known for their clothing and camping/ sporting goods).
* Nearby Wolf Neck Woods State Park offers a number of hiking and nature trails. One should not miss the opportunity to see the rugged Maine coastline and the many quaint towns and fishing villages.

SENTER BED AND BREAKFAST

South Harpswell, Maine 04079
(207) 833-2874
Host: Alfred M. Senter
Rooms: 3 doubles, 1 cottage
Rates: Doubles: $40-50; Cottage: $350 per week
Payment: Personal checks
Children: Welcome
Dogs: Welcome, but not allowed to wander unescorted through the house
Open: All year

Alfred Senter is the hospitable host of an inviting B&B, perched on a picturesque point. This B&B has panoramic views of the ocean as well as access to the water. The village of South Harpswell is only a short drive from Brunswick, Maine (home to Bowdoin College).

When we arrived, we found Alfred tending to his rose garden, where he has well over 50 bushes. He is an avid horticulturist and is always willing to share his knowledge (and possibly a cutting or two) with interested guests. Two good-sized greenhouses are filled with unique varieties of plants and flowers, which he nurtures during the winter months and eventually transfers to his flower beds in the spring. During the summer months, fresh flowers from the gardens are placed in the guest rooms.

Of the three bed chambers available, two face the ocean and the other looks out toward the aromatic rose garden. One cozy bedroom is paneled with wood. A duvet-covered down comforter adorns a bed which looks out onto the ocean. Another room has twin beds covered with white nubbly spreads, simple furnishings, and built-in bookshelves. The remaining room is decorated in a similar fashion. The shared bathroom is unique in that there are two tiled baths with a shared bathtub/shower in the middle. Guests simply close and lock the door on one side and have a full bath at their disposal (just remember to unlock the door when finished).

Alfred truly enjoys people and enjoys recounting his full repertoire of stories. A favorite spot, most conducive to conversation, is the living room with its woodstove. Of course, this spacious room also has panoramic views of the ocean through a plate-glass window.

A full breakfast is quite good and hearty. If guests want an egg and toast, it can be arranged, or if pancakes are more to your liking, then Alfred will whip those up as well. A lighter breakfast of juice and breads is also available. Afterwards, you may want to walk down to the water on the recently completed staircase. Alfred has even thoughtfully included a little bench at the halfway point, for people to rest on and marvel at the picturesque surroundings. Jeff, his golden retriever, may even choose to accompany those who have swimming in mind.

FRISKY FRIVOLITIES:
* The beach is directly in front of the house. Guests can explore the rocky coast, as Bowser retrieves sticks.
* The village of South Harpswell is a summer community. The streets are quiet and the cottages are quaint, making it an ideal area for walks.
* A 15-minute drive from Senter's Bed and Breakfast will bring guests to the town of Brunswick and Bowdoin College's beautiful campus.

THE DRIFTWOOD INN AND COTTAGES

Bailey Island, Maine 04003
(207) 833-5461
Innkeepers: Mr. and Mrs. Charles L. Conrad
Rooms: 4 housekeeping cottages
Rates: Cottages: $190-$310 per week
Payment: Personal checks
Children: Welcome
Dogs: Welcome in the housekeeping cottages only
Open: Mid-May to mid-October

The Driftwood Inn and Cottages is a good example of a classic Maine cottage community. Set upon craggy rocks overlooking a small inlet, the inn has been in continuous operation for over 75 years. Bailey Island is just a short drive from Brunswick, encompassing only one and a quarter square miles. Guests will enjoy exploring this little piece of the Maine coastline and using the housekeeping cottages as a base.

The inn has three gray-shingled, cape-style houses perched on rocks overlooking the water. The rooms housed in these buildings have unfinished wood walls, freshly urethaned hardwood floors, and either maple or iron headboards with simple coverlets on the beds. The furniture is an eclectic combination of simple maple bureaus and straight-back chairs.

People traveling with dogs are welcome in the housekeeping cottages. These are furnished in a similar fashion to the inn's guest rooms. Two are located on a path set back from the water and the others are on a sandy beach. The cottages are a bit rustic but extremely neat and clean. They also happen to be a tremendous bargain for those wishing to enjoy the serenity of the Maine coast without the cost. The cottages not only offer more privacy than the rooms at the inn, but also have cooking facilities. For a modest fee, guests are welcome to dine at the inn.

Organized activities are limited at the inn; however, there is a salt water swimming pool set into the rocks and fishing in the cove. The Driftwater Inn and Cottages provides the perfect spot for a very relaxing, unpretentious vacation.

FRISKY FRIVOLITIES:
* There is an antique store within walking distance of the inn, located in an 1838 barn. It is called Carriage Barn Antiques.
* The picturesque roads around the island lead to many scenic coves and inlets, where there is terrific fishing (the Bailey Island Fishing Tournament is held every August) and picnicking.
* Bowdoin College is 15 minutes from the island. The campus is beautiful and the streets surrounding it are lined with historic homes.

CLOVERLEAF LODGE

RFD 1, Box 330
Bailey Island, Maine 04003
(207) 833-6498
Hosts: Joan and Don Leach
Rooms: 1 or 2 doubles (depending upon the Leach's visiting children)
Rates: $38-48
Payment: Personal checks
Children: Welcome
Dogs: Welcome
Open: March to December

The Cloverleaf Lodge is located on Bailey Island -- the last in a string of islands which begin just outside of Brunswick. The Leaches have spent many summers on this island and finally decided to buy a house and reside here year-round. Their three-story cape-style home, with views of the ocean, has a gazebo on the left side and a porch around the back. They have renovated much of the house and are in the process of landscaping the grounds.

One of the biggest renovation projects involved the kitchen. The Leaches gutted the original kitchen and expanded out through the attached screened-in porch. The windows in this new room have some of the best ocean views. The fireplaced living room is another pleasant place to spend time, either reading a book or visiting with other guests.

A carpeted stairway leads to the two traditional B&B bedrooms. There is always one room available and sometimes two (depending on visiting relatives). The bath is shared. Both chambers are comfortable and traditionally furnished. The front room has a double bed with a Bates bedspread and a small alcove with a pottery sink. A glance through the stenciled tab curtains yields its best feature....a terrific view of the ocean.

The third floor has been converted into a small office and cozy sitting area. The eaves are steep, with large sofas tucked in against them. Once again, the Leaches have maximized their water views by placing large windows at either end of the room. Views of the ocean and the WWII Portland Watch Tower can be had over the tree tops.

Each morning, hearty appetites will be sated with eggs, pancakes, cereal, bacon, or whatever else Joan feels like making. This hearty complimentary meal is enhanced by the conversation and the tranquil ambiance of the scenic location. Visitors to the Cloverleaf Lodge will truly enjoy the B&B experience and the island serenity the Leaches have come to love.

FRISKY FRIVOLITIES:
* There are terrific rocky and sandy beaches for you and Bowser to enjoy.
* The local fishing is good. It is also interesting to explore some of the nearby working harbors to check on the other fishermen's catches.
* The B&B is on a private dirt road. The walks in either direction are peaceful and scenic.

GRANE'S FAIRHAVEN INN

North Bath Road
Bath, Maine 04530
(207) 443-4391
Innkeepers: Jane Wyllie and Gretchen Williams
Rooms: 9 doubles
Rates: $25-70

Payment: Personal checks
Children: Welcome
Dogs: Welcome with advance notice; must be on leashes
Open: All year; open Fridays to Sundays in the winter (not including holidays)

Grane's Fairhaven Inn was built by Pembleton Edgecomb in 1790. His bachelor's home had been a log cabin, but upon his marriage he felt his new family should have a proper home. It would come to be that the Edgecomb family and their relatives would live in this house for over 125 years. Subsequent owners added several rooms, purchased the surrounding acreage, and ultimately renovated the entire estate. Jane and Gretchen bought the home in the fall of 1978, whereupon they converted it into an inn.

Today, this weathered shingled, antique cape is tucked into the side of a hill overlooking beautiful meadows and the distant Kennebeck River. A flagstone pathway leads guests by a half-dozen bird feeders, on the way to the front door. Once inside the foyer, the low ceilings and pumpkin-pine wide board floors set the overall tone for the inn.

The furnishings throughout are comfortable and invite guests to fully relax. Each guest chamber is individually decorated with an eclectic assortment of wicker and pine furniture. The low ceilings, use of Colonial colors, and collection of antique quilts recreate the feeling of the 1700s. The bedrooms have good views of the meadows and wooded hillside. Perhaps the combination of a picturesque setting and the inn's antiquity are the reasons many guests return year after year. One guest was so enamored with the inn that, after her stay, she sent Jane and Gretchen two beautiful quilts.

Grane's Fairhaven is also famous for its delicious and bountiful breakfast selections. Every morning, fresh fruits, hot and cold cereals, muffins, or toast are served. This would be enough for most people; however, Jane and Gretchen then offer one or two additional items. Swiss eggs, orange French toast, pecan waffles, fruit pancakes, bacon, sausage, scrapple, and hash are just a sampling of the choices. For those who can still move after breakfast, there are many activities available in the area. Guests who prefer to let breakfast settle will find either the library or tavern comfortable places for relaxing. At the end of a busy day, many frequently gravitate to the patio and bask in the evening glow.

People have a myriad of reasons for visiting Bath and the southern part of Maine. Boothbay Harbor and Wiscasset are just two of the more popular towns close by. The historic inn, its proximity to interesting attractions, and Jane and Gretchen's warm hospitality, will provide enough reason to spend some time in this peaceful spot.

FRISKY FRIVOLITIES:

* The inn is surrounded by over 27 acres of fields and woodlands for walking with Bowser.
* The road in front of Grane's Fairhaven is relatively uncrowded and great for jogging or bicycling. Walks are always equally as enjoyable.
* Many opt to explore the craggy coastline, paddle a canoe down one of the many nearby rivers, or go for an impromptu blueberry-picking expedition.

THE TRAILING YEW

Monhegan Island, Maine 04852
(207) 596-0440
Innkeeper: Josephine Day
Rooms: 10 singles, 40 doubles
Rates: $36 per person (MAP)
Payment: Personal checks
Children: Welcome
Dogs: Well-behaved dogs welcome (Monhegan Island has a strict leash law)
Open: Mid-May to mid-October

Monhegan Island, originally founded by English explorers around 1600, is located approximately 10 miles off the Maine coastline. This small, rustic, and rocky island retains the same charm that it did over 100 years ago. To this day, the island does not permit off-island automobiles on it, and telephones and electricity (supplied by solar power) are relatively new additions. This sort of lifestyle is not for everyone; however, for those who are intrigued with solitude, deep pine forests, marshlands, and crashing waves, the island and its inn prove to be idyllic.

The Trailing Yew is a haven for artists and naturalists, offering clean and simple accommodations. Located on a hill above Monhegan Harbor, the inn has a terrific view of the ocean. In addition to the main house, there are four out-buildings. Each of the guest rooms comes with an oil lamp for light, a bed, a bureau, and hot and cold running water. Josephine, who has been running the inn for decades, supplies linens and blankets but reminds guests to bring flashlights, as well as a sleeping bag in the spring and fall. The accommodations are not heated and thus a sleeping bag comes in handy on the cooler nights.

After a day exploring the island, guests have usually built up a good appetite. The dinners, served in the main house, are hearty and presented family-style at long dining room tables. There is a selection of fresh fish and usually one meat dish. Breakfast and dinner are included in the price, and lunch is available at an extra charge. The fresh air and opportunity for exercise create hearty appetites. Guests will also find, after a few days on the island, that they have a greater appreciation for the benefits of a simple, yet pure lifestyle. Guests soon discover that the island's ambiance is addictive, and that many of the other guests have been making a sojourn to the Trailing Yew for years.

FRISKY FRIVOLITIES:
* A short distance away are the beach, general store, and gift shops.
* There are paths to meander along all over the island. Pack a picnic lunch and spend the day finding a new craggy cove or hiking to the highest point on the island.
* The island is known for its wildflowers in the spring and for migrating birds in the fall. These are particularly pleasant and quiet times of the year to visit.

THE BRANNON-BUNKER INN

H.C.R. 64 Box 045, Route 129 South
Damariscotta, Maine 04543
(207) 563-5941
Innkeepers: Joe and Jeanne Hovance
Rooms: 8 doubles, 1 suite
Rates: Doubles: $37-55; Suite: $55-90 (off-season rates available)
Payment: MC, VISA
Children: Welcome
Dogs: Welcome
Open: All year

The Brannon-Bunker Inn is located on a rural road just outside the bustling town of Damariscotta. From the house, it is only a short drive to either the ocean, with its lobster boats and historic lighthouses, or to the many picturesque lakes and rivers. Of course, guests might prefer to spend their time relaxing at the inn; a welcoming antique cape surrounded by meadowlands.

Guests enter the Brannon-Bunker through a rounded doorway, which leads into a foyer. Classical music is often playing softly in the background. One first-floor bedroom is filled with country antiques. A multi-colored Vermont quilt is draped over an antique bed, and a rocking chair rests in the corner. Well-worn narrow board floors lead guests to the back of the inn and into another common room with low ceilings. The main focal point here is the fieldstone fireplace. Maroon walls and contrasting white wainscotting complement the sheer, white tie-back curtains. One's attention is easily drawn to the country-style antiques and large dining room table.

A short flight of stairs brings guests up to the other bedrooms. Some of the walls have been stenciled and others are papered in floral or pineapple patterns. Blue or lavender Vermont quilts adorn several of the beds, and the remainder are covered in white nubbly spreads. An eclectic collection of pretty country antiques fills each of these guest quarters. Dried flower wreaths hang throughout the inn and little hand-painted rocking horses say "Welcome." There is also an intimate upstairs sitting area; framed historic memorabilia decorates the walls. The adjacent carriage house contains the remaining guest bedrooms. As in the main inn, these charming rooms are simply decorated and furnished.

In the morning, you may ask Joe and Jeanne about particularly interesting areas to explore, as they are quite good at recommending interesting day trips. A filling breakfast of juices, coffee, fruit, coffee cake, and a variety of homemade muffins will send you on your way.

FRISKY FRIVOLITIES:
* If you have a very well-behaved dog you may want to take him canoeing. Lake Damariscotta and the Pemaquid River are just two of the many options.
* The Pemaquid Beach Park is 15 minutes from the inn. Should you care for more remote activities, then head up the coast to the Pemaquid Light and to one of the coastal lobster shacks.
* The sailing along this portion of the coast is excellent, as are the sights.

THE NEWCASTLE INN

Newcastle, Maine 04553
(207) 563-5685
Innkeepers: Frank and Sylvia Kelley
Rooms: 20 doubles
Rates: $45-65 (special off-season rates available)
Payment: Personal checks
Children: Welcome
Dogs: Smaller dogs are welcome during the off season
Open: All year, except January

Nestled on a tidal river on the edge of the Pemaquid Peninsula, The Newcastle Inn is ideal for extensive wanderings through southern Maine. In fact, the Kelleys received a note from two women who had bicycled along the entire Maine coastline. They wrote that one of their two favorite areas was the beautiful Pemaquid region. While the rivers and lakes are perfect for canoeing and fishing, there are also many antique galleries and historic sites. The Kelleys are great sources for creative outing ideas, as well as providers of restful accommodations and good food.

The inn was built in 1920 and is filled with 18th-century American country antique furniture and knick-knacks. The bedrooms are very traditional and cozy. Some have bedsteads with maple headboards and white Bates spreads, and others have canopies and crocheted coverlets. Guests will find a mix of shared and private baths, all of which are extremely neat and clean. Subtle old-fashioned floral wallpapers and hardwood floors are found throughout the inn and the adjacent carriage house.

The inn's front parlor is also quaintly decorated with a beautiful rug painted on the floor and colorful stenciling on the walls. Across the hall, a small living room is simply furnished with chairs set around a fireplace. Guests frequently congregate here on cool winter evenings.

In the mornings, guests will be treated to a full country breakfast in the dining room, which overlooks the water. Any number of home-cooked treats may find their way from the kitchen each day, including the Kellys famous Maine blueberry blintzes. Dinner is also served in the summertime. One can choose to dine at the inn or perhaps in one of the nearby restaurants.

FRISKY FRIVOLITIES:
* Christmas Cove is a wonderful place for a morning jaunt. It is only a few minutes' drive from the inn.
* Many enjoy a leisurely walk to the town of Damariscotta. The streets will lead visitors along the water and by a number of small stores. Head off in the other direction and a road wends along a river to Lake Damariscotta.
* The Maine coast is dramatically impressive. Many enjoy exploring the coves, craggy points, and the few remaining un-automated lighthouses.

GRACIE'S BED AND BREAKFAST

52 Main Street
Thomaston, Maine 04861
(207) 354-2326
Host: Grace Kirkland
Rooms: 4 doubles
Rates: $32-40
Payment: Personal checks
Children: Welcome with advance notice
Dogs: Welcome with prior approval
Open: March to mid-January

Main Street in Thomaston, although busy with seasonal traffic, is lined with graceful antique sea captains' homes. Gracie's Bed & Breakfast, an 1830 Greek Revival home, is nestled among these majestic buildings. As guests pull up in front of the barn and house, they are likely to be met by Gracie's friendly black lab.

Guests will immediately feel right at home, as the furnishings are comfortable and the decor warming. The foyer has dark hardwood floors covered in woven rugs. Brass sconces are backed by traditional patterned wallpaper, setting the tone for the period antiques. The staircase, with its gracefully curved balustrade, leads to the guest rooms.

The four upstairs chambers are individually and simply decorated. One room, with yellow patterned wallpaper, features a double brass bedstead tucked under the eaves. A rocking chair rests off to the side on hardwood floors. Another room has twin beds covered in matching white cotton spreads, with throw pillows with goose appliques resting against the carved headboards.

Each morning, breakfast is served in the attractive dining room on an antique oak table surrounded by matching chairs. Gracie usually prepares a substantial breakfast of fresh fruit, homemade breads and muffins, eggs, and coffee or tea. Guests should be sure to notice the extensive collection of ceramic owls in the dining room.

FRISKY FRIVOLITIES:
* From Thomaston Harbor you may take a ferry to Vinal Haven, North Haven, or Monhegan islands.
* There are a number of old granite quarries in the area. These are great for swimming.
* Clark Island is a half hour's drive from the inn. Pack a picnic lunch and go out to explore its many trails and look for wildlife.

THE CRAIGNAIR INN

Box 533, Clark Island Road
Spruce Head, Maine 04859
(207) 594-7644
Innkeepers: Norman and Terry Smith
Rooms: 2 singles, 21 doubles, 2 suites
Rates: Singles: $38; Doubles and Suites: $58-70
Payment: MC, VISA
Children: Welcome
Dogs: Welcome
Open: All year

A wonderful thing about the Craignair Inn is its proximity to civilization, yet its overall remote feeling. The natural setting allows guests to thoroughly relax and enjoy the picturesque Maine coastline. Situated at the end of Spruce Head and separated by a spit of land from Clark Island, the inn used to serve as the residence for granite quarry workers. Today, it houses guests who instead prefer to swim in the refreshing waters of the quarries and explore Clark Island.

The inn is delightfully informal with large public rooms. Guests will enjoy the parlor with its roaring woodstove, where they can settle into the well-worn sofas and side chairs. When it comes time to retire, guests will find the rooms to be simply furnished, with quilts covering iron-framed beds, pretty wall hangings, and braided rugs scattered about the hardwood floors. It should also be noted that there are three shared bathrooms per floor, but that doesn't seem to concern most of the house guests.

In the mornings, a full complimentary breakfast of eggs, pancakes, sausage, breads, and juice is served to fortify guests before they set off to explore the area. The dining room has beautiful views of the water and Clark Island, just across the way.

Clark Island is reached by a tiny footbridge and causeway. Once on this mini oasis, you will discover it is a wonderful place for walks and a chance to observe waterfowl and ocean life in their natural environment. After an adventuresome day afield, you will return to find a family-style dinner, which is hearty enough for even the largest of appetites. The single entree dinners may vary from roast beef or fresh fish to scampi or a traditional clambake (on Saturday night). After dinner, some like to gather in the kitchen around the cast iron cook stove and exchange stories about their day.

FRISKY FRIVOLITIES:
* Spruce Head is a tiny village with little roads eventually leading explorers to the water.
* Clark Island is a "must see" with Bowser. There are miles of trails meandering around the island and seemingly endless beaches to roam.
* Many also wish to explore some of the other traditional Maine settings. We recommend a ferry trip to rustic Monhegan Island or a more leisurely drive to Camden.

EDGECOMB-COLES HOUSE

HCR60 Box 3010, 64 High Street
Camden, Maine 04843
(207) 236-2336
Innkeepers: Terry and Louise Price
Rooms: 6 doubles

Rates: $55-130
Payment: Most major credit cards
Children: Over 7 years old are welcome
Dogs: Well-behaved dogs accepted with prior approval
Open: All year

Sitting perched on a hillside overlooking the deep blue waters of Maine is the Edgecomb-Coles House. The home was built in the mid-1800s as a small, traditional New England farmhouse. As the years rolled by, various wings were added until there were more than 20 rooms. Today, the farmhouse is an elegant B&B filled with fine antiques, oriental rugs, and loads of charm.

The Prices have renovated the home and made an effort to retain much of its authenticity. The living room is filled with formal antiques, which complement the grand piano and fireplace. This room exudes a Victorian ambiance even with ornate oriental rugs covering the hardwood floors. Just off the living room is a tiny parlor decorated in maroon and white speckled wallpaper with a contrasting white wainscotting. The red painted staircase separates these two rooms and leads to the guest chambers.

The most spacious bedroom has a commanding view of the water through a picture window. The king-size bed is placed to maximize this view, with a working fireplace off to the side. This is the most popular guest chamber, and guests would be well advised to book it in advance. The other bedrooms are also inviting, with delicate floral wallpapers, sheer tie-back curtains, and lacy comforters. All of the guest quarters exude a light and airy feeling of springtime, achieved through the use of bright colors and contrasting white backgrounds. Fresh flowers and potpourri are thoughtful additions.

After a peaceful night's sleep, guests will awaken to the smell of freshly brewed coffee. After descending the staircase, guests will find a selection of fresh baked breads or muffins and seasonal fruit or juice. Breakfast may be enjoyed in the cozy dining room or taken outside to the garden. From the wicker chairs, views of the rolling lawns and pretty gardens may be enjoyed.

FRISKY FRIVOLITIES:
* The Camden Hills State Park (5,000 acres) is fairly close at hand. It is a terrific place for walking and picnicking.
* Camden is a manageable town to explore on foot and is within walking distance of the inn. The waterfront can be found at the base of the main street, where one may take advantage of the views of the busy harbor.
* After taking a self-guided tour of the historic homes (maps are found at the Chamber of Commerce), visitors may wish to take a ferry to nearby Isleboro and the Grindle Point Lighthouse.

THE HIRAM ALDEN INN

19 Church Street
Belfast, Maine 04915
(207) 338-2151
Innkeepers: Jim and Jackie Lovejoy
Rooms: 1 single, 7 doubles
Rates: $30-45
Payment: Personal checks
Children: Welcome
Dogs: Welcome only with prior approval
Open: All year

The Hiram Alden Inn was built for Hiram O. Alden in 1840. Alden was a local attorney, but he also found the time to be a banker, postmaster, and the co-founder and president of Maine Telegraph. His Greek Revival (with touches of Victorian) home is located on a quiet street in a residential neighborhood.

Since the 1800s, there have been renovations to the house, with attention paid to preserving its architectural and historical heritage. Thus, guests will still be able to appreciate the ornate tin ceilings, hand-carved moldings, marble fireplace mantles, and original fixtures. The Lovejoys are the current occupants and hosts. Jackie and the family's friendly golden retriever will greet guests upon their arrival.

210

Bedrooms are all spacious, enhanced by the high ceilings. Most of the individually decorated chambers are located at the top of the hand-carved stairway. Beds are covered with Bates or crocheted spreads. Our favorite room is decorated in navy blue and white. The wallpaper and drapery patterns match, with reversed color combinations. The fireplace in this room has blue and white tiles set into the mantle. The bathrooms in many cases are shared; however, this bedroom does have its own marble-topped sink. Another guest chamber is most appropriate for families because it offers a double and single bed. The bright floral wallpaper and large windows combine to create a light, airy effect. Dried wreaths add a decorative country touch.

Those who awaken early are welcome to take their coffee or tea to the rocking chairs on the porch. A full country breakfast is served a short time later in the formal dining room. This comfortable room has a large oval table covered with a pretty lace tablecloth. French doors lead into a walk-in butler's pantry. The morning fare varies, but most likely will consist of fresh fruit, juice, and breads or muffins. These are accompanied by either blueberry-nut pancakes, eggs, French toast, and sausage or bacon.

The inn is also open in the winter and offers special packages for those who want to cross-country ski or explore Maine during quieter months of the year. As a final note, the Hiram Alden is particularly conducive to visiting children. The Lovejoys have teenagers who would be happy to baby-sit while mom and dad enjoy an evening out. They also have a crib for the wee ones.

FRISKY FRIVOLITIES:
* A walk downtown is both good exercise and gives you an appreciation for this 18th-century town. There is a small park on the waterfront close to a great family restaurant called Weathervanes.
* Acadia National Park is a short drive away and provides an excellent feeling for both the beautiful forests and the rugged Maine coast.
* There are two festivals that visitors might want to take advantage of: the Bay Festival in July and the Downtown Festival in October.

PENOBSCOT MEADOWS INN

Route 1
Belfast, Maine 04915
(207) 338-5320
Innkeepers: Dini and Bernie Chapnick
Rooms: 6 doubles, 1 studio apartment
Rates: $49-79 (off-season rates available)
Payment: MC, VISA

Children: Welcome
Dogs: Welcome
Open: All year

Very few people have the courage and knowledge to undertake a major renovation, but in 1984 the Chapnicks applied a little of each and restored a turn-of-the-century building into a charming modern-day inn. The grounds around the inn also underwent a facelift as the Chapnicks cleared a path from the inn down to the water. In the process, they took down selected trees in order to create a distant water view.

The building is reminiscent of the Victorian era; the front door has an etched frosted glass window. Step through the entry way and emerge into the foyer bathed in light and gleaming wood. Rose, the Chapnick's friendly 240-pound Great Dane, is sometimes on hand to greet and escort new arrivals to their rooms.

The guest quarters have all been updated, including the modern bathrooms. White walls are a stark contrast to the colorful wall hangings. This simplicity succeeds in drawing one's eye away from the decorations to the antique furniture. One room has an antique bed with a carved pine headboard and matching bureau. A pretty antique quilt lies at the foot of the bed. Rag rugs or area carpets cover the beautiful old hardwood floors. Two of the guest chambers also have water views. A glass hutch on the landing offers a wide selection of books for guests' perusal.

The inn does serve dinner in its intimate dining rooms. Tiny calico fabrics cover the tables and dried or fresh flowers are placed throughout. To say the menu is inspired is an understatement. Appetizer selections may consist of baked mushrooms stuffed with Neufchatel cheese, herbs, and spinach; or tomato-cognac soup. Perhaps a raspberry chicken or ginger jumbo shrimp entree might prove to be an interesting second choice. Top this off with homemade ice cream or perhaps a five-layer mocha cake with Sambuca frosting.

After dinner, guests might want to try a Coffee Nudge (a delicious four-liqueur coffee drink) on the outside porch and enjoy the cool Maine evening. If it is early, one can watch the afterglow from the setting sun.

FRISKY FRIVOLITIES:
* Follow the path down to the water. This is a nice way for you and Bowser to wear off the effects of a long drive. Swimming, retrieving sticks, or enjoying the beautiful shoreline of the Penobscot Bay are all delightful activities.
* City Park consists of 15 acres and is within walking distance of the inn.
* The ferries to Isleboro (one of Maine's exclusive summer colonies) leave daily from Lincolnville Beach. The three-mile crossing takes less than a half hour.

THE PULPIT HARBOR INN

Box 704
North Haven Island, Maine 04853
(207) 867-2219
Innkeepers: Christie and Barney Hallowell
Rooms: 5 doubles
Rates: $35-78
Payment: MC, VISA, personal checks
Children: Welcome
Dogs: Welcome, only with prior approval
Open: All year

North Haven Island is approximately 3 by 9 miles in size and lies 12 miles from the coast of Maine. Originally settled in 1774, the island today has a population of 350 year-round residents. The inn, a refurbished 1850's farmhouse, is surrounded by fields, evergreens, and gardens.

The Pulpit Harbor Inn has five bedrooms; all are appropriately named after their location in the building. Thus, guests may choose from either the Southwest Corner, Northwest Corner, North-South Suite, North-South Chimney, or Back Stairs. Three of the guest rooms have private bathrooms, and the other two share a bath. Each guest chamber is individually and comfortably furnished. Handmade quilts add color to the simple pine and maple furnishings.

Guests will, depending on the weather, eat in any of the three dining rooms. A glassed-in porch, outside terrace, and an informal dining room provide as many changes in atmosphere as there are in menu. The dinner is a fixed price of $16 and features homemade soup, salad (from the inn's garden), and a meat or fresh fish entree (lobster may be ordered with a little advance notice). Wines and other beverages are also available to complement the meal. Guests who are at the inn for an extended period of time may want to try the two other island restaurants as well.

In the morning, a light Continental breakfast of juice, hot beverage, and fresh muffins is served. The day can be spent trying any number of outdoor activities, including golf or tennis. Those who would like to explore the island may want to have a picnic lunch packed for them. This gives guests the opportunity to thoroughly enjoy the natural surroundings and not worry about the time.

FRISKY FRIVOLITIES:
* Guests may bicycle (rentals available) to the tiny town, which contains a post office, yacht club, art gallery, and a couple of small shops.

* Long walks along quiet roads are favorite activities for most visitors to the island.
* North Haven is a wonderful spot for taking in all the natural sights; herons, ospreys, bald eagles, fields of flowers, and beautiful coastal views are a delight to naturalists of all ages.

THE MANOR

Box 276, Battle Avenue
Castine, Maine 04421
(207) 326-4861
Innkeepers: Paul and Sara Brouillard
Rooms: 12 doubles, 1 cottage
Rates: Doubles: $55-95; Cottage: $450 per week
Payment: MC, VISA
Children: Welcome
Dogs: Welcome with prior approval
Open: All year with the exception of Christmas

Five acres of sprawling lawn does not lessen the impressive effect of The Manor, a dark brown shingled "summer cottage," originally built for

Commodore Fuller of the New York Yacht Club. This stately home, constructed at the turn of the century, is now run by the Brouillard family as an inn, one that the Commodore would still be proud of.

Ascending the tree-lined driveway, guests drive under an enormous portico linking the main building to another half its size. In the summertime, Cinzano umbrellas dot an adjacent deck, overlooking the lawn and waters beyond. Climb the massive stone stairs and emerge into a high-ceilinged foyer. Take a moment to wander through the spacious living room with its enormous fieldstone fireplace. The Victorian furnishings are the only pieces that would be appropriate in a home of this size and stature. Beyond the living room is a mahogany bar with a green marble top. Overnight guests, as well as other visitors, like to stop in for afternoon hors d'oeuvres and refreshing libations. During the slower and cooler months of the year, many even remain for the hearty entrees prepared by Paul Brouillard.

The staircase to the guest bedrooms is wide enough for three people to walk abreast comfortably. Antiques fill the hallways as well as the bedrooms. The rooms are as spacious as those on the first floor. Fifteen-foot ceilings tower above walls papered in a variety of prints. One guest bedroom has deep red floral paper and an equally unique antique carved wooden headboard. Another room, with views of the water, is twice the size of most formal living rooms. It has a king-size bed with an old brass headboard and a side twin bed. Each of the guest rooms has been decorated with great flair and style in keeping with the feeling of the era.

There is also a guest cottage on the grounds for those who are traveling as a family or with friends. The cottage is as large as a good-sized house. Guests leave The Manor knowing they have stayed in and experienced an exceptional New England "summer cottage."

FRISKY FRIVOLITIES:
* Walk down through the property, turn right, and follow the road toward the lighthouse at the end of the peninsula.
* If you wander off in the other direction, you will come to the waterfront. Castine is an invigorating town to explore, with interesting old houses and a few small shops. Historic walking tours are available through the Chamber of Commerce.
* The salt air and water are delightful, and many opt to rent a boat and sail to the nearby islands. If you would rather stay ashore, a visit to scenic Blue Hills or the reversing falls is always an interesting day trip.

OAKLAND HOUSE

Herrick's Landing
Sargentville, Maine 04673
(207) 359-8521
Innkeepers: Sylvia and Jim Littlefield
Rooms: 18 cottages
Rates: Cottages: $175-434 (per week-AP)
Payment: Personal checks
Children: Welcome in most accommodations
Dogs: Welcome in cottages only
Open: May to October

In the old days, Herrick's Landing was one of the passenger drop-off points for steamships. The Oakland House was built around an old existing farmhouse and opened as an inn in 1889. Since then, the cottages and the spacious 10-room Shore Oaks building have been added to the original homestead. While many things have changed during the years, the Oakland House has remained in the Herrick family.

Today, those who prefer simple, family-oriented vacations are drawn to this rustic Maine resort. It has become such a tradition with many families that the resort boasts a 70% repeat business. The present owners, the Littlefields, have done their best to maintain the natural ambiance and privacy throughout the vast acreage. The cottages, built at different times over the years, vary in structure from a very rustic, exposed-beam cabin with fieldstone fireplace to a more modern cottage with thermopaned windows, sliding glass doors, and a well-equipped kitchenette. They are all decorated with the same, basic furnishings. Sofas and armchairs have that well-worn look, and simple cotton spreads cover maple bedsteads.

The cottages are completely private. Some are tucked into the woods and others are on the water's edge. Guests will find themselves spending time on either their screened-in porch or deck. Return guests definitely have their preferences for particular accommodations, therefore newcomers should book early and specify the amenities, decor, and location they prefer. For instance, "Hideaway," located on the edge of a field, may be more suited for families with children. "Grindstone" offers the ultimate in privacy, while "Brown Jug" offers views of Eggemoggin Reach and Little Deer Isle.

Guests will eat well during their stay at the Oakland House. Breakfast is served from 8-9:30 a.m. and features freshly made doughnuts, muffins, orange juice, fresh fruit, hot cereal, eggs, pancakes, and French toast. This is complemented by bacon, sausage, and even codfish cakes. Lunches include a choice between two main dishes, salad, rolls, beverage, and dessert. Guests look forward to the weekly lobster bake on the beach.

Guests will also have plenty to do during the day with both fresh and salt water bathing, sailing, fishing, badminton, rowing boats, and extensive walking trails at their disposal.

FRISKY FRIVOLITIES:
* Guests who have the urge to jump in the car and explore the area will find many scenic towns nearby. Bar Harbor, Castine, and Blue Hill are just a few of the places on the "must see" list.
* The water could not be much closer. While you fish, Bowser can paddle around and sun on the sandy beach.
* The inn's grounds are expansive and ideal for walking on with Bowser.

GOOSE COVE LODGE

Deer Isle
Sunset, Maine 04683
(207) 348-2508, 773-7338
Innkeepers: Eleanor and George Pavloff
Rooms: 2 singles, 5 doubles, 3 suites, 11 cottages
Rates: $350-$550 per person, per week (MAP)
Payment: Personal checks
Children: Welcome
Dogs: Welcome with prior approval. The innkeepers have a cat, Puff, and
    two springer spaniels, Gala and Allegro.
Open: May 1 to October 15

The Goose Cove Lodges' exceedingly friendly staff, casual atmosphere, and scenic surroundings combine to create an ideal vacation spot. Friends are made and relationships formed due mostly to the efforts of the Pavloffs. The accommodations, activities, and meals are all geared to encourage guests to join in the fun. The ringing of a bell brings people together for hors d'oeuvres before dinner. Guests trade stories about their day's adventures before going into the dining room for a sumptuous feast, which includes garden fresh vegetables, hearty meat dishes, and homemade desserts. Afterwards, some head off to the game room to play billiards or ping pong. Others wander off to their cozy rooms or cottages.

Rooms can be found in the main lodge or in the cottages nestled into the hillside. The cottages are rustic, with open ceilings exposing rough-hewn beams, natural wood walls, and fieldstone fireplaces. The beds are covered with thick woolly blankets for chilly Maine nights. Hooked rugs cover the hardwood floors. Windows and decks are also perfectly situated to take advantage of the water views and picturesque surroundings.

The Goose Cove Lodge is an ideal place for people who like the outdoors. Hiking and birdwatching are favorite pastimes. There is also a sailing school right on Goose Cove. For a modest fee, children, as well as adults, can learn to sail or practice their tacking in some of the finest waters in the country. The Island Country Club, which is nearby, caters to golfers and tennis players. We could go on and on about the hiking trails and other activities, but we will stop here and let you make a reservation.

FRISKY FRIVOLITIES:
* The lodge supplies a detailed map of hiking trails in the area. Bowser will love meeting new forms of wildlife.
* The cove is a wonderful place for swimming and sunning, after a day exploring Acadia National Park or Mt. Desert Island.
* Visitors to this scenic area will want to see the charming towns of Blue Hill and both Northeast and Southwest Harbor

JOHN PETERS INN

Peters Point, P.O. Box 916
Blue Hill, Maine 04614
(207) 374-2116
Innkeepers: Barbara and Rick Seeger
Rooms: 5 doubles, 1 suite
Rates: Doubles: $65-110; Suite: $75-110

Payment: Personal checks
Children: Welcome
Dogs: Welcome, must get along with the Seegers' dog, Doc
Open: All year

The John Peters Inn is an 1810 Georgian mansion perched on a knoll overlooking the tidal waters of Blue Hill Bay. The inn was bought last year by the Seegers and since then they worked around the clock in order to prepare it for its grand reopening. New plumbing and wiring were installed, bathrooms were updated, walls were knocked down, and guest rooms were decorated with great thought and care. The final result is an extremely elegant country inn.

Guests will most likely be greeted by Barbara Seeger and Doc (an acronym for "disobedient canine" which Barbara coined for the family dog). They will show newcomers into the enormous country kitchen and, through the use of a hidden computer, quickly dispense with check in. Guests will then be led up the stairs, over an assortment of oriental rugs and by many fine antiques, to their spacious rooms.

The guest rooms are as different as they are delightful. Bold formal floral papers have been chosen for some walls, while delicate country wildflower patterns grace others. Barbara has also used stenciling in some of the other rooms. Guests might sleep in the antique bed covered in a handmade Vermont quilt that Barbara had commissioned in Stonington. The quilt came out so beautifully she decided to design the room around it. Another chamber has white tie-back curtains and wicker furniture which creates an open, airy summer house effect. The one room in the inn particularly appropriate for guests with dogs has high ceilings, a fireplace, and multi-paned windows (overlooking the hills). The king-size bed is covered with a goose down comforter that will take the chill off any cool Maine evening.

Dinner is not served at the inn; however, there are many excellent restaurants in the Blue Hill area. Upon returning home later in the evening, many enjoy sitting in the formal living room before one of the two fireplaces, relishing in the fire's glow before retiring.

Guests will find breakfast to be a leisurely affair. Barbara turns out a five star meal, beginning with freshly squeezed juice and moving on to other delicious courses. The morning we were visiting she started with asparagus with hollandaise wrapped in paper-thin egg crepes, followed by waffles with real maple syrup. Breakfast is taken in the formal dining room on chilly days or on the glassed-in sunporch on warm summer mornings.

After breakfast, which can take up to two hours, a walk into town or over the inn's 25 acres is a must. For those who prefer water sports there is a swimming pool for leisurely laps. With or without activity, guests will find their stay at the John Peters Inn rivaling any of the finest inns in New England.

* The grounds are quite expansive and perfect for exploring with Bowser.
* The town of Blue Hill is well within walking distance from the inn. The homes are beautiful and of great historical interest.
* Many others choose to visit the beautiful areas of Mount Desert Island, Acadia National Park, and Camden Hills.

BAYVIEW INN AND HOTEL

111 Eden Street
Bar Harbor, Maine 04609
(207) 288-5861
Manager: John A. Davis, Jr.
Rooms: 32 doubles, 5 suites
Rates: Doubles: $85-175; Suites: $325-375
Payment: All major credit cards, personal checks
Children: Welcome in the hotel (cribs: $10)
Dogs: Welcome in the hotel
Open: May 15 to November 15

The Bayview Inn is a 1930's Georgian-style mansion, set on the edge of Frenchman's Bay. When the inn was opened to the public in 1983, the Davises wanted to ensure that the decor remained in keeping with its heritage. This they have accomplished with great flair, and have also extended this ambiance to the newer additions. Today, there are three sections to this mini-resort: the more modern hotel, two-to-three bedroom townhouses, and the old inn.

The elegant and airy hotel exudes sophistication. As guests enter through the double glass doors, they can catch glimpses of the ocean through the windows at the far end of the lounge. This is also an ideal place to spend the late afternoon watching sailboats cruising over the midnight blue Maine waters.

Many of the bedrooms are also graced with views of the ocean. Bell hops escort guests to their quarters along thickly carpeted hallways. The spacious bed chambers utilize seafoam greens and dusty pinks in the opulent wallpapers, incorporating flowers and partridges. The furnishings are stately. Fine reproduction armoires house color televisions, finials grace the bedsteads, and soft armchairs are provided for total relaxation. All of the bathrooms are large and modern. Guests will appreciate the thick towels, bath salts, fragrant soaps, and shampoos. One of the more striking aspects about the bayside bed chambers is the expansive view of the water. This effect is achieved through the French doors and windows running the length of the wall.

A swimming pool, set on the rocks above Frenchman's Bay, is available to guests. An exercise room will help work off calories consumed in one of the fine restaurants located on the premises. Drinks may be enjoyed on The Terrace, while breezes off the water cool the warm summer's night.

FRISKY FRIVOLITIES:
* There are 33,000 acres in Acadia National Park. Hiking, boating, and swimming are favorite pastimes. There are over 100 miles of hiking trails and close to 50 miles of carriage roads. The latter are appropriate for jogging and horseback riding.
* Cadillac Mountain is the highest point on the Atlantic coastline (in the United States). The athletic are welcome to clamber up to the top.
* A beautiful drive leads visitors out to Schoodic Point, located at the end of Schoodic Peninsula. Here visitors will be treated to incredible views of the Bay of Fundy and the mountains.

THE CROCKER HOUSE COUNTRY INN

Hancock Point, Maine 04640
(207) 422-6806
Innkeepers: Elizabeth and Richard Malaby
Rooms: 10 doubles
Rates: $50-68
Payment: AE, MC, VISA, personal checks
Children: "Truly well-mannered children are welcome."
Dogs: Welcome
Open: May 1 to Thanksgiving

The Crocker House Country Inn lies at the end of small but picturesque Hancock Point. Originally built in 1884, the inn has been a landmark
since the days when Hancock was both a busy ship-building town and a stop
for the Bar Harbor Ferry. Richard Malaby discovered the inn back in 1980,
when his brother read about it in the newspaper. After several visits, he fell in
love with the town and the inn, despite the tremendous amount of work it would
eventually take to completely restore it. Finally, in 1986, after several years of
concentrating on the restaurant, the Malabys completely overhauled the guest
rooms and added private bathrooms. The inn is now able to accommodate
guests as well as restaurant patrons.

The decor varies from room to room, but guests can expect wide-pine
floors with braided throw rugs or wall-to-wall carpeting. Some guest chambers
have delicate English country wallpapers and others are graced with decorative
stenciling. Tab curtains and exposed wood beams further enhance the overall
simple country elegance. White wicker chairs and comfortable rockers are
placed to take advantage of a view or quaint alcove. Potpourri in decorative jars
and vases of dried flowers add a personal touch. The bedsteads usually have
finial headboards and are adorned with white nubbly spreads. The existing
bathrooms have all been updated. Some have showers and others have claw-
footed tubs. Fragrant soaps and shampoos are provided.

Each morning, inn guests are treated to a delicious hearty breakfast.
This may include an overstuffed omelet, cereal, pancakes, fruit, juice, and
freshly brewed coffee (the Malabys even had our favorite - Hazelnut). After a
casual day exploring this cozy little summer community or other regional
attractions, guests will have worked off breakfast and be ready for dinner.

The restaurant is open to both guests and the public at dinner time.
Dinners are even more elaborate than breakfast and a bit more formal.
Everything from the presentation to the service is first rate. Appetizers vary
from pate mousse truffe to oysters Rockefeller to artichoke bottoms with crab
meat. Entrees include poached salmon, local grey sole meuniere (similar to
Dover sole), and broiled swordfish. The homemade pastries, cakes, and rich
mousses have weakened many a strong will.

After-dinner drinks can be enjoyed in the cozy sitting room with its woodstove. As much as it is a favorite gathering spot after dinner, guests have also been known to while away a cold Maine day in here, just reading and listening to the bell buoys ringing in the harbor. The Crocker House Country Inn is a delightful place for a romantic weekend or an extended vacation. As pretty as the inn is, one of the best features is the true hospitality and friendliness the Malabys exude.

FRISKY FRIVOLITIES:
* There are several winding country roads that take you by the clay tennis courts, the tiny yacht club, the second smallest post office in the United States, and last but not least, the beautiful waters of Frenchman's Bay.
* Cadillac Mountain, Schoodic Point, and Acadia National Park are just a short drive away.
* Often when visitors come to Maine they have a tendency to only see the established "sights." We also recommend exploring the back roads that lead to many charming fishing ports and small New England villages (i.e. Corea)

LE DOMAINE

Route 1, Box 496
Hancock, Maine 04640
(207) 422-3395
Innkeeper: Nicole L. Purslow
Rooms: 7 doubles
Rates: $75-95 (MAP)
Payment: All major credit cards
Children: Welcome
Dogs: Welcome
Open: June to Columbus Day

A bit of France has found its way into northern Maine in the form of an intimate French restaurant and B&B. Le Domaine has an unassuming facade, but once inside, you will immediately be enveloped by its French provincial warmth.

Downstairs is a restaurant and comfortable sitting area. White wicker chairs and couches are covered with red Pierre Deux pillows. Hardwood floors shimmer under the tables set with red tablecloths and white overlays, china, and crystal. A fire is often blazing in the raised hearth, as courses of beautifully prepared food are served. The various entree selections range from quail on toast to Lapin aux Pruneaux (the specialty of Le Domaine). The exquisite meals are a true testament to Nicole's Cordon Bleu schooling. After-dinner drinks, from the mahogany bar, can be enjoyed in the sitting room and then it is off to bed.

The tiny guest rooms have been appropriately named after herbs (the inn has an extensive herb garden). Elegant and subtle chintz fabrics cover the beds and window seat cushions, and frame the windows. Pale blues, yellows, greens, and lavenders are used in varying combinations. The guest quarters and baths are newly renovated. Crabtree and Evelyn seashell soaps await bathers. An appropriate bedroom for guests with a dog is to the rear of the inn, as it has an outside entrance and private redwood deck overlooking the lavish flower, herb, and vegetable gardens.

In the morning, you may take your Continental breakfast of fresh Maine blueberries and raspberries, complemented by croissants and home-made jam and honey, on the deck. A stroll across the grounds is a pleasant way to begin the day. A bench set amidst the gardens provides wonderful views of the rock gardens and of the vines growing up the expansive redwood trellis. Enormous shade trees filter the warm morning sun and entice guests to spend more time at this charming inn.

FRISKY FRIVOLITIES:
* Just down the road lie Winter Harbor and Schoodic Point, offering terrific hiking and water sports.
* North of Ellsworth, you will find an extensive lake and river region where fishermen and naturalists alike enjoy the abundance of pickerel, trout, and landlocked salmon.
* Many enjoy driving to the end of Hancock Point, where walks along the water, in this private little community, are peaceful.

LINCOLN HOUSE COUNTRY INN

Dennysville, Maine 04628
(207) 726-3953
Innkeepers: Mary Carol and Jerry Haggerty
Rooms: 5 doubles, 1 single
Rates: $56 per person (MAP)
Payment: Personal checks
Children: Very well-behaved children welcome

Dogs: Welcome only with prior approval
Open: All year except Thanksgiving and Christmas

The Lincoln House Country Inn was built by Judge Theodore Lincoln in 1787. This handsome classic Georgian Colonial lies in the midst of 95 wooded acres. In 1976, Jerry and Mary Haggerty satisfied a longtime yearning by buying the dilapidated home and transforming it into a country inn. Although they finished refurbishing the inn quite some time ago, there is always new wallpaper to put up and wainscottings to paint. Despite the continual maintenance involved, it has all been worthwhile, as the inn has been included in the National Register of Historic Places.

Kinapiw, the Haggerty's large but friendly Irish wolfhound, is usually on hand to greet newcomers. The library, where guests check in, is an impressive room. This is not due as much to its size as it is to its feeling of history. Wide-board floors extend to the large cooking fireplace, which still houses iron cauldrons. There is an interesting collection of books, a *Times Herald* paper stating "Truman Announces War Over," and a number of other historical artifacts. Guests will find the living room, with its Steinway piano, sofas, and high-backed chairs, to be equally as inviting.

There are two narrow staircases leading to the six guest rooms. One staircase is just off the living room and the more formal staircase is found in the entry way. The bed chambers are individually decorated and furnished with country antiques. Wide-pine floors (some are painted) are covered with rag rugs. The bathrooms are shared; one even has an enormous claw-footed tub. Separate sinks can be found in some of the bedrooms. A few of the guest rooms have fireplaces (non-working) and others have woodstoves.

The small dining room is an intimate setting. Tables are simply set and face a charming hearth. Each night, Mary Carol offers different dinner entrees. The fixed price of $16 includes an appetizer, soup, homemade breads, entree, and dessert. The main courses range from shrimp creole and lobster newburg to veal amelio and roast strip loin with bearnaise sauce. After dinner, many guests gravitate out to the tavern. It is a terrific little pub that is great fun for drinks, darts, board games, and conversation.

FRISKY FRIVOLITIES:
* The inn has 95 acres of land for exploring or cross-country skiing. An abundance of wildlife surrounds the inn — a special treat for guests.
* Campobello, Roosevelt's famous retreat, is just a short distance away.
* The river offers excellent canoeing opportunities. During spawning season, the Atlantic salmon can be seen heading upstream to lay their eggs.

THE PHENIX INN

20 West Market Square
Bangor, Maine 04401
(207) 947-3850
Manager: Alan R. Jenkins
Rooms: 12 singles, 21 doubles, 2 suites
Rates: Singles: $42-52; Doubles: $58-64; Suites: $65-68
Payment: Major credit cards
Children: Welcome (under 12 free)
Dogs: Welcome
Open: All year

The Phenix Inn, built in 1873, is located in a four-story commercial building in downtown Bangor. It was a gracious building in its time; however, a variety of unconscientious owners led to years of neglect. The last occupant, a music store, sold the building to the Phenix management, who completely refurbished this historical landmark and opened it to guests.

Once in the lobby, guests will be drawn in by the warm combination of stained wood and forest green decor. The mahogany antiques and interesting framed paintings are at home among the comfortable leather chairs and sofas. An elevator whisks guests to their bedrooms. These chambers vary in size from small singles to spacious queen-bedded rooms. They are all decorated in much the same manner, utilizing a mixture of antiques and good quality reproductions. Canopy and standard beds are covered with Bates spreads; writing desks and color televisions are off to the side. We especially liked the very spacious queen canopy bedrooms, with reproduction antiques and wall-mounted faux marble sinks. The spacious modern bathrooms have large showers and faux marble sinks with brass fixtures.

The breakfast room is simply furnished with butcher block tables. In the morning, guests are offered a Continental breakfast of juice, muffins, and coffee/tea for an additional charge of $1.50. The Phenix Inn offers visitors comfortable accommodations amid handsome furnishings. It is ideally located for exploring the Downeast region of Maine.

FRISKY FRIVOLITIES:
* Bangor is bisected by the Penobscot River. Visitors to the area can be found doing everything from fly fishing for salmon to canoeing along this river.
* Bangor has a number of excellent cross-country skiing areas just outside its borders.
* A self-guided walking tour of historical Bangor is always interesting. Free maps are available from the Chamber of Commerce.

226

THE HERBERT INN

P.O. Box 67
Kingfield, Maine 04947
(207) 265-2000
Owner: Bud Dick
Rooms: 5 singles, 12 doubles, 3 suites
Rates: Doubles: $45-65; Suites: $90-125 (off-season rates and packageplans
  available)
Payment: AE, MC, VISA
Children: Welcome
Dogs: Small dogs welcome, not to be left alone in the room
Open: All year

Herbert Wing, a man with political aspirations for governorship of
Maine, constructed The Herbert Hotel in 1918. He wanted to create an opulent
building, using only the choicest materials, in an effort to woo the region's most
influential people. Today's guests will be pleased he took the time and spent the
money necessary to create this architectural gem.

Kingfield is known for its proximity to Sugarloaf Mountain and thus
attracts its fair share of skiers. Many of these people seem to gravitate to The
Herbert Inn. It has a reputation for good hearty meals, charming guest rooms,
and a friendly staff. We also believe it has a distinctly Western flavor,
reminiscent of something one might find in Aspen, Colorado.

The rooms are newly renovated. The old brass sconces and headboards have been polished and the walls have been repapered in a variety of
traditional prints. Original pieces of furniture have been dusted off and fixed
to further recreate an authentic feeling. The bathrooms all have steambaths,
which are a blessing to aching bones after a long day of skiing or exploring.
Some bathrooms even have old-fashioned telephones. (Mr. Wing wanted the
very best, so in 1918 the Western Electric Company wired the hotel. The
Herbert Hotel was reknown as the only hotel north of Boston where guests
could receive a call at their dining room table.) Today's guests will find bottled
spring water on their dressers and lollipops on their pillows.

Descending the circular staircase on the way to dinner, guests will
notice the old-fashioned telephone booths (another example of the antique
telephone system). The dining room, with its reproduction Hunter ceiling fans
and French crystal shades, has been beautifully restored to further reflect a
bygone era. The food, though, is contemporary, innovative, and award win-
ning. Guests can expect a menu featuring duckling, scallops Madiera, The
Herbert ribs, or veal Edinburgh, as well as an extensive wine list. After dinner,

guests may wish to retire to the living room and enjoy an after-dinner drink in front of the crackling fireplace, while listening to the melodies from the grand piano. The oak woodwork in this room is particularly lustrous. This is due to a very expensive process called "fuming," where wood is placed in an airtight room and exposed to ammonia vapors until the appropriate color is achieved. It is rarely seen today due to its great cost.

For those who desire more activity after dinner, the Healthworks Spa has exercise equipment. There is also a masseur, hot tub, and steam room.

FRISKY FRIVOLITIES:
* There are a number of swimming holes and little known fishing spots that the staff would be happy to share with guests.
* The Appalachian Trail also meanders through the area. The chef will pack a picnic lunch and send you off on a day's adventure.
* The fall foliage is especially magnificent on the seven surrounding mountains, each of which is over 4,000 feet.

COUNTRY CLUB INN

P.O. Box 680
Rangeley, Maine 04970
(207) 864-3831
Hosts: Sue and Bob Crory
Rooms: 25 doubles
Rates: $59-68 per person double occupancy (MAP)
Payment: MC, VISA, personal checks
Children: Welcome
Dogs: Welcome, charge of $5 per dog
Open: Mid-May to mid-October, December 26 through March

Guests will surely love the Country Club Inn's panoramic views of the Rangeley Lakes and distant mountains from atop the 2,000-foot promontory. The inn was originally built in 1920s by a group of wealthy sportsmen, who discovered that the lakes were perfect for fly fishing. Some years later, the Crorys' search for their own small resort was finally answered, when they discovered the Country Club Inn.

As arriving guests ascend the last knoll to the inn, they will pass the 18-hole golf course. Check-in takes place in the informal living room. This is a cavernous room with a cathedral ceiling, enormous fieldstone fireplace, comfortable sofas, and arm chairs. The television is usually tuned to a golf match. The adjacent dining room has spectacular views through the plate-glass windows. The delicious entrees that are served are almost secondary to the 180-degree view.

Guests will enjoy the same impressive views from their bedroom as are found in the dining room. These chambers are attractively decorated with delicate floral wallpapers, quilted bedspreads, and wall-to-wall carpeting. The bathrooms are private and well appointed. Comfortable armchairs are situated to take advantage of the views through the small picture windows. The rooms also open out onto flagstone terraces overlooking the fields of blueberries and Rangeley Lake.

The Country Club Inn is an active place. Other than golf, the inn offers a number of activities for all ages. Lawn games consist of bocci and horseshoes. Swimming is always popular in the lake as well as in the pool. The Crorys' also like to sponsor theme parties and bingo nights.

FRISKY FRIVOLITIES:
* After an energetic walk down to the lake, you might want to swim, fish, or explore more thoroughly by canoe.
* Bowser should understand that golf balls are not to be retrieved; however, he will enjoy the wide open space that is perfect for retrieving tennis balls.
* Hiking is a favorite pastime in the area. The workout is excellent either along the Appalachian or Bald Mountain trails.

THE RANGELEY INN

Main Street
Rangeley, Maine 04970-0398
(800) MAINE-800 or (207) 864-3341
Innkeepers: Fay and Ed Carpenter
Rooms: 10 singles, 40 doubles, 1 suite, 4 housekeeping units
Rates: Doubles: $49-80; Suites: $75-99
Payment: AE, MC, VISA, personal checks
Children: Welcome (cribs: $6)
Dogs: Welcome, $6 per night
Open: All year

The Rangeley Inn has been a popular stop for almost as long as the Rangeley Lake region has been a stomping ground for fishermen and hunters. Set on Main Street, it is close to restaurants, shopping, and lake activities. An inviting front porch spans the full length of the inn. Two wings stretch back towards the water and a motor lodge complex.

Over the last year, the Carpenters have completed the inn's renovations and redecoration. In fact, during our visit, they were hosting an open-house so that visitors could see the rooms and also read about the historically significant events that have affected Rangeley and the inn. Guests will still find the original hardwood floors, brass sconces, and wood paneling. The difference is that the wood and brass now gleam, a fresh coat of paint and wallpaper bring the walls to life, and the furnishings have been updated. Brass bedsteads or hand-carved headboards support beds covered in Bates spreads. Antique armoires with attached mirrors house clothing. Rocking chairs are set near bedside tables and brass lamps. The private bathrooms have old-fashioned pull-chain toilets, porcelain sinks, and claw-footed bathtubs.

The accommodations in the motor lodge are also popular because of their proximity to the lake. These are definitely motel units and have separate outside entrances. During the warmer months, guests will enjoy relaxing along the water's edge or on the front deck. During the winter months, many can be found indoors in the inn's wood-beamed pub, the lobby's Colonial-wallpapered sitting area (complete with fireplace), or in the spacious dining room. The dining room fare ranges from seafood and local fish to beef and chicken dishes.

FRISKY FRIVOLITIES:
* Terrific cross-country skiing is available at several of the nearby resorts or on the sprawling fields.

* The Bigelow Preserve is a 30,000-acre forest alongside Flagstaff Lake that is great fun to visit (you can also hike on the Appalachian Trail).
* Rangeley Lake Park is famous for its beautiful scenery, trout and salmon fishing, and good swimming.

THE DOUGLASS PLACE

U.S. Route 2, Star Route, Box 90
Bethel, Maine 04217
(207) 824-2229
Innkeepers: Barbara and Dana Douglass
Rooms: 5 doubles
Rates: $26-35
Payment: Personal checks
Children: Welcome
Dogs: Well-behaved dogs welcome
Open: All year

The Douglass Place is a rambling farmhouse that the Douglass family has lived in and enjoyed for many years. They have raised their children here, married them here, and welcome their grandchildren back. Evidence of the many generations lie on the kitchen door frame, where the children's and grandchildren's heights are penciled in.

The Douglass Place is actually two houses. The back portion was built as a traditional New England farmhouse in 1791, and a century later a "prosperous farmer" added the Victorian front. The back stairway, off the kitchen, leads guests to the bedrooms in the rear of the house. These chambers can be characterized by their low ceilings and wide board floors. Simple, white Bates spreads adorn the beds, and country farmhouse antiques fill the rooms. The guest quarters in the newer section of the house have higher ceilings and a combination of English antiques and simpler country furnishings. Old-fashioned floral papers adorn the walls. Guests will feel, before too long, as if they are visiting friends of the Douglasses. This is due not only to the many personal touches and family momentos scattered about the guest rooms, but also to the warmth and kindness the Douglasses exude.

The living room has a 1940's television, a fireplace, and a collection of mahogany English antiques. Well-worn sofas and tables are mixed in with the more formal pieces. There are photographs of the Douglass' children, and a wall of silver cups and trays. The paneled den is also a cozy spot. A game room houses a pool table and assorted board games for indoor recreation.

Breakfast features English and fresh baked muffins, orange juice, coffee, and best of all, "good conversation." The Douglasses are delightful hosts, who are as ready to tell their guests about the history of the area as they are to share their home with them.

FRISKY FRIVOLITIES:
* The Appalachian Trail runs through the Bethel region. Pack a picnic lunch and head off for either a day of hiking or possibly some invigorating cross-country skiing.
* The Evans Notch District has a variety of hikes available, from the Roost Trail Loop of 1.2 miles to Caribou Mountain of 6.3 miles. Hikers will encounter waterfalls, valley views, and possibly a caribou.
* Just north of Bethel is Grafton Notch State Park, where you can see the Mother Walker or Screw Auger Falls. Here you will find unusual natural bridges crossing the gorges.

THE BETHEL INN AND COUNTRY CLUB

Bethel, Maine 04217
(207) 824-2175
Owner: Dick Rasor
Rooms: 70 doubles, 40 new luxury townhouses

232

Rates: $54-103 per person double occupancy (MAP) (package plans and
    off-season rates available)
Payment: All major credit cards, personal checks
Children: Welcome
Dogs: Well-behaved dogs accepted with advance notice
Open: All year

The Bethel Inn & Country Club is the very essence of what one would expect from a classic Maine resort. It is comprised of five Colonial-style buildings surrounded by acres and acres of land. The property also has a new Geoffrey Cornish golf course and a year-round recreation center (just recently completed).

Guest bedrooms are located in both the main inn and the outbuildings. Fireplaces are found in many of the spacious rooms with fabulous mountain views, as well as in the suites with cozy living rooms. The basic theme for the guest quarters is Colonial, with furnishings consisting of Windsor chairs, skirted armchairs, and white nubbly bedspreads and quilts. All of the rooms also have modern conveniences such as private baths, telephones, and clock radios.

The public rooms are equally interesting and inviting. Fireplaces are found in most of the common rooms and are kept well stoked on brisk Maine days. The main dining room has large picture windows offering beautiful views; however, guests may prefer to take their meals on the equally attractive screened-in veranda. For those looking for a more casual dinner atmosphere, the Mill Brook Tavern serves a reasonably priced light fare.

Most come to the Bethel Inn to take advantage of all the activities the resort offers. Golf and tennis as well as swimming in the outdoor pool are just a few of the available options. Guests who prefer to be near the water may utilize the Sunfish, canoes, and sandy beach at the lake. Of course, shuffle-board, horseshoes, and other lawn games are available. Should the weather turn inclement, many indoor games are offered in addition to the complete Nautilus facilities, hot tubs, and saunas in the new recreation center.

FRISKY FRIVOLITIES:

* There are a number of country walks in and around the inn. One particularly appealing one is in the Hastings/Wild River area of the White Mountain National Forest. There is a suspension bridge and the remains of a turn-of-the-century lumbering town.
* There are cross-country ski trails at the inn and in the White Mountains.
* This small town houses Gould Academy. There are also a number of well-preserved homes; many of them are listed on the National Register of Historic Places. All of these places are within walking distance of the inn.

THE WATERFORD INNE

Box 49, Chadbourne Road
East Waterford, Maine 04233
(207) 583-4037
Innkeepers: Barbara and Rosalie Vanderzanden
Rooms: 9 doubles
Rates: $45-75
Payment: Personal checks
Children: Welcome (no cribs available)
Dogs: Welcome with prior approval ($5 fee required)
Open: May to February

The Waterford Inne is an 1825 farmhouse located along an old stagecoach route in the Oxford Hills. The inn, set amid 10 acres of woods and fields and bordered by a large pond, is an idyllic setting for those looking for a "country inn" experience. The farmhouse has been recently restored and extra "homey" touches have been added by Barbara and her mother Rosalie.

Once inside, the ambiance of the 1800s comes alive with wide pumpkin pine board floors, beamed ceilings, narrow staircases, and old-fashioned hearths. These architectural features are complemented with brass trivets, sconces, antique furniture, and stenciling. There are two common rooms filled to capacity with handsome furnishings, including Queen Anne-style tables, a tall secretary, a harvest table, and a rocking chair. The colors vary from almond walls with forest green trim to a more traditional room with beamed ceilings and barn-board walls.

The five upstairs bedrooms and four in the old converted woodshed are decorated in keeping with the 1800's theme. Antiques predominate here, as in the common rooms. The wallpaper is a stenciled pattern, the comforters attractive, and the bouquets of flowers are always fresh. For those wanting a little more space, there is even a suite with a fireplace and private porch.

Barbara and Rosalie prepare "gourmet home-cooked" meals with fresh vegetables from their garden. These are served in an intimate dining room. In the morning, guests may expect a Continental breakfast of freshly baked hot muffins and breads. Meals are prepared in the bright and cheery kitchen with its sunlit windows, painted fruit decorating the walls, and woodstove.

FRISKY FRIVOLITIES:
* From high on this hillside, you can wander over to the white birch groves or down to the base of the road where there is a stream and waterfall.

234

* After some shopping and antiquing (the barn next door is full of antiques) you may want to try out some of the excellent cross-country skiing.
* Swimming and boating are available on many of the nearby lakes and streams.

WESTWAYS ON KEZAR LAKE

Box 175, Route 5
Center Lovell, Maine 04016
(207) 928-2663
Innkeeper: Nancy C. Tripp
Rooms: 7 doubles, 6 cottages and houses
Rates: Doubles: $67-132 (MAP); Cottages: $550-1,200 (weekly)
Payment: AE, MC, VISA, personal checks
Children: Welcome
Dogs: Welcome in houses and cottages (also permitted in the inn during
 quiet times of the year
Open: All year with exception of November and April

The Westways on Kezar Lake was originally built as a corporate retreat for the Diamond Match Company in the 1920s. This cedar-shingled manor rests on the shores of Kezar Lake, amidst a 100-acre forest of giant pines. Wonderful views can be had of the White Mountains off in the distance.

The main road leads guests down a long dirt drive to the lodge. The houses and more rustic cottages are set back from, but still have views of, the lake. Brook House is particularly well located next to a running brook. Three bedrooms and one-and-a-half baths create enough space for a good-sized family or a group of friends. The kitchen does feature a dishwasher, gas stove, and full-size refrigerator. Entertaining is easy in either the living room or on the screened-in porch, overlooking the stream and forest of birches and pines. The cottages are simply furnished with wicker rocking chairs, comfortable sofas, and plain comforters on the beds.

The larger and more elaborate houses lie just down the road from the cottages. These sleep from 6 to 14 people comfortably. Some have cathedral ceilings and fieldstone fireplaces. Wrap-around decks or screened-in porches allow outdoor flexibility. Modern kitchens and laundry facilities are added conveniences. There is even a small recreation room in one of the houses.

Guests traveling with very well-behaved dogs, during the off-season, may stay in a room in the lodge. Hardwood floors and beamed ceilings set the overall mood. These seven guest rooms have more of an elegant summer-house feeling. The furnishings are mostly antique and include handcarved bedsteads, maple furniture, and Queen Anne armoires. Fine quality reproduction art hangs on the walls alongside hunt prints. The beautiful views of the lake are alluring.

The main draws to Westways are the surroundings and peaceful environment. For the more energetic, there are tennis courts, table tennis, racquetball, canoeing, sailing, and a two-lane bowling alley.

FRISKY FRIVOLITIES:

* Cross-country ski trails, as well as walking paths, lead all over the property.
* Take Bowser for a refreshing swim in the lake on hot summer days, but please keep him away from the main swimming beach.
* Try a day of fishing along the shores of Kezar Lake.

OLDE ROWLEY INN

Route 35
North Waterford, Maine 04267
(207) 583-4143
Innkeepers: Pamela R. and Lucien P. Leja
Rooms: 4 doubles
Rates: $46-55
Payment: AE, MC, VISA, personal checks
Children: Welcome with prior arrangement
Dogs: Welcome, with prior approval
Open: All year

The Olde Rowley Inn stands today as it did almost 200 years ago. When it was first built in 1790, it was used as a stagecoach stop. Guests will find that it still caters to travelers by offering clean, comfortable accommodations and good food. The town of North Waterford is comprised of the inn, a general store, and a handful of other buildings. Even in these progressive times, the town has managed to hold onto its charming small town feeling. The rambling inn is made up of three connected buildings: the original barn, carriage house, and farmhouse. It has been painted a rich barn red with yellow trim and black shutters. The Lejas are busy restoring the old home, when they are not running a restaurant and catering to overnight guests. When we visited we found Lucien busy sheetrocking the back portion of the kitchen, while loaves of bread cooled on the front counter.

There are a number of common rooms in the house, each seemingly situated on a different level. Throughout the inn, guests will notice the wide king-pine floors, exposed beam ceilings, and fireplaces (most are in working order). The keeping room is particularly quaint, with its collection of country antiques, comfortably cushioned side chairs, and a table for board games and puzzles. Guests who are waiting for dinner will usually do so in a small parlor with long cushioned benches.

The three dining rooms are located in the barn and carriage house. The walls are stenciled and tables are neatly set with floral cotton tablecloths and tin lanterns. The diners are able to choose from quite an extensive menu. Selections run the gamut from veal and fish to pasta and beef. Those fortunate enough to be staying in the four guest rooms need only excuse themselves from the table and retire to their bedrooms.

The guest quarters are inviting and cozy. The bedroom and bathroom walls have been stenciled in a variety of bright colors. One chamber in particular is reminiscent of springtime with its blue and yellow stenciling complementing the floral bedspread. The blue bathroom has a reversed color scheme with white and yellow stenciling. A narrow staircase leads to the upstairs rooms, where guests will discover more pretty period furniture and antique bedsteads, all set on canted and creaky floorboards.

After a restful night's sleep, guests will awaken to a full breakfast. The selections vary, but may include blueberry pancakes, eggs (any style), fruit, and juice.

FRISKY FRIVOLITIES:

* This rural part of Maine offers many simple summer activities such as hiking and swimming in clear mountain lakes and streams.
* This area is popular for bike riding. If Bowser enjoys this type of activity, then let him join you for an afternoon jaunt.
* Cross-country skiing is a favorite pastime in this area, and Bowser will surely enjoy the opportunity to bound through the snow.

APPENDIX

BED AND BREAKFAST SERVICES

CONNECTICUT

Bed and Breakfast, Ltd.
P.O. Box 216
New Haven, CT 06513
(203) 469-3260

Covered Bridge B&B
Box 380
West Cornwall, CT 06796
(203) 672-6052

Covered Bridge B&B
Reservation Service
Maple Avenue, P.O. Box 701
Norfolk, CT 06058
(203) 542-5944

Four Seasons International
11 Bridlepath Road
West Simsbury, CT 06092
(203) 658-2181

Nautilus B&B
133 Phoenix Drive
Groton, CT 06340
(203) 448-1538

Nutmeg B&B
222 Girard Ave.
Hartford, CT 06105
(203) 236-6698

Seacoast Landings
133 Neptune Drive
Groton, CT 06340
(203) 442-1940

RHODE ISLAND

Ana's Home Connection
5 Fowler Ave,
Newport, RI 02840
(401) 849-2489

B&B of Rhode Island
P.O. Box 3291
Newport, RI 02840
(401) 849-1298

Castle Keep
44 Evert Street
Newport, RI 02840
(401) 846-0362

Guest House Association
of Newport
P.O. Box 981
Newport, RI 02840
(401) 846-5444

MASSACHUSETTS

Around Plymouth Bay
P.O. Box 6211
Plymouth, MA 02360
(617) 747-5075

B&B Agency Of Boston, Inc.
47 Commercial Wharf
Boston, MA 02110

B&B a la Cambridge
& Greater Boston
P.O. Box 665
Cambridge, MA 02140
(617) 576-1492

B&B Associates Bay Colony, Ltd.
P.O. Box 166
Boston, MA 02157
(617) 449-5302

B&B Brookline/Boston
Box 732
Brookline, MA 02146
(617) 227-2292

B&B Cape Cod
P.O. Box 341
West Hyannisport, MA 02672
(617) 775-2772

B&B Exchange
382 Washington Ave.
Chelsea, MA 02150
(617) 884-6087

B&B House Guests, Cape Cod
Box AR
Dennis, MA 02638
(617) 398-0787

B&B in Minuteman County
8 Carraige Drive
Lexington, MA 02173
(617) 861-7063

B&B in New England
Main Street
Williamsburg, MA 01096-0211
(413) 268-7244

B&B Marblehead and North Shore
54 Amherst Road
Beverly, MA 01915
(617) 921-1336

Be Our Guest, B&B, Ltd.
P.O. Box 1333
Plymouth, MA 02360
(617) 837-9867 or 545-6680

Berkshire B&B Homes
P.O. Box 211
Williamsburg, MA 01096
(413) 268-7244

Betina's B&B
P.O. Box 585
Cambridge, MA 02238
(617) 497-9166
1-800-624-6654 (outside Mass)

Boston B&B, Inc.
16 Ballard Street
Newton. MA 02159
(617) 332-4199

Christian Hospitality B&B of New
England
636 Union Street
Duxbury, MA 02332
(617) 834-8528

Educator's Inn
P.O. Box 663
Lynnfield, MA 01940
(617) 334-6144

Folstone B&B
P.O. Box 931
Boylston, MA 01505-0931
(617) 869-2687

Greater Boston Hospitality
P.O. Box 1142
Brookline, MA 02146
(617) 227-5430

Greater Springfield B&B
25 Bellevue Ave
Springfield,MA 01108
(413) 739-7400

Host Homes Of Boston
P.O. Box 117
Newton, MA 02159
(617) 244-1308

New England B&B, Inc.
1045 Center Street
Newton Center, MA 02159
(617) 244-2112

Orleans B&B Assoc.
59 Bridge Road
P.O. Box 1312
Orleans, MA 02653
(617) 255-3824

Pineapple Hospitality, Inc.
100 Cottage Street
New Bedford, MA 02740
(617) 990-1696

The B&B Folks
73 Providence Road
Westford, MA 01886
(617) 692-3232

University B&B, Ltd.
12 Churchill Street
Brookline, MA 02146
(617) 738-1424

VERMONT

American B&B in New England
P.O. 983
St. Albans, VT 05478

Green Mountain B&B
Stage Road
Benson, VT 05731
(802) 537-2081

Vermont B&B
Box 139, Browns Trace
Jericho, VT 05465
(802) 899-2354

Vermont B&B
P.O. Box 1
East Fairfield, VT 05448
(802) 827-3827

NEW HAMPSHIRE

New Hampshire B&B
RFD #3, Box 53
Laconia, N.H. 03246
(603) 279-8348

Valley B&B
Box 1190
No. Conway, N.H. 03860
(207) 935-3799

MAINE

B&B Down East, Ltd.
Box 547, Macomber Mill Road
Eastbrook, ME 04634
(207) 565-3517

B&B of Maine
32 Colonial Village
Falmouth, ME 04105
(207) 781-4528

ADDITIONAL NEW ENGLAND ACCOMMODATIONS ACCEPTING DOGS

CONNECTICUT

AVON:	Avon Old Farms Hotel	(203)677-1651
	Jct of Rte. 44 and 10	
BRANFORD:	Branford Motor Inn	(203)488-8314
	375 East Main St.	
BRIDGEPORT:	Days Inn	(203)366-5421
	815 Lafayette Blvd.	
	Marriott	(203)378-1400
	180 Hawley Lane	
DANBURY:	Ramada Inn	(203)792-3800
	(exit 8 off I-84)	
	Holiday Inn	(203)792-4000
	80 Newton Rd.	
DARIEN:	Holiday Inn	(203)655-8211
	50 Ledge Rd.	
GREENWICH:	Sheraton	(203)637-3691
	1114 Post Rd.	
HARTFORD:	Ramada Hotel Downtown	(203)528-9703
	100 East River Dr.	
	Holiday Inn Downtown	(203)549-2400
	50 Morgan St.	
	Mariott Farmington	(203)678-1000
	15 Farm Springs Rd.	
	Summit	(203)278-2000
	5 Constitution Plaza	
LAKEVILLE:	Iron Masters	(203)435-9844
	Main St.	
	Sharon Motor Lodge	(203)364-0036
	Rte. 41	
MERIDEN:	Howard Johnson's	(203)628-0921
	30 Laming St.	
MILFORD:	Holiday Inn	(203)878-6561
	1212 Boston Post Rd.	
MYSTIC:	Ramada Inn	(203)536-4281
	North of exit 90 on Rte. 27	

NEW BRITAIN:	Holiday Inn	(203)747-6876
	400 New Britain Ave.	
NEW HAVEN:	Holiday Inn	(203)777-6221
	30 Whalley Ave.	
NEW LONDON:	Red Roof Inn	(203)444-0001
	707 Colman St.	
NORWALK:	Holiday Inn	(203)853-3477
	789 Connecticut Ave.	
NORWICH:	Sheraton	(203)889-5201
	1 Sheraton Plaza	
OLD SAYBROOK:	Howard Johnson's	(203)388-5716
	100 Essex Rd.	
PUTNAM:	King's Inn	(203)928-7961
	Exit 96 off I-395	
STAMFORD:	Ramada Inn	(203)327-4300
	19 Clark's Hill Ave.	
	Le Pavillion	(203)357-8100
	60 Strawberry Hill Ave.	
	Sheraton Hotel and Towers	(203)967-2222
	1 First Stamford Pl.	
VERNON:	Howard Johnson's	(203)875-0781
	451 Hartford Turnpike	
WATERBURY:	Best Western Red Bull Inn	(203)597-8000
	Schrafft's Drive	
	Holiday Inn	(203)575-1500
	88 Union St.	
WETHERSFIELD:	Ramada Inn	(203)563-2311
	1330 Silas Deane Highway	
WINDSOR LOCKS:	Howard Johnson's	(203)623-9811
	Center St.	
	Ramada Inn	(203)623-9411
	161 Bridge St.	
	Koala Inn	(203)623-9417
	185 Ella T Grasso Tpke	
	Ramada Inn Bradley	(203)623-9494
	5 Ella T Grasso Tpke	

RHODE ISLAND

MIDDLETOWN	Howard Johnson's 351 West Main Rd.	(401)849-2000
NEWPORT:	Holiday Inn Crowne Plaza 25 America Cup Ave.	(401)849-1000
PROVIDENCE:	Marriott Charles and Orms Streets	(401)272-2400
	Holiday Inn Downtown 21 Atwells Ave.	(401)831-3900
	Sheraton Tara Airport Inn 1850 Post Rd.	(401)738-4000
WARWICK:	Rhode Island Inn 2081 Post Rd.	(401)739-0600
	Sheraton Motor Inn 1850 Post Rd.	(401)738-4000

MASSACHUSETTS

AMHERST:	Howard Johnson's 401 Russel St	(413)586-0114
ANDOVER:	Koala Inn 131 River Rd.	(617)685-6200
	Boston Marriott Andover Old River Rd.	(617)975-3600
BOSTON:	Boston Park Plaza Hotel One Park Plaza/Arington St.	(617)426-2000
	Copley Plaza 138 St. James Ave.	(617)267-5300
	Hilton-Back Bay 40 Dalton St.	(617)236-1100
	Hilton-Logan Airport 75 Service Rd.-Logan Airport	(617)569-9300
	Marriott-Long Wharf 296 State St.	(617)227-0800
	Sheraton Boston Hotel 39 Dalton St.	(617)236-2000
	The Westin Hotel, Copley Place 10 Huntington Ave.	(617)262-9600

BRAINTREE:	Holiday Inn-Randolph	(617)961-1000
	1374 North Main St.	
	Sheraton Tara	(617)848-0600
	37 Forbes Rd.	
BROCKTON:	Carlton House Motor Inn	(617)588-3333
	1005 Belmont St.	
	Holiday Inn	(617)588-6300
	Westgate Drive	
BURLINGTON:	Marriott	(617)229-6565
	Jct. Rte. 128 and 3A	
	Howard Johnson's	(617)272-6550
	98 Middlesex Turnpike	
CAMBRIDGE:	Howard Johnson's	(617)492-7777
	777 Memorial Drive	
	Royal Sonesta	(617)491-3600
	5 Cambridge Parkway	
CONCORD:	Howard Johnson's	(617)369-6100
	740 Elm St.	
DANVERS:	Howard Johnson's	(617)774-8045
	Jct. Rte. 1 and Rte. 114	
DEDHAM:	Holiday Inn	(617)329-1000
	55 Ariadne Steet	
EASTHAM:	Town Crier	(617)255-4000
	Rte. 6	
EDGARTOWN:	Governor Bradford Inn	(617)627-9510
	128 Main St.	
FRAMINGHAM:	Sheraton Tara	(617)879-7200
	1657 Worcester Rd.	
GREAT BARRINGTON:	Monument Mountain	(413)528-3272
	249 Stockbridge Rd.	
GREENFIELD:	Howard Johnson's	(413)774-2211
	125 Mohawk Trail	
	Candle Light	(413)772-0101
	208 Mohawk Trail	
HAVERHILL:	Howard Johnson's	(617)373-1511
	401 Lowell Ave.	
HOLYOKE:	Holiday Inn	(413)534-3311
	245 Whiting Farms Rd.	
HYANNIS:	Holiday Inn	(617)775-6600
	Rte. 132	
	Iyanough Hills Motor Lodge	(617)771-4804
	Iyanough Rd.	

	Hyannis Harborview Iyanough Rd.	(617)775-4420
	Sheraton-Hyannis Rte. 132	(617)771-3000
LAWRENCE:	Holiday Inn 333 Winthrop Ave.	(617)686-9411
LOWELL:	Holiday Inn 95 Main St.	(617)851-7301
	Hilton 50 Warren St.	(617)452-1200
	Quality Inn Heritage 10 Independence Dr.	(617)256-0800
METHUEN:	Methuen Inn 159 Pelham St.	(617)686-2971
NEWTON:	Marriott 2345 Commonwealth Ave.	(617)969-1000
	Howard Johnson's 320 Washington St.	(617)969-3010
PEABODY:	The Victorian Motor Inn 229 Andover St.	(617)531-8800
PITTSFIELD:	Hilton Inn-Berkshire Berkshire Common	(413)499-2000
PLYMOUTH:	The Gov. Bradford Motor Inn Water and Brewster Streets	(617)746-6200
	The Governor Carver Motor Inn 25 Summer St.	(617)746-7100
PROVINCETOWN:	Holiday Inn Rte. 6A	(617)487-1711
SCIUATE:	Clipper Ship Motor Lodge Front St.	(617)545-5550
SHARON	Sharon Motel Rte. 1	(617)668-2155
SOUTH YARMOUTH:	Riverview Motor Lodge 37 Neptune Lane	(617)394-9801
SPRINGFIELD:	Best Western Black Horse 500 Riverdale St.	(617)733-2161
	Quality Inn 296 Burnett Rd.	(413)592-7751
	Sheraton Inn 1080 Riverdale St.	(413)781-8750
WOBURN:	Holiday Inn 19 Commerce Way	(617)935-7110

WESTMINSTER:	Best WesternWestminsterVillage	(617)874-5911
	Highway 2	
WORCESTER:	Marriott	(617)791-1600
	10 Lincoln Square	
	Budgetel Inn	(617)832-7000
	444 Southbridge St.	
	Quality Inn Downtown	(617)791-2291
	70 Southbridge St.	

VERMONT

BENNINGTON:	Bennington Motor Inn	(802)442-5479
	143 West Main St.	
	Catamount Motel	(802)442-5977
	500 South St.	
	Fife N' Drum	(802)442-4074
	Rte 7	
	Ramada Inn	(802)442-8145
	Rte 7 and Kochner Dr.	
BRANDON:	Brandon Motor Lodge	(802)247-9594
	Rte 7	
BRATTLEBORO:	Quality Inn	(802)254-8701
	Putney Rd.	
BURLINGTON:	Anchorage	(802)658-3351
	108 Dorset St.	
	Econo Lodge	(802)863-1125
	1076 Williston Rd.	
	Holiday Inn	(802)863-6363
	1068 Williston Rd.	
	Howard Johnson's	(802)863-5541
	Rte 2 and I-89	
	Ramada Inn	(802)658-0250
	1117 Williston Rd.	
	Radisson	(802)658-6500
	Burlington Square	
	Sheraton Inn	(802)862-6576
	870 Williston Rd.	
KILLINGTON:	Edelweiss	(802)775-5577
	Rte 4	
	Sherburne-Killington Motel	(802)773-9535
	Rte 4	

	The Tyrol Motel	(802)773-7485
	Rte 4	
	Val Roc	(802)422-3881
	Rte 4	
LUDLOW:	Timber Inn Motel	(802)228-8666
	South Main St.	
LYNDONVILLE:	Lynburke Motel	(802)626-3346
	Rte. 5 and Rte 114	
NORWICH:	Inn at Norwich	(802)649-1143
	225 Main St.	
ST. ALBANS:	Cadillac	(802)524-2191
	213 Main St.	
ST.JOHNSBURY:	Holiday	(802)748-8192
	25 Hastings St.	
	Yankee Traveler	(802)748-3156
	65 Portland St.	
SHAFTSBURY:	Hillbrook Motel	(802)442-4095
	Rte. 7A	
	Iron Kettle	(802)442-4316
	Rte 7A	
SPRINGFIELD:	Howard Johnson's	(802)885-4516
	Rte. 5 and Rte 11	
STOWE:	Mountain Rd. Motel	(802)253-4566
	Rte 108	
	The Snowdrift Motel	(802)253-7305
	Rte 108	
VERGENNES:	Skyview Motel	(802)877-3410
	Rte. 7	
WATERBURY:	Holiday Inn	(802)244-7822
	Blush Hill Rd.	
WHITE RIVER JUNCTION:	Holiday Inn	(802)295-7537
	Rte. 5	
	Howard Johnson	(802)295-3015
	Rte. 5	
WOODSTOCK:	Quechee Gorge	(802)295-7600
	Rte. 4	

NEW HAMPSHIRE

BARTLETT:	The Villager Motel	(603)374-2742
	Rte. 302	
BETHLEHEM:	The Wayside Inn	(603)869-3364
	Rte. 302	
CONCORD:	Capitol Motor Inn	(603)224-4011
	Gulf St.	
	Ramada Inn	(603)224-9534
	172 North Main St.	
	Brick Tower Motor Inn	(603)224-9565
	414 South Main St.	
CONWAY:	Saco River Motor Lodge	(603)447-3720
	Rte. 302	
DOVER:	Friendship Inn	(603)742-4100
	Silver St.	
EAST MADISON:	Purity Spring Resort	(603)367-8896
	Rte 153	
GORHAM:	Town and Country Motor Inn	(603)466-3315
	Rte. 2	
	Mt. Madison Motel	(603)466-3622
	365 Upper Main St.	
HANOVER:	Chieftain	(603)643-2550
	Rte. 10	
KEENE:	Winding Brook Lodge	(603)352-3111
	Park Ave.	
	Ramada Inn	(603)357-3038
	401 Winchester St.	
MANCHESTER:	Sheraton Wayfarer Inn	(603)622-3766
	Jct.Rte.s 3 and 101	
	Koala Inn	(603)668-6110
	55 John Devine Drive	
	Holiday Inn West	(603)669-2660
	21 Front St.	
	Howard Johnson's	(603)668-2600
	298 Queen City Ave.	
MEREDITH:	Rob Roy	(603)476-5571
	Rte. 25	
NASHUA:	Hilton at Merrimack	(603)424-6181
	Best WesternHallmarkMotor Inn	(603)888-1200
	220 DW Highway South	
NEWPORT:	Newport	(603)863-1440

NEW LONDON:	Hide-Away Lodge	(603)526-4861
	Little Sunapee Rd.	
PLYMOUTH:	King's Court Inn	(603)536-3520
	RFD 1	
PITTSBURG:	The Glen	(603)538-6500
	Off Rte. 3	
PORTSMOUTH:	Charter House Motor Hotel	(207)439-2000
ROCHESTER:	Cardinal Ranch	(603)332-1902
	Rte. 11	
SUNAPEE:	Burkehaven	(603)763-2788
	Burkehaven Hill Rd.	
	Mt. Sunapee	(603)763-5592
	Rte. 103 and 103B	
WHITEFIELD:	Mountain View House	(603)837-2511
	Mountain View Rd.	

MAINE

AUBURN:	Best Western Manor Inn	(207)783-1454
	Rte. 202	
AUGUSTA:	Best Western Senator Inn	(207)622-5804
	Western Ave.	
BANGOR:	Best Western White House	(207)862-3737
	I-95 and Coldbrook Rd exit	
	Holiday Inn - Main St.	(207)947-8651
	500 Main St.	
	Holiday Inn	(207)947-0101
	404 Oldin Rd.	
	Ramada Inn	(207)947-6961
	357 Oldin Rd.	
	Hilton Inn	(207)947-6721
	308 Godfrey Blvd.	
	Quality Inn Chateau	(207)942-6301
	482 Oldin Rd.	
BAR HARBOR:	Frenchman's Bay	(207)288-3321
	Eden St.	
BATH:	Holiday Inn	(207)443-9741
	139 Western Ave.	
BELFAST:	Belfast Motor Inn	(207)338-2740
	Searsport Ave.	
	Wonderview Cottages	(207)338-1455
	Searsport Ave.	

BELGRADE:	Woodland Camps	(207)495-2251
	Point Rd.	
BETHEL:	L'Auberge	(207)824-2774
BOOTHBAY	Ocean Gate Motor Inn	(207)633-3321
HARBOR:	Rte. 27	
	Boothbay Harbor Inn	(207)633-6302
	37 Atlantic Ave.	
	Smuggler's Cove Motor Inn	(207)633-2800
	Rte. 96	
BRIGHTON:	Pleasant Mountain Inn	(207)647-2431
	Mountain Rd	
BUCKSPORT:	Spring Fountain	(207)469-3139
	Rte. 1	
ELLSWORTH:	Holiday Inn	(207)667-9641
	Rte. 1	
	White Birches	(207)667-3621
	Rte. 1	
FREEPORT:	Freeport Inn	(207)865-3106
	Rte. 1	
	Eagle	(207)865-3371
	Rte. 1	
GRAND LAKE	Leen's Cottages	(207)796-5575
STREAM:	Rte. 1	
	Weatherby's	(207)796-5558
HOULTON:	Shiretown	(207)532-9421
	North Rd.	
JACKMAN:	Briarwood Mountain Lodg e	(207)668-7756
	Rte. 201	
	Sky Lodge	(207)668-2171
	Rte. 201	
KENNEBUNK:	Kennebunk Inn 1799	(207)985-3351
	45 Main St.	
KENNEBUNKPORT:	The Shawmut Inn	(207)967-3931
	Turbot's Creek Rd.	
NEWPORT:	Lovely's Motel	(207)368-4311
	Rte. 2	
NORTH ANSON:	Embden Resorts	(207)566-7501
	West Shore Drive	
PORTLAND:	Best Western Executive Inn	(207)773-8181
	645 Congress St.	
	Best Western-John Martin's	(207)774-6151
	Main St.	

	Comfort Inn	(207)775-0409
	90 Main Mall Rd.	
	Sheraton Tara Hotel	(207)775-6161
	363 Main Mall Rd.	
PRESQUE ISLE:	Keddy's Motor Inn	(207)764-3321
	Rte. 1	
	Northeastland	(207)768-5321
	436 Main St.	
RUMFORD:	Madison Motor Inn	(207)364-7973
	Rte. 2	
SANFORD:	Bar-H-Motel	(207)324-4662
	Rte. 109	
SEARSPORT:	Inn at the Yardarm	(207)548-2404
	East Main St.	
SKOHEGAN:	Somerset Motor Lodge	(207)474-2227
	422 Madison Ave.	
	Belmont	(207)474-8315
	425 Madison Ave.	
WATERVILLE:	Atrium	(207)873-2777
	332 Main St.	
	Holiday Inn	(207)873-0111
	375 Upper Main St.	
WELLS:	Watercrest Motel and Cottages	(207)646-2202

INDEX

1785 Inn, The 144
1860 House, The 123
Andover Inn 41
Applewood Farms Inn 3
Arlington Inn, The 84
Barrows House 88
Bayview Inn and Hotel 220
Benjamin Prescott Inn, The 170
Berkson Farms 130
Bethel Inn and Country Club,
  The 232
Brannon-Bunker Inn, The 203
Calico Cat Guest House, The 19
Captain Jefferds Inn, The 188
Captain R. Flanders 72
Cartway House, The 151
Centennial House, The 30
Charles Hotel, The 46
Cloverleaf Lodge 199
Colony, The 192
Corner House Inn, The 154
Country Club Inn 228
Coveside Cottages 187
Craignair Inn, The 207
Crocker House Country Inn,
  The 221
Darling Family Inn, The 113
Deerfield Inn 31
Dexter's Inn and Tennis Club 165
Dockside Guest Quarters 186
Douglass Place, The 231
Dr. Shiverick House, The 70
Driftwood Inn and Cottages,
  The 198
Edencroft Manor 159

Edgecomb-Coles House 208
Ellery Park House 21
Essex Street Inn, The 39
Exeter Inn, The 179
Four Columns Inn, The 119
Four Gables, The 17
Four Seasons Hotel 49
Four-in-Hand, The 81
Gelston House, The 8
Goose Cove Lodge 217
Gracie's B&B 206
Grane's Fairhaven Inn 200
Green Mountain Inn 126
Green River B&B 85
Greenhurst Inn 97
Hanover Inn, The 162
Hapgood Cottage B&B 107
Harbor Village 60
Hargood House, The 63
Hartness House 108
Hawthorne Hill B&B 57
Hayes House, The 117
Herbert Inn, The 227
Hilltop Inn, The 158
Hiram Alden Inn, The 210
Hobson House 161
Homewood Inn 194
Hotel Meridien 47
Hugging Bear Inn 110
Inn at Chester, The 6
Inn at Christian Shore B&B,
  The 182
Inn at Crotched Mountain, The 171
Inn at Sunderland, The 87
Inn at Weathersfield, The 105

Inn on South Street, The 191
Inn on the Common, The 128
Isaac Randall House, The 195
Isaac Springfield House 148
Ivanhoe Country House 29
Jared Coffin House 73
John Hancock Inn, The 167
John Peter's Inn 218
Johnny Seesaw's 114
Kedron Valley Inn 101
Kona Mansion Inn and
  Cottages 152
Lafayette Hotel, The 50
Lake Shore Farm 176
Lamb and Lion, The 61
Larchwood Inn 18
Le Domaine 223
Lincoln House Country Inn 224
Little Harbor Guest House 56
Loch Lyme Lodge and
  Cottages 164
Lord Jeffery Inn, The 34
Madison Beach Hotel, The 5
Manor, The 214
Meadow Farm and B&B 178
Middlebury Inn, The 91
Millbrook Lodge 94
Morgan House, The 27
Morrill Place Inn, The 40
Mountain Meadows Lodge 100
Mountain-Fare Inn, The 157
Munro-Hawkin's House, The 82
Newcastle Inn, The 205
Northway House 155
Notch Brook Resort 120
Oakland House 216
October Pumpkin B&B 90
Old Cutter Inn, The 136
Old Lyme Inn 4
Old Red Inn and Cottages,
  The 142
Old Riverton Inn 11

Old Tavern at Grafton, The 115
Olde Rowley Inn 236
One Aker Farm B&B 127
Penobscot Meadows Inn 211
Phenix Inn, The 226
Philbrook Farm Inn 141
Phillips House B&B 76
Point Way Inn 69
Poplar Manor 98
Pulpit Harbor Inn, The 213
Quimby Country 137
Rabbit Hill Inn 134
Ram in the Thicket, The 173
Rangeley Inn, The 230
Rasberry Ink 54
Red Inn 65
Ritz Carlton Hotel, The 52
Rockhouse Mountain Farm Inn 147
Seaside, The 190
Senter B&B 197
Sheafe Street Inn 181
Sherman-Berry House 44
Shore Acres Inn and
  Restaurant 133
Silvermine Tavern 13
Snowvillage Inn 145
South Village 95
Stephen Daniels House, The 43
Stepping Stones 174
Stone Hearth Inn, The 110
Strong House Inn 93
Summer House, The 58
Ten Acres Lodge 124
Three Church Street 103
Tin Whistle Inn 150
Toll Gate Hill Inn and
  Restaurant 12
Topnotch at Stowe 121
Town Farms Inn 9
Trailing Yew, The 202
Tyler Place on Lake
  Champlain 131

Victorian, The 36
Village Inn of Woodstock,
  The 104
Village Inn, The 62
Walker House 26
Waterford Inne,
  The 234
Watermark Inn 67

Westways on Kezar Lake 235
Whale Inn, The 33
Whetstone Inn 80
White Wind Inn 66
Williams Inn, The 25
Windsor House, The 37
Woodbound Inn 168
Woodbox, The 75

TRAVELING WITH MAN'S BEST FRIEND

If you are unable to find this book in your local stores and wish to order one or more copies, please write to the publisher:

Dawbert Press, Inc.
P.O. Box 2758
Duxbury, Massachusetts 02331

Send me _____ copies at $ 10.95 each.

Traveling With Man's Best Friend is a selective guide to New England's finer B&Bs, inns, and resort hotels that welcome you and your dog. Unfortunately, as extensive as our research has been, we may have missed a few places that should have been included. If this book is to be a complete guide on the accommodations that will accept dogs, we will need your assistance. Should you discover an interesting B&B, inn, or hotel that we have not included in our 1987 edition, please send us its name, address, and telephone number. If, after researching your suggestion, we include that entry in our next edition of Traveling With Man's Best Friend, we will be more than happy to send you a complimentary copy of that edition.

Please send entries to:
Dawbert Press, Inc., P.O. Box 2758, Duxbury, Mass. 02331
Thank you for your help!

617
934-7202